THE WAY
OF
UNITY

Essential Principles and
Preconditions for Peace

THE WAY
—— OF ——
UNITY

Essential Principles and Preconditions for Peace

ROBERT ATKINSON, PHD

Light
on
Light
p r e s s

ADVANCE PRAISE
FOR
THE WAY OF UNITY

The Way of Unity is a brave, rich, profound book written with elegance and deep prayer for the future of our tormented world. It will help everyone who comes to it renew their commitment to constant spiritual practice in service of the birth of a new humanity out of the ashes of the old and it will serve as a guide to all those of us who dream groundedly of a universal unified and unifying vision of the divine that can empower directly at the time we most need it. It is a call to all human beings to establish a world of peace, harmony and justice.

~ Andrew Harvey, founder and director of the Institute for Sacred Activism, and author of The Essential Mystics, Radical Passion, and (with Carolyn Baker) Radical Regeneration

The new book from the pen of Robert Atkinson is a call to peace coming at this very critical moment in the history of humanity. It supplements and crowns all current efforts to inspire the move toward peace at the time when the darkest clouds gather on the horizon. The vision projected by this book could be the spark that ignites the ever-present even if widely neglected flame of peace in the heart of humanity. We are a global society oriented at the deepest level of insight and consciousness toward oneness with each other and with nature. The flickering but never extinguished flame of creating a peaceful and whole world can be and must be rekindled and this book does just that.

~ Ervin Laszlo, world's leading systems scientist, philosopher, and author of over 100 books, including The Great Upshift and The Wisdom Principles

The Way of Unity is founded on universal wisdom teachings, now in-formed by breakthrough scientific discoveries with evidence at all scales of existence. This emergent understanding is of a living and loving Universe whose innate interdependence evolves throughout its essential wholeness. The book's call that 'love is the sacred activism of our time' is empowered by this realisation; both of the unitive reality of our Universe, and our fundamental role and purpose within the radical diversity and inherent belonging of its vast web of life. This truly is the sacred mission of our time!

~ Dr Jude Currivan, cosmologist, author of The Story of Gaia, and co-founder of WholeWorld-View

Unity is what the world needs now. It is the remedy for a divided humanity. This book has come at the perfect time, offering a prescription for all our ills. Read it, take it to heart, and put its principles into action.

~ Jack Canfield, Coauthor of the Chicken Soup for the Soul® series and The Success Principles™

In The Way of Unity, author Robert Atkinson presents a comprehensive blueprint to guide humankind to the long cherished goal of peace on Earth. The foundation to this lofty achievement is a profound shift from our fragmented worldview to the consciousness of our fundamental unity. Atkinson asserts that this understanding, activated through the unitive principles of his Baháʼí faith, will inevitably follow nature's pattern to bring us into the fruits of our true wholeness: a global civilization based on mutual respect and fairness. The Way of Unity should be required reading for all who seek a hopeful vision of world peace.

~ Rev. Deborah Moldow, Interfaith Minister, Director, Evolutionary Leaders Circle of the Source of Synergy Foundation, Founder, Garden of Light

The Way of Unity offers comprehensive insight into the truism: Synthesis Is. Unity Must be Created. Bob is a living demonstration of unitive consciousness and offers deep insights into the shift of consciousness that humanity is experiencing, from a separative worldview to a whole systems, unitive worldview. He gives voice to the Spirit of Peace, also known as the Spirit of Equilibrium, and lays out a practical vision that inspires and informs us to take action to realize peace. Highly recommended for all peacebuilders and spiritual seekers!

~ Dot Maver, Founding President, National Peace Academy, co-founder of the Global Silent Minute, and co-author of Conscious Education: The Bridge to Freedom

Human beings are born with an innate potential for unity, yet we continue to witness deep division across our world. In The Way of Unity, Dr. Bob Atkinson skillfully guides us on the essential journey of personal and collective transformation. Through his wisdom, the path to unity—and ultimately, to peace—feels not only possible, but within reach.

~ Emily Hine, Peace and mindfulness consultant, social entrepreneur, teacher, author, inspirational speaker, and nonprofit fundraiser

Robert Atkinson has gifted us a luminous map for these transformative times. In a world aching to remember its wholeness, The Way of Unity offers both a vision and a pathway—grounded in wisdom, guided by love, and alive with evolutionary promise. This is not just a book about peace—it is a transmission of peace, a gentle yet powerful invitation to align our lives with the deepest truth: we belong to each other. Through a sweeping synthesis of cosmology, sacred traditions, and real-world models of social transformation, he illustrates how unity is both the origin and destiny of life—a sacred pattern from which peace naturally flows. With clarity and conviction, Atkinson positions The Way of Unity as a spiritual call, a practical guide, and a compelling model for peacebuilding that is already being implemented by communities worldwide. He calls readers not merely to believe in peace, but to become peace through a lifelong practice of wholeness, justice, and compassionate action. For those longing to midwife a new world, this book is both compass and companion. May it be widely read, deeply received, and boldly lived.

~ Dr. Julie Krull, host of the Dr. Julie Show: All Things Connected, psychotherapist, president of Good of the Whole, and author of the award-winning book Fractured Grace

The well-being of mankind, its peace and security,
are unattainable unless and until its unity is firmly established.

~ Bahá'u'lláh

TABLE OF CONTENTS

Preface: The Way to Peace Has No Shortcut, But There Is a Way Forward .. i

Introduction: A Wholistic Vision of Peace ix

PART 1. UNDERSTANDING UNITY

1. Unity Characterizes the Hidden Wholeness of the Universe 1

   Unitive Consciousness as Our Archetypal Inheritance

   The Cosmology of Unity

   Unity-in-Diversity and Diversity-in-Unity

2. Unity Is the Source and Direction of Evolution 21

   The Universe Is a Marvel of Wholeness and Unity

   Evolution's Trajectory Fulfills an Age-Old Vision

   The Time for Unity Has Come

3. A Trinity of Unitive Principles 31

   The Wholeness Principle

   The Evolution Principle

   The Consciousness Principle

PART 2. UNITY IS THE REMEDY FOR A DIVIDED HUMANITY

4. The Emerging Unitive Age 47

   Ways of Understanding the Changeless and the Changing

   The Unitive Nature of Humanity's Spiritual Evolution

   Unitive Consciousness Will Be the Norm in the Unitive Age

5. Peace Is the Natural Outcome of the Way of Unity 65

   Nine Unitive Principles as Preconditions for Peace

   The Unity of the Human Family Is the Culminating Condition for
   World Peace

   Additional Expressions of the Unitive Age

6. Unity-in-Action for the Betterment of the World 111
 A Unitive Approach to Social Change
 Capacity Building, Empowerment, and Coherence for Deeper
 Impact
 Models of Social Action for Building Communities of Peace

PART 3. UNITY IN ALL SPHERES IS THE ONLY WAY TO PEACE

7. The Way of Unity to Inner Peace... 141
 Nurturing Peace in Our Hearts
 Developing Inner Capacities
 Striving for Spiritual Distinction
8. The Way of Unity to Interpersonal Peace.............................. 153
 Becoming a Source of Social Good
 Compassionate Consultation and Collaboration
 Social Justice to Bring About Unity
9. The Way of Unity to World Peace 167
 An Ever-Advancing Civilization
 The Ethics of Globalization
 Unitive Global Governance

Study Guide.. 189
 Chapter Spotlights & Questions for Consultation......................... 189
 Keys to the Evolutionary Process Leading to Peace on Earth 227
Acknowledgments.. 239
Endnotes & Additional Resources 241
About the Author 289
Message From the Publisher 291

PREFACE

The Way to Peace Has No Shortcut, But There Is a Way Forward

Prophets, sages, wise leaders, and visionaries have been talking about peace for millennia. And peace action organizations and global peace movements have been doing more than talking about peace for centuries.

To bring about a lasting global peace, something more is needed, something that opens the hearts of all people to the urgency of remembering, reclaiming, and living by our innate state of unity, harmony, and wholeness that connects us all and keeps us in peaceful relationship with all beings on our planetary home. This inner knowing seems to have been out of reach for eons.

Remembering who we really are leads us into and through an arduous transformative journey that confirms what we all share at our essence. This provides us with the needed hope – and assurance – that we deeply want to be aligned with all that is already being done in an emergent process of creating the conditions for lasting peace.

This book sets us off on a journey beginning with personal peace, following the way of unity in all its steps, guiding us from family peace to community peace to national peace, and finding its fulfillment in world peace.

To achieve this ultimate goal, in our complex, divided times, what is called for is an all-inclusive, comprehensive way to peace that clarifies an organic process that the entire human family, young and old, rich and poor, can relate to, embrace, and help bring into reality.

Lasting peace can only be the result of a long, conscious evolutionary process that requires building out the necessary preconditions for global harmony. From this foundation and framework, the realization of the unity of the human family in all its rich diversity can become manifest.

Critical to both this evolutionary process to transform consciousness and to satisfy our need to align with the energies of the universe, is individual and group meditation. The more meditation in the world, the more peaceful the world will be. Yet, no matter how inclusive, well-intended, and focused this practice is, meditation alone will not bring about world peace.

All efforts toward inner peace and well-being for raising and transforming individual and group consciousness can only result in peace on Earth if they are consciously coupled with a cumulatively expanding outer process of transforming all social structures to support the oneness of humanity and all life.

A shift in consciousness is the first step needed in an extensive process of global renewal. A *unitive consciousness* – seeing all things as an indivisible wholeness – is the goal that will bring into focus all that is possible when a unitive perspective is applied in all endeavors.

When this process of elevating consciousness toward wholeness is fully accomplished, it will still take decades, if not centuries, for a totally transformed multi-level local, regional, national, and global infrastructure to be built out and put into effect that would support this unitive consciousness and its continuing growth and development.

Personal, group, community, regional, national, and global efforts toward this goal of unity and peace are all essential as they complement each other and help humanity recognize the interconnectedness of all peacebuilding efforts independently and interdependently working toward their convergence.

Our challenge today is not only to raise the frequency of our collective consciousness to a unitive outlook, but also, with that as our foundation, to build an infrastructure of families, communities, societies, and nations that will encourage, support, and sustain the process of achieving global unity through the realization of the unity of the human family.

This call to action initiates and guides the spiritual regeneration of individuals, communities, institutions, and social structures. It needs to be consciously and universally agreed upon as the goal to be achieved in the next stage of our collective evolution.

No matter how dark and foreboding things may look at any moment, all that is happening is part of a process of ups and downs that together contribute to collective progress. This, by necessity, includes the breaking down of old ways.

When the world starts to feel chaotic, competitive, and conflicted, it doesn't have to feel out of control. The transformation going on around us is about turning the apparent tensions we perceive into the natural flow of opposing forces merging and becoming balanced components of a unified whole. We do this by learning to reflect the cooperation and harmony all around us. How we react to the world we live in is our choice.

Winter's decline is followed by the budding of new life. Coming right along is a spiritual springtime with new collaborative ways of being that will slowly but deliberately transform the world into the full blossoming of our innate virtues.

Though everything happening now is following natural cycles of decline and renewal, even with long-standing structures being torn down for unclear or self-centered reasons, the ominous contrast of worldviews appears greater than ever. The contrast between disunity and unity feels so out of balance. The lack of peace has rarely been so evident.

Seeing only what is happening in the day-to-day world can easily evoke hopelessness. Yet, this is a time when we simply cannot give up on world peace. We must not lose sight of the entire process we are in the midst of, as it is continuing to unfold every moment.

This book resolves the ever-shifting contrast of opposites by offering an evolutionary perspective that keeps its focus on the whole. This will lead to a world that works for the benefit of all, as Martin Luther King Jr. understood. His vision for change went well beyond the conflict of the moment, noting that it will be a long process for the "arc of the moral universe" to unfold in its fullness, but that when it does, it will be a living expression of "justice," affirming that progress is inevitable, no matter how long it takes.

This perspective emerges from trust in a higher source. It is founded upon spiritual values and principles that are timeless, universal, and inclusive. It is based on an unfaltering faith in humanity's highest nature to carry out its sacred purpose in the world, no matter what gets in its way.

This book represents the radical hope of a wholistic understanding from the Baháʼí teachings, embodying universal wisdom delivered in a modern, visionary, world-changing container when applied in real-life settings. I've attempted to convey the heart of what the Baháʼí tradition has brought to the world, to interfaith dialogue, to interspirituality, to universal principles, sacred activism, and the evolving vision of Wholeness and peace.

I've also drawn from the spiritual teachings of the world's wisdom traditions. Central to this approach is the concept of a *unitive consciousness*, what I think of as a consciousness that brings about and maintains unity in all endeavors.

The challenge at hand is to offset the prominent pessimistic world view – fueled by rogue impulses creating a climate of fear meant to sustain and expand all existing imbalances – with the more optimistic world view inspired by the simultaneous rise of unitive thinking, being, and acting that embraces the entire human family for the betterment of the whole.

This book is set in the context of the struggle between these two starkly contrasting worldviews unfolding right before our eyes. Disorder and destruction will result from the former prevailing. World peace is the ultimate destiny of the latter, if – and only if – humanity as a whole fully accepts and carries out its cooperative role in making that happen.

To ensure that this contrast is as clear as possible, a wholistic perspective is framed by what I refer to as *the way of unity*. Developed throughout the book, the way of unity encompasses a worldview, a philosophy, a methodology, a dynamic process, and an approach toward all aspects of life. It is a way of being and doing, guided by principles, values, beliefs, and actions that bring about and maintain the goal of unity and harmony in all settings. The way of unity rests upon a unitive consciousness to simultaneously bring about:

- inner peace by personally aligning with the unitive forces of the evolutionary impulse through our own focused spiritual practice
- interpersonal peace by being a source of social good and contributing to strong and vibrant unified communities,
- world peace by contributing to the renewal of local, national, global infrastructures supporting an ever-advancing civilization.

At the heart of how I see the way of unity is a dynamic, evolving strategy that includes a collaborative learning process utilizing relevant guidance, the art and practice of consultation, social action, reflection, and growth. This is the way unity unfolds, is strengthened, and is manifest in the world. It is an expression of cooperation and solidarity that transcends divisions and offers hope in place of despair.

This collaborative learning process builds the essential components of a culture of peace that contribute to bringing about the harmony and balance of the entire human family. There may be no other way to build unified communities and create a peaceful world than by each circle of unity living by unitive principles that facilitate inclusivity and belonging while bringing about the eventual merging of all circles of unity into one unified circle of Wholeness.

This process resembles the natural growth and development of a living organism. Chance and chaos are avoided, coherence between all component parts is essential, and continuity of action is maintained. On the social level, this collaborative learning process builds communities of peace.

We are the agents of change for an organic renewal process of society. We can assist the natural flow happening right now under our feet. There is an innate strategy to this renewal process. With a deliberate persistence, the tentacles of renewal, firmly rooted, are coming to life once again, in a cyclical reawakening, to replace decaying structures with fresh fibers of life-giving tenderness and beauty, to eventually bloom into their fullness.

Organic renewal chooses to move at its own pace, because it knows its outcome is assured. It doesn't resist anything around it, because it is busy building towards its own innate potential of a future not yet stolen. It is focused solely on building its own networks of care, cooperation, and sharing, by safeguarding the common good.

Such organic renewal spreads invisibly, through networks that are self-sustaining and growth-producing through the strength of its own unity-in-diversity. This describes the mycelial networks that are always weaving their wholeness beneath the surface of the ground.

Whether we realize it or not, we are all part of such a mycelial network. Humanity is its own mycelium network, patiently, insistently weaving our own wholeness. We too are meant to endure whatever is happening above the surface. This is our time to emerge, to rise up in new growth with a fresh force to put forward.

The existence of such a process of organic renewal should provide us with hope, instead of despair, with conviction that can lead us onward. Organic renewal doesn't fight against what assails us; it builds toward what inspires us, toward the vision we hold most dear.

The equivalent of mycelium networks in the social world, how a natural process of organic renewal translates to the social world we live in, lies in our commitment to renew and recreate the entire infrastructure of social relationships upon a new foundation of universal harmony and unity achieved through an ongoing process of growth and transformation involving the full participation of the entire human family. Carrying out our mycelial functions in the social world could mean building out vibrant, resilient, inclusive, deeply connected, peaceful communities right where we are.

We are in the early stages of creating the world anew. The old systems are not working. They are easily disrupted. They appear to be beyond repair. Yet, the vision of building lasting peace that has given us hope for eons can only be achieved community by community. Just as organic mycelial networks, this process is globally scalable, evidence based, and the work of the way of unity.

This book is focused on the early stages of an emergent process of individually, collectively, and collaboratively building the foundation and framework for a unitive perspective on recognizing all things as interconnected and Whole.

This calls for a note on formatting. A select few words that are considered sacred terms, like Creator and Source, or a direct representation or expression of the divine, like Changeless, Wholeness, Whole, Universe, and Earth are therefore capitalized. Italics are used to identify writings from the sacred texts of various spiritual traditions. Rather than interrupt the flow of reading, all references can be found at the end in the Endnote section, with quotes and concepts found by their page number and identified by author mentioned or main concept referenced.

Throughout the book, unity is the way, but not the ultimate goal. Unity, rather, is the process used to achieve the preconditions for the greater goal of realizing peace. All the world's ills are but symptoms of the disease of disunity. While conscientiously and unflinchingly following the way of unity is surely the longest and most personally demanding way, it may nevertheless be the only viable way to lasting and sustainable world peace.

The way of unity is presented here as a new path synthesizing and integrating the wisdom of the ages with practical solutions to the needs of today. Unity, as both a process and a plan, is not just a way of talking about peace and identifying foundational principles needed to support an infrastructure for nurturing and maintaining a peaceful world, but a way of acting to build peace step by step through the application of a model of coherence that is already being implemented in thousands of communities worldwide.

INTRODUCTION

A Wholistic Vision of Peace

In the beginning, there was love. In the beginning, there was wholeness. In the beginning, there was unity. In the beginning, there was peace.

Unity – peace in action – is an evolving principle in which ever-expanding circles will eventually merge into one Whole. A unitive world view reflects the understanding that all things in the entirety of existence make up an interdependent whole, a oneness in which everything in the whole is an inseparable part.

Many of the world's spiritual traditions embrace a reality in which all things were created from an original Wholeness, through the treasury of love. The mother of all principles guiding the evolution of the Universe is love-in-action. Unity among and between all created things is the purest expression of this wholeness-in-motion.

From this sacred unity at the beginning of creation to the very early days of humanity's infancy, before divisions arose among neighboring communities, all things existed in relative harmony and balance.

In those earliest days, while there was unity, the First Peoples observed the innate harmony and wholeness around them, integrated this into the unitive narratives that guided their lives and held the community together. This gave them a shared purpose, and maintained their individual and collective well-being, as we know from their wholistic ways of thinking that have survived millennia.

Cosmologist Jude Currivan, in her award-winning film, "A Radical Guide to Reality," confirms that scientific breakthroughs are now discovering and converging with Indigenous and other wisdom teachings to reveal that our entire Universe exists and evolves as a wholly unified entity with everything interrelated and interdependent.

Eventually, as tensions, conflicts, and divisions among the human family became extenuated, a separation from the Creator became evident for many while others were challenged to maintain a wholistic worldview. Harmony and unity became sought after ideals.

Peace on Earth remains a vision shared by most of the world's spiritual traditions. To get to this promised time, we are going through periods of transformation leading us toward unity and wholeness.

Humanity follows developmental stages just like all other life forms. During the transformations of our collective childhood and adolescence, people focused more on their differences. Our stories turned into divisive narratives that supported separation. We have seen growth, expansion, confusion, turmoil, and conflict on greater and greater levels.

This is finally giving way to a dawning consciousness of global integration. Humanity is glimpsing the culmination of its turbulent adolescence and approaching its long-awaited coming of age. The next step in humanity's evolution is becoming clearer.

It is now time to recognize the oneness and wholeness of human relationships. This leap of consciousness depends upon seeing all things as one, where there is no "other" left to exclude from the circle of the human family and the web of life.

Humanity's age of collective maturity, what I am calling the Unitive Age, is upon us. This is the time to come together through a unitive consciousness that brings about and maintains unity on all levels and in all relationships.

BUILDING PEACE ON A SCALE YET TO BE EXPERIENCED

Out of necessity, we have come to the point in our collective evolution where we stand in a unique position to realize and establish unity – and peace – on a global scale.

Evolution – and history – do not occur in a straight line but in a nonlinear, spiral-like process. This leaves divisions and separation overlapping with a transformative process meant to lead us toward greater and greater levels of unity, until the oneness of all things is realized.

The emergence of the Unitive Age is the culmination of an evolutionary flow brought about by periodic leaps of consciousness throughout humanity's history. The origin of this current leap in consciousness may be traced back to a time of widespread discord, division, and inequality in the mid-19th century.

Conditions having reached an unprecedented level of imbalance, disharmony, and oppression created the need for and brought about many unifying human rights initiatives – the end of slavery, the advancement of women's rights, the first Parliament of the World's Religions leading to the interfaith and interspiritual movement, the ongoing civil rights movement, and many other unitive efforts – signaling the dawn of a new consciousness.

Since that time, a focus on unity as the way of healing the ills of an ailing humanity has been more apparent. Unity is the central organizing principle that all progress in the world depends upon. It is the natural outcome of an organic process of restoring seemingly opposing forces to their inherent wholeness.

Unity is the glue maintaining the wholeness-in-motion of all things. At the mystic heart of all sacred traditions – and now at the leading edge of the latest scientific findings – is the knowledge that a hidden thread of wholeness connects and unites all things in existence. Love is its underlying expression in the world. Love is the sacred activism of our time.

INITIAL SIGNS OF AN EMERGING UNITIVE AGE

The Unitive Age – when the unity of the human family will be realized – will not be fully achieved until this wholeness is the basis for all our endeavors. Unity on a global scale, in all social, cultural, and economic spheres, requires living by common foundational values and central organizing principles that bring about the oneness of humanity.

Unity on this widest scale will be achieved progressively. Through a purging process of ups and downs, the Unitive Age will come about gradually after a thorough renewal has resulted in a unitive consciousness being the norm.

We are entering a time when the equality of women and men will be fully realized, when the elimination of the extremes of wealth and poverty will be fully realized, when freedom from all forms of prejudice will be fully realized, when harmony between science and spirituality will be fully realized, and when the protection of nature as a divine trust will be fully realized.

This will be a time when narratives are unitive, when justice is unitive, when education is unitive, when economics is unitive, when all relationships are unitive, and when local, state, national, and global governance is unitive, all endeavors being approached to bring about unity.

These unitive principles, especially a unitive system of global governance, depend upon the undertaking of a dynamic, evolving process of growth and transformation to arrive at a truly inclusive and equitable governing structure for all members of the human family. They are all preconditions to peace, intricately tied together.

The clearest, yet most challenging, way to peace in the world is the way of unity. Sustainable peace is the natural outcome of the entire human family living in harmony and unity with each other and all life. All eight billion of us on this planet are needed to take our place in any of the emerging riverbeds to peace, from local community engagement to global causes, initiatives, and movements. We each have our own unique role to play – and story to tell – at this critical juncture in the ever-unfolding process of bringing about peace on Earth. What is your story of how and why inner and outer peace is important to you?

I was well into my adult life before I realized that my entire life has been a subtle quest to find an elusive peace, both inner and outer. I didn't remember the story my mother told about my birth until there came a time when my own life experience could explain it.

She had related to me when I was quite young her story of being in the hospital giving birth: "The streets were filled with parades of celebration the day you were born."

The celebration was not for me being born, of course, but for the atomic bomb dropped on Hiroshima, turning a world at war into a nuclear village. And, as hoped, into a world at peace. I was born into this conflicted moment of devastation and destruction, pain and loss, as never before experienced, leading to protests of nuclear weapons, that at the same time prompted spontaneous celebrations for the promise of world peace. This created a deep, yet hidden, thread in my life, the impact of which has only gradually become apparent for the inner and outer contradictions it has presented me.

With my life deeply linked to Hiroshima, as a teacher on an around the world Semester at Sea voyage in 2002, I came full circle visiting that sacred spot and sharing a moving moment of connection with our tour guide whose family had survived that fateful day I was born.

Founding One Planet Peace Forum in 2019 also brings me full circle. Working and collaborating with many others in this effort, focusing on peacebuilding and the processes needed for this, has identified some gaps that I'm hopeful this book will fill to some degree in illumining how sustainable world peace will be achieved.

UNITIVE PRINCIPLES THAT FORM PRECONDITIONS TO PEACE

To be realistic, world peace through world unity will be built upon many preconditions in a long, arduous journey to wholeness and true interdependence. Our collective peacebuilding efforts depend upon undertaking a process of implementing the necessary principles in all levels of society, as unity itself is the ultimate precondition to peace.

Three elements are also needed to complete this ongoing dynamic progress: *knowledge* of the unitive principles and their necessity for peace, *volition* to commit to their conscious implementation in the world, and the *action* taken now to carry this out.

Peace on Earth needs a plan, a strategy, for global transformative change that is scalable throughout society, from local to regional to national to global. This book offers a glimpse into how such a plan has been implemented by thousands of communities around the world for over a century.

In addition to being referred to as a principle-based approach, a process, and a methodology, *the way of unity* is also inspired by two models characterizing the essence of the world's spiritual traditions. Detailed in chapter 4, both models end with the 6th century tradition of Islam and need an ongoing narrative brought into alignment with our times.

Offering a possible update and continuation of these models into the present, a consideration of the mid-19th century Bahá'í tradition is proposed, with its method, purpose, and goal of bringing about world peace through world unity as the remedy for a divided humanity. The Bahá'í teachings are my primary inspiration, source of guidance, and point of reference for conveying a perspective on unity at all levels as the way to peace.

This story can only be told effectively by referring directly to the source of those principles, practices, and methodologies that are guiding its effort to undertake social action for building communities of peace connected by a shared vision and purpose, to consciously create a global culture of unity.

I also bring in a variety of perspectives to round out this vital question of our essential oneness by offering adequate references to understand and appreciate the depth, scope, and potential impact in the world of *the way of unity*.

I am proposing a serious consideration of the way of unity as an approach we can all aspire to, and as a method and process we can apply for achieving humanity's long-promised goal of living together in peace on this Earth.

The purpose of this book is to offer a fresh, new perspective on what the world needs most right now – a viable, vision-driven, evidence-based, spiritually grounded, wholistic way to peace. It strives to confirm the power of unitive principles and values to empower and build capacities in individuals and communities needed to sustain long-term progress. It shows that these principles are not just conceptual dreams but rather realities that have already been put into action and are being lived out in communities worldwide through social action initiatives inspired by these unitive principles.

The Way of Unity has three main parts. Part 1 explores the nature of unity and how biological unity mirrors cosmological unity, both vital expressions – and reflections – of a greater unity we seek to realize and establish in all our diverse relationships on Earth. Part 2 explores why unity is the remedy for a divided humanity, how we are individually and collectively evolving toward a time when unitive consciousness will be the norm, what unitive principles are creating the conditions for lasting peace, and how thousands of communities worldwide are implementing them in building social coherence. Part 3 offers reflections on how the way of unity in all spheres of life is the way to peace, and how we can each play our part in contributing to bringing about inner peace, interpersonal peace, and world peace.

The process of peacebuilding consists of achieving a set of evolutionary preconditions, each one an interconnected unitive principle contributing to the infrastructure necessary for building and maintaining peace on Earth. This consists of two simultaneous, progressive processes – one, the widely accepted *emergence and establishment* of a unitive consciousness that will become the groundwork for world unity, and the other, the complete *consolidation* of this unitive consciousness, with the implementation of changes needed based on unitive principles at all levels of society. This will signal the realization of the unity of the human family, will complete the preconditions for the Unitive Age, and will usher in the promised time when peace on Earth will prevail.

This process is already underway in the Bahá'í world community. It is founded upon equitable relationships where resources are not concentrated in the hands of a few, but all have access to in ensuring personal, community, and global well-being and harmony. Even when there is resistance and backlash, this is the world toward which humanity is moving.

The purpose of this book is to illustrate the coherence of these themes:

- Humanity's spiritual evolution, including ancient and modern sacred traditions, consists of one evolutionary process of ebb and flow, as do all other systems of evolution.

- The fulfillment of this singular process, guided by one unifying Source, depends upon unity-in-action by a unified global society working together in harmony and cooperation.

- Only the collective and collaborative effort of all unitive movements of our time working in harmony will lead to the intended outcome of this evolutionary process: peace on Earth.

The way of unity leads to world peace by creating the conditions for realizing the unity of the human family, the final step of a long evolutionary process leading to an age of peace. Yet, this will require unprecedented interfaith, interspiritual, and interdisciplinary dialogue and social discourse in communities worldwide on how humanity's shared spiritual heritage, universal values, and common destiny can address and resolve the many challenges plaguing the world in our time.

PART 1

Understanding Unity

CHAPTER 1

Unity Characterizes the Hidden Wholeness of the Universe

There is an inherent unity to the Universe. All the planets in the sky above have been created to be in perfect alignment with each other. All the cells and organs in the human body have been created to be in perfect alignment with each other. These macro and micro levels were designed to fit perfectly together expressing harmony, balance, and unity.

All things came into being through the supreme attractive force of Love. All of Creation is a sacred wholeness-in-motion, the embodiment of Love-in-action. The cause of the existence of the entire Creation *is* Love-in-action, the force that maintains unity throughout.

From its inception, an archetypal unity pervaded the entire Cosmos. This original wholeness was the essence of the Cosmos, with all beings emerging out of the same elemental substance, bound together by the same power of attraction.

This attractive force of unity manifests coherence between all atoms of the component parts of Creation, from mineral to vegetable to the animal kingdom and beyond, as expressed in the love emanating from the human heart.

From a unitive perspective, with humanity as a prominent figure in the story of Creation's ongoing evolution, within which all things originate from the same source and are therefore one, the most natural goal toward which we can evolve is to reflect the archetypal unity all around us. This is indeed how we grow and develop toward maturity, individually as well as collectively. Our consciousness expands, becomes more inclusive and comprehensive, takes on wider and wider perspectives, and finally grasps the wholeness of all things.

UNITIVE CONSCIOUSNESS AS OUR ARCHETYPAL INHERITANCE

We are born as whole beings into a world characterized by division. The innate unitive potential within us takes much of the maximum human lifetime to fully realize, which explains the perplexing situation of unity being both sought after and always existing.

The wholistic nature of the parts and their whole is not to be lost in its seeming duality. The parts of the whole are never separate from the whole. The very nature of the parts of a whole is that they exist to form and express a greater unity. The parts need not create dualistic, opposing relationships. Nothing already within the whole can form an opposition that cannot be resolved.

There is a natural evolutionary process and direction to our consciousness that moves us toward unity and wholeness, despite the illusory divisions that try to keep us apart. This is why an ongoing process of personal and collective transformations has been created, to facilitate the bringing about of unity on greater and greater levels, ultimately resolving separation and leading us toward the unity of the human family and all living things.

Unity is defined as being whole, undivided, integrated, joined together, in agreement, or at one with someone or something, and usually results from the experience or knowledge of cooperation, accord, and harmony. Unity also implies being included with others, or the felt assurance of belonging. Yet, this refers only to interactions with others and does not account for the inherent unity, or wholeness, of the entire Creation all around us.

In the beginning, when everything was created, unity was the organizing principle. The whole had a quality that went beyond the parts. The meaning of the whole was in the parts and in the harmony of all their relationships. This wholeness became hidden as distinction and differentiation among things became greater and greater. Yet all things, macro and micro, in their essential nature, continued to reflect each other in form, structure, processes, and purpose. In this way, all things corresponded to each other, adding to the ways all things in all of Creation are interconnected, interdependent, and Whole.

This mirroring of all things is known in perennial philosophy as the Hermetic principle, "As above, so below, all things accomplishing the miracles of the One thing." The "One thing" is the Source that created all things to be in harmony.

The organizing principle of Wholeness defines and directs a singular evolutionary impulse in which all things in existence are connected to – and reflected in – each other. This could have been what Plato envisioned when he said, "Perhaps there is a pattern set up in the heavens for one who desires to see it, and having seen it, to find one in himself."

The First Peoples of the Americas could be said to have accessed this unitive consciousness – the awareness of a greater harmony and unity all around and within us – as they observed harmony around them and embedded this understanding in their narratives designed to bring about and maintain unity in their community.

Unitive consciousness, consciousness that understands and contributes to the inherent and intended unity of all things, emanates from and is the primary characteristic of the primal force of Love. It is our archetypal state of consciousness that is always within us. Yet, our greatest challenge in this world may be to bring this innate unitive consciousness forth and into our conscious awareness. This usually happens through personal experiences that unite us with all things.

In unitive consciousness, unity is infinite, ongoing, and all there is. Once achieved, unitive consciousness becomes our desired mode of being, defining our quality of life and connecting us on a deep level with all other things. Humanity's greatest challenge may be to reclaim the perennial wisdom that upholds a vision of the inherent wholeness of a living Universe. This archetype of wholeness embraces all things in loving unity.

This is not a clear, easy path to follow. Yet, it is a healing path. An example of "As above, so below," the stages of human development mirror the cyclical flow of the seasons, each with their core oppositions to resolve and transcend through a process of differentiation and integration in its growth and fulfillment, as discussed in *Global Unitive Healing*.

The integrative nature of all levels of evolution creates identifiable patterns containing a built-in tension to the orderly flow of all things, resulting in pairs of oppositions that require the attractive force of love to maintain the harmony and balance of the whole. We see this in all pairs of so-called opposites, yin and yang, feminine and masculine, light and dark. They are all complementary parts of one whole, co-existing as interdependent systems within the whole, designed to maintain its own Wholeness.

This unity at the base of our understanding of reality provides us with the vivid imagery of a deeply rooted tree from which its trunk has spread many branches. Their unity can be traced from every branch to every root. As Plato imagined, mirroring the pattern "set up in the heavens," a similar pattern exists within us to guide us through a series of challenges, toward the discovery of our own unitive consciousness.

This is a pattern consisting of innate archetypes meant to be drawn out through real life circumstances and experiences. Living out this archetypal pattern, with transformation at its core, brings their purpose and meaning to our consciousness. Understood as a means of merging opposites into a new unbroken, unified whole, many ways of knowing, including mythology, mysticism, ritual, and psychology, share variations on the same three-part pattern leading to a restoration of wholeness.

As explained in my book, *A New Story of Wholeness*, beyond the familiar narrative pattern of beginning – middle – end, this pattern goes to the deeper level of *beginning – muddle – resolution*. The muddle is the crisis, or challenge, appearing as an opportunity, to prepare us for completing our personal transformative journey to wholeness.

The greater purpose of this universal pattern of transformation is to bring the diverse parts of the whole, even opposing forces within the whole, into balance and harmony to re-establish the unity of the undivided wholeness. This ensures the highest level of functioning of the whole.

It is through the experience of this archetypal pattern of transformation embedded within our unconscious that unity is realized as the intended outcome of our quest. This deeper understanding of the nature of unity also assures us that the guiding force of the Whole has created a process specifically intended to maintain unity on all levels of existence.

Just as important, this universal pattern connects personal transformation to collective transformation. Individual transformation carries within it a collective function of contributing to the betterment of the world—what Kabbalists call Tikkun Olam, the work of repairing the world, or restoring the world to wholeness. When we do this work of restoring the world to wholeness, we are peacebuilders. This desire, this calling, comes naturally to all who have consciously experienced this transformative pattern.

The remarkable thing about all this necessary work is that wholeness and unity, the intended outcome of our evolutionary journey, its accompanying awareness, unitive consciousness – *and* peace – are all the time within us, as an archetypal endowment. Unity is the innate force drawing us toward restoring the world to wholeness.

The bond that will most deeply unite human hearts is the perfect unity and love that binds the oneness of reality together. Unity does not occur on its own, but is rather a state that is achieved through a conscious choice and the desire to be in solidarity with others. Unity founded upon love is the greatest strength available to us.

THE COSMOLOGY OF UNITY

Cosmology now confirms Plato's view of patterns "set up in the heavens," illustrating a synchronistic order to all things that can guide us toward harmony, unity, and peace. An open-hearted understanding of the workings of the Universe provides a realization of its essential balance and cooperative nature.

Reframing the implicit chaos of a big bang, cosmologist Jude Currivan says the beginning of the Universe occurred with a fine-tuned and ongoing "big breath" lovingly and purposively giving order to an evolving creation that expanded from a simple state to its current complexity and diversity as a fully "unified and innately sentient entity."

So precise was the creation of existence, she says, that had the relationships between its physical attributes and associated numerical constants they embed been any different "from what they are by only a minute amount, our Universe would never have been able to even exist, let alone go on and evolve."

Implied in this explanation of the balanced wholeness of the Universe is that Creation itself represents the most exact and meticulous expression of unity there is. As Currivan says, the remarkably "unified nature and the extreme order" of its evolutionary impulse reveals "the potency of its unified oneness."

Indeed, of *The Seven Mysteries of Life*, Guy Murchie says the omnipresence of life "denies that any impervious boundary has ever been found between any of the kingdoms or, for that matter, between life and nonlife, which leads inescapably to the conclusion that all rocks and seas and worlds, and consequently the entire Universe, must in some sense be alive."

The Universe as a living superorganism with no borderlines between any of its parts vividly expresses the inherent unity of existence that is manifest at every one of its levels. As difficult as this may be to fathom, this further implies a single unifying agency organizing the deep order of its wholeness.

In 1980, quantum physicist David Bohm envisioned this living, unified, superorganism of all creation as the *holomovement*, or the wholeness-in-motion of the whole Universe. This gives all of creation the properties of inherent balance and a deep sense of order, meaning, and purpose.

Like the wholistic Hermetic principle, "as above, so below," Bohm envisioned the holomovement as consisting of two parallel orders, each one contributing to the balanced, unified flow of evolution. The Implicate Order, at the core of our Universe, is a field of unitive consciousness that creates, orders, and directs our world. He called its manifestation in the material Universe the Explicate Order. The holomovement weaves the two together.

Another way to view these two aspects of reality could be as interconnected, interdependent rivers, one the Changeless order (directed by the Creator) and the other the changing order (with its own free will). The Changeless always flows in balance, harmony, unity, and peace. The changing order, designed to reflect this greater unity and peace, flows on its own, with many twists and turns on its way toward mirroring the Changeless. For many millennia, the changing order has maintained its sovereignty, resisting the inevitable.

The critically important understanding, especially for our time, is that this view of the two mirroring aspects of one reality means that unity and peace are the *natural state* of the Changeless, while the changing order has unity and peace as its *intended outcome*. From an evolutionary perspective, the even more important implication is that there will be a time when the two rivers merge into one unitive reality.

This time will come only when we have chosen to live with a unitive consciousness, applied unitive principles in all our endeavors, and have built out local, regional, national, and international structures for maintaining peaceful relationships.

The unitive patterns necessary for achieving this are within us, just as the acorn contains within it the tree it becomes. We contain within us the DNA that guides our growth and evolution toward our intended unity, wholeness, and peace. This wholistic perspective of the unitive nature of existence is confirmed in the views of many spiritual traditions.

Most recently, from the Bahá'í teachings, 'Abdu'l-Bahá uses a metaphor to express the complementarity (as above, so below) principle:

> "*This endless universe is like the human body, and all its parts are connected one with another, linked together in the utmost perfection... they mutually assist, reinforce, and influence each other.*"

Said a little differently, and even more clearly, he sets this in the context of the greatest unity:

> "*The sign of Divine Unity is present and visible in all things.*"

The Chandogya Upanishads address this inherent unity:

> "*In the beginning was only Being, One without a second. Out of himself he brought forth the cosmos and entered into everything in it. There is nothing that does not come from him.*"

Indigenous wisdom echoes this understanding:

> "*All things are the works of the Great Spirit... the Great Spirit is within all things: the trees, the grasses, the rivers, the mountains, and the four-legged and winged peoples.*"

The Buddha also confirms the mystery of wholeness and unity at the heart of creation:

"As all things originate from one Essence, so they are developing according to one law, and they are destined to one aim."

Such spiritual mysteries abound, yet our understanding of them continues to evolve as human consciousness unfolds toward wholeness. A greater unity is seen as our consciousness recognizes nothing else except divinity in all things.

True reality is the unity that exists in the diversity of its many appearances. Reality is the harmonious balance of – and between – the one and the many, an evolutionary goal, or destination, to be reached, and to be manifested in the world as universal peace.

Humanity is on a journey toward the realization of the divine unity of all things. Our intended unity is realized by walking a path of opposition. As we transcend the seeming pluralities of life in the changing order, we come to recognize a sacred unity, even in the diversity all around us. This is how the changing order merges with the Changeless. Connecting with *"this endless universe"* solidifies our own identity of unity, as we realize our own reflection of the divine in all things around us.

The inherent unity of the entire existence is only fully realized through our own mirroring of this greater unity. We transcend our own perceived limitations when we look upon all things with our own innate unitive consciousness, becoming one with all things as all things become one with us. This is the circle that completes the unity of existence, when all things are perceived as reflections of one and the same underlying spiritual reality.

When the diversity of all things is seen as emanations of divine love, we sense a living solidarity and unity with all things that can transform the world into a paradise. This unitive consciousness is the inner force that consolidates our identity of unity into a profound gratitude for all things, bringing contentment, joy, wonderment, and bewilderment into a harmonious and balanced flow of wholeness. This further results in a fully engaged personality committed to contributing to the betterment of the world.

The true unity beyond all appearance is the sacred unity pervading all of existence. All things mirror the whole. Through the organization of the One unknowable essence, all things consist of this Oneness, undivided. The many, even in their diversity, form a oneness achieved through the vantage point of unitive consciousness.

UNITY-IN-DIVERSITY AND DIVERSITY-IN-UNITY

The wholeness-in-motion of the entire Universe, brought into being by Love-in-action, can also be understood as the archetypal expression of peace. This peace exists within a grand unity-in-diversity of a phenomenal range of components making up all of Creation.

Peace in the changing order, however, where we still struggle to realize the unity of the human family, requires a deep commitment and an ongoing effort to live by the principles that will establish the preconditions needed for the healing of a divided humanity.

A few of these unitive principles are *gender equality*, *economic equity*, *freedom from prejudice of all kinds*, and *unitive justice* locally and globally. These are the necessary preconditions for bringing about the unity of the human family, which is the final condition for world peace.

But love is what most deeply connects the human family. Love is the foundation, framework, and thread weaving lasting unity on this Earth. Yet, unity always consists of parts that are inherently diverse. Each part is needed for carrying out a different function to maintain harmony and balance within the whole.

The greatest challenge we have, the necessity of our time, is realizing this peaceful unity-in-diversity within the human family. Though approaching its collective maturity, humanity has a long way to go toward realizing its full and intended unity-in-diversity.

Our clearest model of how unity-in-diversity is meant to work is within us. The human body itself is an organic expression of the whole maintaining its undivided wholeness, health, and well-being when all is functioning as intended. Throughout its many years of growth and maturation, the human body is a diverse system designed to function as a harmonious whole while growing into its fullness. However, it will not reach its fruition without the harmony and unity required to maintain its wellness.

Starting off as two cells becoming one, then undergoing a process of cell division and differentiation in the womb, our body evolves into perhaps the most complex expression of unity-in-diversity in the natural world, a system where its eventual 30 trillion different cells and some 80 different organs, each with a unique purpose, function together as one.

Each cell and organ perform their vital life-sustaining roles as essential components in a multi-layered unity of purpose working together in harmony and balance to maintain their inherent wholeness-in-motion, or innate state of health.

The health and well-being of the human body and the body of humanity are both contingent upon the unity of every cell and every organ, of all members and communities, within the whole working together as one. Both are whole systems operating according to the primary principle of cooperation ensuring the healthy functioning of the whole.

Unity means inclusion of all the parts and the full cooperation of the entire whole. True unity cannot exist where there is exclusion of any kind, for any reason. This is why humanity achieving its inherent potential of unity-in-diversity – a prerequisite to lasting universal peace – is an ongoing evolutionary process that may well take decades or even centuries of concerted, willful, cooperative social action.

Humanity's long history of prejudice, hatred, genocide, and warfare, all maintaining forced separation and exclusion, illustrates that all of humanity's problems and crises arise from wanting to keep some members of the human family apart from others, based solely on perceived differences of appearance or belief.

This is a process Bahá'u'lláh explains concisely in the imagery of an original wholeness knocked out of balance and needing to be healed: "*Regard the world as the human body which, though at its creation whole and perfect, has been afflicted, through various causes, with grave disorders and maladies.*"

Having fell for eons under the incapable treatment of misguided physicians, "*who gave full reign to their personal desires,*" Bahá'u'lláh goes on to add that the "*remedy,*" "*the mightiest instrument for the healing of all the world is the union of all its peoples.*"

The unitive nature of the Changeless realm is manifest in its Wholeness. With a tendency toward various selfish desires, the challenge of living in this changing world is to mirror the inherent unity of the greater wholeness all around us. Attaining the wholeness of its unity-in-diversity is the remedy for an ailing humanity. Wholeness is experienced in the qualities of harmony, completeness, balance, and unity within and among all its parts.

Being created "*whole and perfect*" means having the innate capacity to develop and evolve into a complex system that is complete on its own and within which all its parts function in balance and harmony as one unified whole.

Utilizing our own collective will, it is completely within humanity's power to choose to function as a unified whole, and realize our greater potential, with all the parts equally vital and essential in carrying out their common purpose. The leap in consciousness required for this depends upon the conscious evolution of all eight billion of us.

This evolution of consciousness toward a greater state of maturity does not occur uniformly but in small pockets that expand and eventually become connected to form a universal awareness that supports and facilitates the good of the whole.

Unitive consciousness is the ground upon which unity-in-diversity on the grandest scale stands. Unity-in-diversity is only complete when all the component parts know from their own experience that they belong within the human family.

Unity-in-diversity can only exist when the plurality of all things is understood, appreciated, and embraced. A culture of peace is built upon the acceptance and interdependence of pluralities, as in *e pluribus unum* – out of many, one. We are long past the time in our collective evolution for this choice to be a luxury; it is now a necessity for any and all exclusion to be reversed and remedied in order that "all our relations" become one family.

The degree of disunity that has too long divided us usually results from someone seeing their own perceived personal interests as more important than the good of the whole. There are still many who are simply not open to engaging in any kind of a mutual process that would restore unity.

Unity is a principle to be attained, a process that unfolds over time, always moving toward the fullest expression of what already exists within a unitive consciousness. The process of unity, always being understood relative to where we are, is like the process of crossing a continuum from division to unity. The farther we are on the division side of the continuum, the greater the disunity. The farther we are on the unity side of the continuum, the greater the unity.

Seeing things through a divided consciousness, all things appear to be separate, as trees in a forest. Viewing the same thing with a unitive consciousness, a greater unity is recognized: all the trees may appear separate above ground yet are known to be united below ground. Connected by a mutually supportive root system and mycelium network of nutrition and communication, the trees of the forest are components of a greater Whole, always in unity.

The distinction of degrees of unity depending on our consciousness may be what 'Abdu'l-Bahá, son and authorized interpreter of Bahá'u'lláh's teachings, describes as the limited unity of *human unity* and the greater unity of *spiritual unity*.

While the common form of unity, the solidarity experienced in most relationships and gatherings, is *human unity*, this is like a body without its fullest animation. *Spiritual unity* comes from a deeper, universal source, emanating from the divine part of us that has access to the very source of unity, and is like *"the spirit animating the body."*

Spiritual unity, 'Abdu'l-Bahá says, *"is a perfect unity. It creates such a condition in mankind that each one will make sacrifices for the other... in behalf of another's good."* This recalls the teachings of Jesus Christ: *"Greater love has no one than this: to lay down one's life for one's friends."*

Spiritual unity takes us to the farthest reaches of the continuum between division and unity. *Human unity* is what is possible utilizing just the powers of our mind. *Spiritual unity* transcends this by tapping into our soul powers that connect us to a greater degree of unity. *Spiritual unity* is a direct reflection of the Changeless, carrying out only what will benefit the whole. This is the most direct route to unity and peace.

Spiritual unity is often what we strive for, without knowing what it looks like or where it comes from. It is what would come natural with a unitive consciousness but is beyond the reach of what can be achieved in practice when a divided consciousness prevails. Any action taken just from a *human unity* perspective is useful, though limited, as this would be a purely practical response, a step on the way to the greater unity that is possible from a *spiritual unity* perspective.

When an individual or community operates from a *human unity* perspective, separation persists. But when operating from a place of *spiritual unity*, all is interconnected and whole. A state of oneness and wholeness pervades all thought and interaction when *spiritual unity* is experienced.

This is where unity of thought and unity of action become possible. The highest degree of unity-in-diversity, when the entire human family is seen, treated, and respected as one, is only possible at the stage of *spiritual unity*, with unitive consciousness.

At this time in humanity's collective evolution, every community seeking unity is made up of individuals with different understandings of what unity consists of and how it is achieved. A common form of disunity that can occur in any intentional, voluntary community is when an individual does not agree with something for some reason. This may often be a difference of understanding becoming enough of a challenge, or test of faith, for the individual that they choose to re-evaluate their association with that community and may even withdraw from it, as it appears to be too much of a conflict of conscience for them.

This separation often results from a misunderstanding or misapplication on the part of one or both parties of what true, spiritual unity requires in a particular circumstance. The outcome of disunity is usually an indication of different stages of consciousness in conflict, or that the practice of consultation has not been utilized to address and resolve these differences of opinion.

The opposite of this can also occur under similar circumstances when an individual chooses to act in violation of a community principle that endangers the well-being of the whole. Most communities, including spiritual and religious communities, have the means to prevent any further splintering or division from occurring by sanctioning the individual, or in some cases suspending the person temporarily or indefinitely. This could also include removing the individual from membership in the community.

Though it may appear ironic in these circumstances that a community can use a mechanism to remove a member to maintain its unity, this is not what it appears to be. If there is a divided consciousness, there will be efforts to challenge or even undermine unity and these cannot be ignored. Those mechanisms are needed safeguards under current circumstances to build and maintain unity.

A community's values, principles, beliefs, and even its boundaries to define what is acceptable within the community, are especially vital to understand and uphold when they are meant to apply to and take in the entire human family. This is exactly where the lesson of the good of the whole being above the good of the individual becomes most vital to learn and put into practice.

Such an inherent mechanism common in religious communities is a *covenant* between the members of the community. A covenant is a binding agreement founded upon commonly accepted principles designed to bring about and maintain unity.

An example, unique in the annals of religious history for its comprehensive nature, is the Bahá'í international community in which the Covenant is designed to "preserve the unity" of the community, "maintain the integrity" of the teachings, and "guarantee the progress" and ensure "the continuation of authority and leadership" by providing provisions for maintaining an administrative order into the future. This is a model that ensures the organic wholeness of the community while sowing the seeds for a just and unified system of governance that can be replicated to a global scale.

The existence of such a covenant certainly does not guarantee that no one will attempt to by-pass, circumvent, or even override it through any individual perceptions of personal imperatives. It does, however, provide a safeguard protecting the unity of the community, ensuring that the community's guiding principles will be preserved, that its clearly defined process for dialogue and learning about their implementation in the world will prevail, and that the entire range of the cultural diversity of the human family will be acknowledged and honored.

Ultimately, the Bahá'í Covenant represents a divine thread connecting humanity with all the forces of sacred unity flowing throughout the Universe, a magnetic and motivating power attracting all to its unifying impulse, guiding us toward deeds of unity-in-action. Most essential here is our own attitude toward such a sacred covenant, as well as the openness on the part of all involved to the purpose and role of spiritual transformation in the process of arriving at and maintaining unity-in-diversity especially, again, when it involves the entire human family.

Perhaps this is why unity-in-diversity, with our collective divided consciousness, is so elusive. We have all the tools needed to resolve differences of disunity, but not all are ready or willing to take the necessary steps to make this happen. Such reconciliation seems impossible in our time because we are still not yet at a point of collective maturity when a unitive consciousness prevails, when *spiritual unity* is more common, and when the vision of complete unity-in-diversity is fully realized.

Yet, as the expression of unitive consciousness is being continually nourished by the profound loving purpose and whole-hearted participation of so many in thousands of communities around the world contributing to the betterment of the whole, our opportunity to usher in the Unitive Age has arrived. The time foretold by many of the world's sacred traditions, when peace on Earth will prevail, when the two riverbeds of the Changeless and changing orders will merge into one reality, is within reach.

This flowering of our unitive consciousness is anticipated in psychology as well. According to developmental psychologist Erik Erikson, we are collectively evolving toward a more mature "wider, more inclusive identity" that will transcend our limited, exclusive, and superiority-oriented collective adolescent identity. This will be a time when individually and collectively we take on "a new and all-human identity" with a wider loyalty, a broadening of affiliations, without giving up any legitimate allegiances, yet subordinating national interests for the greater good of a unified world.

"Unity-in-Diversity" is not just a slogan or a buzz phrase. It's a way of explaining the principle of the oneness of humanity. It honors all the natural and unique forms of diversity that exist within the human family, from every ethnic group to each individual temperament. Diversity in the cultural and personal realms is just as vital and essential to the well-being of humanity as it is in the realm of the human gene pool.

Unity-in-diversity acknowledges a moral responsibility on the grandest scale – through an understanding of our inherent *spiritual unity* – to nurture and safeguard diversity in all its expressions and forms.

If we understood the true nature of the human being, there would be no reason or excuse to exclude anyone from any circle of unity. The forces propelling new forms of global interconnection and interdependence demand that we widen the circle of our belonging to transcend oppositional identities of "us" and "them" that breed mistrust and reinforce competition. Our true nature leaves no excuse to exclude anyone from any circle of unity. Unity-in-diversity rests upon the sacredness of all beings. Basing our actions on this universal identity would contribute significantly to eliminating prejudice, injustice, and inequality.

Unity-in-diversity needs difference, difficulty, and sometimes even discord to help us realize the integration of all its component parts. Unity-in-diversity does not mean uniformity, nor sameness. It does not allow for estrangement or imposed separation. Unity-in-diversity is an underlying principle of our existence, even while things appear separate and distinct. This makes unity-in-diversity an ever-evolving ideal, a process depending upon progress. Sometimes, challenging circumstances, like loss and natural catastrophes, can help bring about a deeper realization of our ultimate connectedness.

There will come a time when the fully realized unity-in-diversity of the entire human family will be complete. This evolutionary destination will be reached when the whole of humanity lives – and acts – with a unitive consciousness in all things we do in this world.

We can assist this process by carrying out our lives helping each other in whatever ways we can, because what is good for the whole is good for one and all. 'Abdu'l-Bahá notes a natural, organic reason for this:

"The diversity in the human family should be the cause of love and harmony, as it is in music where many different notes blend together in the making of a perfect chord."

This is an understanding that can make sense to all members of the human family. Whether it is kids in a neighborhood occupied by gangs, ordinary people on the street with little or no control of anything in their lives, or people who may feel like they have never belonged, everyone has something in their current life situation that connects them to this vision of equality and equity.

All human beings, whatever the reality of their own world, can connect to the universal spiritual principle of the Golden Rule writ large, what all individuals and communities find their highest wish realized in. The purpose of unitive principles is to bring people of all backgrounds, regardless of differences, together as one human family.

This is being carried out now in many communities around the world in neighborhoods of all economic levels and in all living situations. As this universal process continues to reach a critical mass, the natural outcome of *unity-in-diversity* will be *unity-in-belonging*.

Just as peace can only be achieved through unity, unity can only be achieved through diversity. *Unity-in-diversity* requires *diversity-in-unity*, where variations and differences come together as one, in harmony and cooperation to benefit and enrich the whole.

CHAPTER 2

Unity Is the Source *and* Direction of Evolution

We seem to have a disconnect between our up-close view of things and a big-picture perspective. Our world is in the midst of overwhelming crises and calamities, widespread distress and turmoil. Yet from a distance, as we behold the breathtaking beauty of our fragile habitation from outer space, as have many astronauts, it is as if we are glimpsing the divinely created unity of our planet.

Scientists concur that "our planet is sustained by an intricate and mysterious web of interdependency... an overarching unity," within which "all things are connected."

Why is there such a discrepancy from these different viewpoints? Perhaps because most of us are detached from the beauty and wisdom of nature. Our reflection on nature's cycles and patterns might confirm for us that both are true at the same time. Up close, we see the violence and suffering that we can't see from afar. All things here are changing while all things divine are Changeless.

Evolution's trajectory is guiding us toward a re-awakening of our original wholeness to complete a cycle of renewal and fulfill an age-old vision. The way of unity, focusing on the beauty, harmony, and balance of the greater whole, is the way to peace.

THE UNIVERSE IS A MARVEL OF WHOLENESS AND UNITY

Unity is the origin and goal of a Creation formed out of love, since this is the essential nature of its Creator. The attractive force of love binds all things in unity, and for those whose faith tradition embraces a relational Creator, this love ultimately binds us to the divine source of love. As affirmed by Bahá'u'lláh:

> "I loved thy creation, hence I created thee. Wherefore, do thou love Me, that I may name thy name and fill thy soul with the Spirit of life."

This divine love unfolds and reveals the inner mysteries of the Universe without the slightest word being uttered. 'Abdu'l-Bahá adds to this theme:

> "The greatest bestowal of God is love. Love is the source of all the bestowals of God. Until love takes possession of the heart, no other divine bounty can be revealed in it."

In this context, the grandeur and perfection of the entire Creation is a unified wholeness-in-motion. All created things have come into being as a reflection of that love and unity. As we observe and investigate the nature of existence all around us, and grasp the intricacies of all created things, we discover this absolute order on our own. This awareness carries with it an invisible power of divine love that sustains us in all things.

A unitive world view reflects the understanding that all things in all of existence make up an interdependent whole, a oneness in which everything in the whole is an inseparable part, each an expression of the other, all having originated from one source.

In unitive consciousness, reality is one, and all seeming differences, differentiations, and distinctions are imaginary. Even apparent opposites –

like yin and yang, feminine and masculine – are complementary, interrelated halves of the same whole, balancing, integrating, uniting, and transcending their assumed duality. The separation between us and everything else vanishes in unitive consciousness. History's polar tensions are resolved with a higher level of consciousness than that which created them.

This wholistic vision gives us a better understanding and appreciation of a Universe conceived and created in wholeness, unity, and love. Evolution, individually and collectively, begins and ends in wholeness and unity.

Biology mirrors cosmology. An innate peacefulness exists in the organic harmony of the wholeness-in-motion within us and all around us. This cosmology of peace is just as vital to appreciate and honor in peacebuilding as it is in all our interpersonal relationships. Underlying the apparent opposition and tension of the Universe, there is a splendor to behold in its inherent and absolute harmony, unity, and oneness.

EVOLUTION'S TRAJECTORY FULFILLS AN AGE-OLD VISION

Only a wholistic view of creation, in which its evolutionary progress is seen as an organic process of built-in cyclical ups and downs, can explain how a dying, divided order can be replaced with what in our time can best be called the Unitive Age.

The evolutionary flow of Creation is built upon repeating cycles of birth, growth, maturity, decline, and renewal. But the form and duration of each cycle is interdependently determined by the intermingling of human receptivity and resistance to the process.

In social cycles, those benefiting the most from the growth phase tend to remain attached to that while the maturity and decline phases take their course, prolonging the renewal phase. But we can always be assured that while evolution is by no means a straight line, the wholeness of Creation is undeniable, and its cycles inevitably bring about renewal.

This has been true in every age and cycle, with new life that has recreated all things. These cycles of organic renewal are in a state of perpetual motion. When one has run its course, a new cycle is inaugurated.

In the universal regeneration of all things is the greatest of all partnerships, that between the Creator and all created things. This is manifest in the mutual dance of all creatures to the same divinely inspired symphony, the common purpose by which all things advance civilization to its next level of collective evolution. Renewal sustains the order of the universe.

The organic process of decline and renewal is described in the Bahá'í writings as the "arc of descent" and the "arc of ascent." As 'Abdu'l-Bahá describes, "*All creation ... is compelled to obey the law of motion; it must either ascend or descend.*"

The inherent nature of all living things is to grow, develop, and change. The movement and sequence of all things, determined by a universal attractive force, means life itself is motion, a universal, dynamic, ever-flowing energy.

Humanity's own process of development follows these arcs as well, growing and declining, ascending and descending. The special endowment of our spiritual nature provides us with a hidden potential to be realized when we consciously nurture our own arc of ascent, with its built-in centripetal motion toward wholeness and unity.

More poetically, in the world of existence, human beings have been placed at the end of the night of plurality and at the beginning of the day of unity, because we encompass all the degrees of imperfection while potentially possessing all the degrees of perfection.

With an innate potential, *and* the free will to move either towards darkness or light, we also have access to a universal source of assistance meant to guide us toward advancement in spiritual and transcendental realms. Thus do our inherent potentialities become manifest, as we evolve into a complex system that is complete on its own and within which all its parts function in balance and harmony as a unified whole.

This is where we are in this historic moment. After having lived with a consciousness of duality and separation for an extended period, we can now envision that humanity is entering a Unitive Age leading to harmony and peace, built upon a unitive consciousness. Living into a consciousness of wholeness brings about unity within and among us. Living *by* this in all things we encounter is the best guarantee of the realization of our intended unity-in-diversity.

Unitive consciousness is achieved by directly experiencing the wholeness-in-motion in our own lives and in our relationship to all things around us. It is a realization of all things being deeply interconnected and that our inherent potential cannot be fully realized without this experience of the greater wholeness all around us. As Thich Nhat Hanh wrote in *Cultivating the Mind of Love*, "If you really touch one flower deeply, you touch the whole cosmos... When you touch one, you touch many."

Integrating this experience of a greater wholeness becomes the understanding that we most want to pass on to others. This desire to "give back" and "lift up" others in whatever ways we can unites us with humanity's common purpose. This pattern defines a life lived deeply, confirms that all are governed by the same natural law, shows how evolution in all realms is tied together, and why all of Creation is an indivisible wholeness.

As 'Abdu'l-Bahá expressed it, "*The wonderful Law of Attraction, Harmony, and Unity holds together this marvelous Creation.*" This indicates that beyond our own power of positive thoughts attracting us to and connecting us with others there is a unifying force of attraction, what some call Love, within creation itself that is the very cause of life, connecting, harmonizing, and unifying all things in the entire creation. Unity and Love are the twin inseparable forces tying all things together as one.

Humanity's spiritual evolution is directed toward unity, the physical manifestation of wholeness. Its apex of consciousness will be reached when we collectively reflect the perfect harmony, unity, and wholeness already existing in all the diversity of creation. Unity of purpose is central to the evolutionary impulse. As evolution is cyclical, there have been many peaks and valleys along the way. But there has never been a time before this when world unity – and with it, world peace – was within reach.

In the 21st century, as many multi-faith organizations and interfaith seminaries have come into being, as well as many more multi-national collaborations, a threshold has been crossed from which there is no return, revolutionizing relationships among all peoples.

THE TIME FOR UNITY HAS COME

The natural outcome of unity expressed to its fullest extent in the world is peace. Unity and peace are what most characterized the original wholeness-in-motion of the entire creation "in the beginning." A natural cycle has been followed from this beginning to where we are now, having passed through millennia of discord and disruption.

Our time now calls for a focus on unity, to reclaim our wholeness and rebuild a world structured to achieve and maintain harmony and unity in all endeavors. Unity most characterizes the spirit of our age, just as did the Ten Commandments and the Beatitudes for their time.

The way of unity is designed specifically to achieve a wider, deeper unity on a global scale in the social, cultural, and economic spheres by adopting and living by common values and principles that assist us in becoming one human family. Sustainable peace on Earth is the universal Golden Rule writ large, carried out on all relational levels simultaneously.

Lasting peace is much more than an end to war. The next stage of our evolution is a huge leap from where we seem to be today. Only unity within, among, and across all the diverse expressions of life, and in all interpersonal and social relationships, will create the fertile ground needed for sustainable justice, true harmony, and enduring peace.

Our promised destiny requires an evolution of consciousness that will bring us all to the realization of the oneness of all created things, a conscious awareness that then needs to be acted upon. This means identifying and working with the building blocks of an evolving consciousness that can turn this vision of oneness, harmony, cooperation, and unity into the reality we seek.

It is up to us to assist the process of individual and collective evolution toward the goal of peace. Rev. Michael Bernard Beckwith says, "peace is a quality within us," and that world peace is dependent upon tapping into that part of our brain which is loving by nature. This is done by entering what he calls "peace consciousness," which he sees emerging as a new paradigm "on an increasingly global scale."

Developing to its fullest a peace consciousness that is manifested throughout the world in all interactions and relationships at all levels, especially at the global level and through a system of governance, is a long, committed, and focused step-by-step process. It will take some time to nurture, sustain, and guarantee this realization through a deep, embodied understanding of what real unity means.

A seed does not turn into a flower even in its allotted time without the proper conditions and the fulfillment of its inherent developmental stages required for its blossoming. Embedded within its genes is a pattern built upon intended actions leading it toward a reality already within the seed. So it is for the seed of humanity. Our evolution toward our intended future includes carrying out and achieving, even with conditions hindering its progress, certain prerequisite steps and necessary stages.

When peace consciousness – an awareness and mindset that peace is attainable through achieving a sequence of preconditions in the world – is added in regular increments to our normal developmental process, this can ensure and even speed up that process toward our promised destiny, a full flowering and peaceful existence of the human family. There is no distinction to be made between unitive consciousness, peace consciousness, nor universal consciousness, as all clearly indicate the dawn of a great unity.

James O'Dea, who has written about becoming a 21st century peace ambassador, sees the long and convulsive collective evolutionary process culminating in peace as well on its way, with a "blossoming of citizen activism" to go along with our "increasing awareness of our interdependence." Building "a culture of peace comes from a whole-systems perspective, which sees all things as interconnected and influencing each other."

This whole systems perspective, as well as the spirit of this age, is captured by the Universal House of Justice, governing body of the Bahá'í international community, in their 1985 statement *The Promise of World Peace*:

> "The Great Peace towards which people of goodwill throughout the centuries have inclined their hearts, of which seers and poets for countless generations have expressed their vision, and for which from age to age the sacred scriptures... have constantly held the promise, is now at long last within the reach of the nations... World peace is not only possible but inevitable. It is the next stage in the evolution of this planet."

Far from meaning we can sit back and watch this happen, this evolutionary impulse carries a purpose to even these turbulent times, affirms the eventual outcome, renews hope, and—most significantly—raises a call to action.

How we realize this vision of the ages is dependent upon each of us. We must take on our responsibility as proactive midwives assisting this birthing process to bring about a gentle as possible rebirth of the planet. The vision of "peace on Earth" is the goal of evolutionary advancements in an inner and outer process consisting of many interrelated steps, each dependent upon the others, always unfolding toward unity on more inclusive levels.

We are now in the midst of a process guided by two interdependent wings. First, the evolution of a unitive consciousness, built upon the principle of the oneness of humanity and a set of unifying principles supporting this, is preparing individual hearts and minds. Second, the means for collective well-being through an equitable and just system of global organization to foster world unity is the foundation being built out upon which those fully conscious hearts and minds will construct a culture of peace.

Finding our own way to support this evolutionary process through compassionate action every day of our lives, applying the wisdom, practices, and tools we have acquired along our journey, is most vital now. The work of the day, the action most needed to be taken by each of us, is work across boundaries, across differences. Each step taken in our everyday interactions toward anyone different from us in any way is a step toward removing barriers that have been put up between us by others.

Joining hands across differences is the sacred activism needed now. Taking this action will establish a sense of belonging to the community of the whole. This is love in action, the work of a generation that won't happen without us. All the superficial, illusory boundaries and differences between us need to be consciously broken down, dismantled, and crossed so we can experience no separation between any of us, as human beings. We have been made for compassionate, altruistic loving relationships and interactions. This is what humanity's evolution has been guiding us toward.

As Shoghi Effendi, grandson of 'Abdu'l-Bahá and guardian of the Bahá'í Faith (1921 – 1957), shared in this vision prior to World War II, the unity of humanity is "the hallmark of the stage which human society is now approaching... World unity is the goal towards which a harassed humanity is striving. Nation-building has come to an end... A world, growing to maturity, must recognize the oneness and wholeness of human relationships, and establish once for all the machinery that can best incarnate this fundamental principle of its life."

The step in this dynamic process immediately beyond world unity is world peace. Though this is a long journey, and involves many sidesteps, there are forces that continue to move humanity towards an age of peace.

What is notable, and most remarkable, about the coming into existence of the Bahá'í Faith when it did in the mid-19th century is that it did so with the unprecedented principle of the oneness of humanity at the heart of its teachings. Out of this has emerged a dynamic learning process for facilitating personal and collective transformation, calling at the same time for the activation of global citizenship.

This organic process for global renewal lies waiting for close examination as a model that can be applied for bringing to completion humanity's current transformation of consciousness. Spiritual energies have been released to quicken the hearts of humanity and take shape in the world of thoughts and actions.

Achieving world peace is both an inner and outer process that depends upon a long term commitment to an unfolding evolutionary process built upon living by an interconnected, interdependent series of unifying principles that facilitate a sustainable local, national, and international structure supporting global peace.

CHAPTER 3

A Trinity of Unitive Principles

A unitive principle is a principle, or fundamental truth, that brings about and maintains unity. Three essential principles explain the nature of reality and our place, role, and purpose in the Universe. These three principles, central to *the way of unity*, focus on the nature of mysticism, or *wholeness*, the nature of religion, or spiritual *evolution*, and the nature of the world, or how we understand the world through our ever-evolving *consciousness* of it.

What is needed to offset and redirect the divisions throughout society is a reconstruction of these three primary elements of reality to clarify the unitive nature of the reality of all things. A wholistic vision of peace on Earth, which takes the whole into consideration first, rather than any of its parts, requires the adoption of the central organizing principle of the oneness of humanity in both belief and practice before it can be achieved.

Unity of purpose is central to the evolutionary impulse. The Unitive Age we are entering is the climax of a long evolutionary process founded upon a vision of reality as one. A closer look at each of the three components – *wholeness, evolution,* and *consciousness* – that are central to the nature of reality will help support humanity's evolution of consciousness by speeding up the process of bringing about the unitive consciousness we are evolving toward.

THE WHOLENESS PRINCIPLE

All things are tied together by an invisible web of wholeness. This realization is found through the power that Teilhard de Chardin refers to as a "single energy at play in the world."

Reality—the entire Creation and everything in it—is always a unified wholeness-in-motion. This wholistic, nondual principle is at the heart of the world's mystic traditions. Because of this unified organization, consciousness evolves by the pull of this single energy toward this inherent unity. This is also why we innately respond to guiding principles that help us grasp the unity and wholeness of the reality we live in.

The challenge is seeing the whole through its parts, bringing those parts back together as a unified whole. Uniting a divided consciousness into a consciousness of wholeness largely depends upon *experiencing* the wholeness that is always all around us.

As physician and spiritual teacher Deepak Chopra notes, "Wholeness lies beyond any kind of split or fragmentation. Wholeness is everything. It is the One, the All, or Brahman, as it was known in Vedic India. Wholeness offers only the experience of yourself as whole: as pure existence and pure consciousness."

This understanding brings us into the reality of the inherent unity of all things. Consciousness, he says, ties everything in the entire Universe together; it gives light its brightness and color, creates images in our mind's eye, and adds meaning to everything.

Our overarching challenge in healing the false separation which causes all suffering is making a complete shift in how we relate to reality. By focusing on the one reality, which is complete, whole, and unified always, with everything existing within it, we connect ourselves to the peace already inherent in this grand unity all around us.

The innate goal of the evolution of consciousness is to replace the acquired illusion of separation with the undivided Wholeness of the many within the One. This is not easily accomplished, since, for most of us, including mystics and mythic heroes and heroines, the journey from separation to unity and wholeness takes us through a Dark Night of the Soul, a period of intense struggle and purification that precedes a deep transformative experience, as described by St. John of the Cross.

Without the tension and struggle at the heart of this pattern, transformation would not be possible, nor would the renewal that aligns us with a greater whole around us. This process mirrors the cycles of nature, consisting of the familiar *birth-death-rebirth*. Transformation can be understood as a simultaneous process of *destruction* (breaking down) and *construction* (building up), or *disintegration* and *integration*.

Change and transformation in this world is ongoing, inherent to life on both the personal and collective levels, and essential to social progress. Adversity is necessary for transcending duality. The illusion of separation among the parts of the whole creates the opportunity for bringing them back together. Unity is the result of the conscious confrontation of opposing forces, signaling the completion of the process of transformation. Difficulties are meant to be overcome and resolved, because this is what leads us back to wholeness and a deeper unity.

Wholeness, oneness, and unity make contradictions complementary. The goal of the transformation process is the synthesis and union of seeming opposites, as they merge into one whole. Far from being an accident, transformation is essential to ongoing progress.

The *law of opposition* is key to understanding the process of transformation. As Carl Jung puts it, "There is no balance, no system of self-regulation, without opposition... Nothing so promotes the growth of consciousness as this inner confrontation of opposites."

From a wholistic perspective, opposites complement each other as interdependent components of the same whole. They serve the regulative function of maintaining the unity of the whole. Because we live in a dualistic world, the process of merging the opposites through transformation is necessary in our lives to complete our journey toward wholeness. The way to wholeness is clear but not easy.

Jung calls the way to wholeness "a *longissima via* (longest way), not straight but snake-like, a path that unites the opposites... a path whose labyrinthine twists and turns are not lacking in terrors..." This also describes the individuation process, where we meet up with those experiences that cost us an enormous amount of effort. This necessary terrain, with its "fateful detours," and "twists and turns," leads us to and through the understanding that opposition and adversity could not be more meaningful in uniting the opposites they magnify and in guiding us toward wholeness.

Many of the world's wisdom traditions foretell a time of unity, harmony, and peace on Earth. They also indicate, as does Jung, that to get to this promised time, we will need to go through this transformative process leading us to unity and wholeness. This process is well under way now on both the individual and collective levels at the same time, and for a very important reason: this archetypal process affirms that a great transition is unfolding, transforming the way we relate to each other and the world we share.

The current stressful condition in the world is part of an oft-repeated natural phase in an organic process leading irresistibly to the deeper unity of the human family, which has passed through its evolutionary stages of infancy and childhood and is now completing its turbulent adolescence approaching its long-awaited coming of age.

This organic, developmental perspective gives us an abiding sense of hope that engages us with the process we are participating in, to assist it toward its fulfillment. Humanity's current turmoil during this time of transition will pass. A time will come when we live with a common purpose in a just, prosperous, and peaceful world.

Such a systems view, or a wholistic perspective, enables us to see all things as a whole first, as tied together, operating *as a whole*, rather than as separate, competing entities. This lessens the "enormous amount of effort" required when we see our difficulties as separate from what we perceive as best for us. In wholeness, all things are in unity.

The transformation taking place in the journey to wholeness is a two-fold process of purging and reshaping everything we know for the wholeness of all things to be realized. We are at the end of one cycle and the beginning of another, as Archbishop Desmond Tutu noted,

> "The atomized homogenous groups that existed in the past are
> no longer the truth of our world... We must recognize that we are
> part of one group, one family—the human family. Our survival
> depends on it."

The work needed now, focusing on the whole first, creates a foundation based on harmony and cooperation. Living by principles that unite, we see all things as tied together in one reality. This wholistic vision allows us to see a future leading to peace on Earth. The mystery of oneness at the heart of Creation shows that all things are counter-balancing parts of the same unified whole, energized and held together by the same force throughout the Universe, known by many names, among them Love and Grace.

The Wholeness Principle states: *Reality is one, and all of Creation is a whole.* Wholeness, and its inherent unity, is the underlying principle defining reality.

THE EVOLUTION PRINCIPLE

Our understanding of evolution, how things develop according to their inner nature, and whether there is an underlying direction and order to this, unfolds gradually. We understand the world we live in, its movement and direction, by the consciousness we bring to it.

Evolution's path has never been a straight line. It unfolds with built-in ups and downs, spiraling toward renewal. Even with side-steps, or back-sliding, evolution's direction always, eventually, moves toward the good of the whole. Ken Wilber's Integral Theory notes there is a direction to culture in which stages of growth unfold purposefully. He says, "Like all other living systems, we humans are in the process of growing toward our own highest potential." Seeing evolution as "Spirit-in-action," this is "destined to carry all of us straight to the Divine."

Along these lines, a wholistic look at the entirety of cultural evolution, including what is yet to come, can be viewed as a process beginning with early communities being able to achieve unity on a small scale because of their commonly held beliefs and traditions practiced communally that kept them together. They lived with an overarching consciousness of their *oneness* as well as the wholeness of all things around them.

But as societies became more complex and geographically spread out, conflict was experienced, difference and discord became harder to integrate, and a consciousness of *duality* emerged, leading to greater and greater struggle and chaos in society. This shift in consciousness is seen in the many millennia of diverse communities dealing with differences in ways that escalated into systemic practices of segregation, prejudice, oppression, racism, conquest, genocide, and ultimately war.

This wholistic view consists not only of a purposeful direction to social evolution, as Wilber says, toward the Divine, or the good of the whole, but also incorporates a cyclical process that would bring the prevailing order back to unity, but this time on the grandest scale of all. Out of necessity for our collective survival, humanity is now faced with an unprecedented challenge: to establish unity on the global level. This phase of our cultural evolution will require us to reclaim our intended consciousness of *oneness*.

As proposed in my 2017 book, *The Story of Our Time*, the three essential steps in this process include: moving from unity to plurality, and, at some point, back to unity, or *wholeness* followed by *duality* followed by *wholeness*.

Humanity's process of evolution has been leading us to our greatest need— and opportunity—to transcend a prevailing, unsustainable consciousness that divides, creates hierarchies, and endangers our very survival. We face a crisis of consciousness threatening the evolutionary impulse and distorting how we relate to each other and the environment.

A large part of this present crisis goes back a century and three-quarters to the misunderstanding of Charles Darwin's theory of evolution. Social Darwinists turned evolution upside down, focusing only on the survival of the fittest and the competition needed to sustain that. This fueled generations of oppression, which led to segregation, racism, genocide, and most wars.

However, what Darwin had to say about social evolution is largely overlooked and ignored in all of this. In 1859, his groundbreaking *The Origin of Species* brought biological evolution into popular discourse. As a former divinity school student, he also embraced the idea that all life comes from the same source and is part of the great Tree of Life.

His pioneering work opened the door to an awareness that all things evolve, even on the social and cultural level. In this higher-level interactive realm, he places a much greater emphasis on cooperation than competition. In 1871, in *The Descent of Man*, Darwin clearly stated his view of social evolution built upon cooperation at each level:

> "As man advances in civilization, and small tribes are united into larger communities, the simplest reason would tell each individual that he ought to extend his social instincts and sympathies to all members of the same nation, though personally unknown to him. This point being reached, there is only an artificial barrier to prevent his sympathies extending to the men of all nations and races."

Social evolution is directed toward a familiar and long-desired outcome, extending the natural law of cooperation and the Golden Rule from the individual level to the global level. Yet, Darwin's grand vision of social evolution would require a leap of individual consciousness leading to a leap in collective consciousness.

Interestingly, to illustrate how science and spirituality are in harmony, around the same time, the Bahá'í writings reconciled the two prevailing views of evolution and divine creation by first providing a perspective that merged both into a view of evolution explaining how all life evolves gradually, as 'Abdu'l-Bahá explained:

> "... the growth and development of all beings proceeds by gradual degrees. This is the universal and divinely ordained law and the natural order. The seed does not suddenly become the tree; the embryo does not at once become the man... all these grow and develop gradually until they attain the limit of perfection... The law of God is one; the evolution of existence is one; the divine order is one. All beings great and small are subject to one law and one order."

Seeing all things in existence as an interconnected whole, a oneness in which everything in the whole is an inseparable part, provides the needed context from which to draw out the principles that further explain and support all three main components of reality as characterizing the unified wholeness of reality. This perspective of oneness describes a divine order within which all things in existence follow one interconnected process of evolution. This view of reality represents a wholistic view of biological and social evolution in which all things are equally dependent upon one Creator. Evolution is purposeful, leading to larger and larger circles of cooperation.

Such a wholistic view of evolution as determined by universal law, a design which all things follow, is a principle now confirmed by science. A 2016 article in *Science* entitled "What is the Most Astounding Fact about the

Universe?" stated that the most astounding fact about the Universe is that the entire Universe obeys the same fundamental laws of nature.

Social evolution seems to be leading toward larger and larger circles of unity. Social evolution's purpose may be to build cooperation and unity across ever-expanding circles, resulting in deeper and wider unity over time, as seen in the proliferation of international organizations like the United Nations.

The laws of Nature express observable and constant patterns which tie all things together in an indivisible oneness. Embracing everything is an interconnected whole. A wholistic view sees the whole first, and evolution as a single great process encompassing the entire creation. A big picture view of evolution notices its ups and downs and acknowledges that it does not happen in a straight, smooth, linear fashion.

Social evolution includes—and is sustained by—seemingly opposing forces interacting with each other to facilitate a process of transformation that is needed to expand circles of harmony. Opposition is a catalyst to transformation. Adversity is built into the process of evolution. Unity is the outcome of this natural process of restoring those seemingly opposing forces to their wholeness.

The Evolution Principle states: *Evolution is directional, ever moving toward wider circles of unity.* In all realms, all things are tied together, and evolve through a unitive process of growth, maturation, decline, and eventual renewal, always toward an inner potential.

Times of struggle, like we see all over the world now, temporarily impede progress. But they are followed by a transformation of consciousness bringing about periodic growth spurts, as the Parliament of the World's Religions said in their 1993 document, *Towards a Global Ethic*: "Earth cannot be changed for the better unless the *consciousness* of individuals is changed." This expresses an eternal process of transformation that facilitates evolution on both the collective and individual levels. And this is where the consciousness principle takes over.

THE CONSCIOUSNESS PRINCIPLE

Consciousness is the dynamic unfolding of a systematic awareness of ourselves in relation to others and the world, and how we make sense of it all. The consciousness we strive for is all the time innate, embedded in our unconscious mind, as archetypes, waiting to be called forth, to light our way, and to guide us toward the truth we seek.

Achieving our innate potential is the greatest challenge we face as humans. Though subject to the same natural law as all of Creation, the fulfillment of consciousness is not guaranteed; it does not come easily. A conscious effort is required to expand our consciousness, as we explore greater and greater levels of self, society, the mysteries of life, and the wonders of the Universe.

The degree to which we achieve our innate potential depends entirely upon the individual initiative we take to actively investigate reality. While myriad distractions capture our attention and pull us in other directions, mysterious forces are always operating to liberate our consciousness from previously restricted stages and propel it onward in its evolution. Whether we attribute this experience to a divine Source, natural forces, or supernatural phenomena, nothing expands our consciousness more than the proactive, intentional, open-hearted search for truth. Now, more than ever, with so much disinformation everywhere we turn, it is the independent investigation of reality that will unleash our fullest potential, leading to the spiritualization of human consciousness.

Born into a mystery, when we least expect it, that unseen realm all around us seems to sneak up on us and pull at our heartstrings. As Elizabeth Gilbert wrote in *Eat, Pray, Love*, hidden somewhere within us is "the itch, the mad and relentless urge to want to understand the workings of existence." When acknowledged, this can become a single-minded quest nothing can deter us from. Its destination is inner peace, serenity, and a quiet mind.

This is a universal potential, yet its opposite, what the Vedanta and Buddhist teachings call *maya*, our tendency to be swayed by what turns out to be an illusion or a deception, still prevents most of humanity from recognizing reality in its true form. Because we get distracted, we must search for this reality, Gilbert says, as we would for water if our head were on fire. To seek truth is to connect with what is beyond ourselves.

There are built-in cognitive structures that guide our way on this journey, what Jung calls archetypes, or types of inherited behavior, that provide us with our innate potential, giving us more strength and courage every step of the way. These archetypes are really quite remarkable, as Jung explains, "The collective unconscious contains the whole spiritual heritage of humanity's evolution, born anew in the brain structure of every individual."

One of the first of these archetypes that human beings ever experienced is the Call, a theme as old as story itself. It is ubiquitous to all literature and the most common basis for all narrative plots. Classic mythology and fairy tales are framed by the motif of search. All the world's mythic heroes and heroines were the original seekers after truth, leading them down a path they were called, by design, to follow.

The archetype of the Call consists of a quest that separates us from the familiar and signals that our destiny is unfolding. Its purpose is to expand our consciousness, by guiding us along a path leading to the realization of our potential, through transformation and renewal. There may be no more important need of our time than the call to an awakened consciousness. As consciousness evolves, it changes the way we see everything, helping us to grasp the sacred nature of reality.

Guiding our search for truth, as we seek integration, communion, and wholeness, is the most powerful force in the Universe – love. Once the quest of the soul, or life of the spirit, begins, through our discernment of everything we encounter, we come closer to the Creator.

The world's sacred traditions assure us of this: "*Seek and ye shall find…*" (Christian tradition). "*If thou shalt seek the Lord, thou shalt find him…*" (Jewish tradition). "*The nature of the one Reality must be known by one's own clear spiritual perception; it cannot be known through a pundit...*" (Shankara, Hindu Vedanta).

In the Islamic tradition: "*He who approaches near to Me one span, I will approach near to him one cubit...*" And from the Bahá'í tradition, we get an answer to what the seeking will reveal to us: "*If we investigate the religions to discover the principles underlying their foundations, we will find they agree, for the fundamental reality of them is one and not multiple.*"

In our time, the search for truth, the investigation of reality, has been made a primary spiritual principle, and the most important of all human rights. In our quest to expand our consciousness, we find that the goal of our search is the boundless consciousness that unites us with all beings, all of creation, and with divinity itself. We come to realize that the whole is *in* the part, the part is *of* the whole, and both are one, as did William Blake in "Auguries of Innocence:"

To see a world in a grain of sand

And a heaven in a wild flower,

Hold infinity in the palm of your hand

And eternity in a moment.

If we look into the world's sacred traditions, we will find many practices and tools designed to help us experience this realization, whether it is prayer, meditation, deepening in the sacred writings, remembrance of God, yoga, ritual, initiation, whirling dance, vision quest, upholding the highest ethical standards, pilgrimage, seeing with the eye of oneness, service to others, and so many more. The conscious effort of such spiritual practice, to diligently seek and find, removes the blinders from our eyes.

While there are those who hold on to a self-centered consciousness built on the illusion of separation, there are also those who desire to live by a mature consciousness supporting the evolutionary impulse toward wholeness and unity. This dichotomy results in a battle of consciousnesses.

At this moment in time, humanity seems to be in a crisis of consciousness where harsh divisions arise when some choose to place any of the of parts above the good of the whole. Yet, all differences are of gradation rather than irreconcilable.

A unitive consciousness is the natural outcome of fulfilling our individual and collective potential. We are all capable of living into a consciousness of wholeness. The evolution of consciousness occurs within a continuum along which all states of consciousness co-exist in the same whole.

Envisioning consciousness as a continuum allows us to see a borderless movement, or flow, in which all variations of consciousness are interconnected and interdependent, as links of a chain. One side, directed by a *dualistic consciousness*, is characterized by hierarchies, systems of injustice, stereotyping, discrimination, and violence, ending up with genocide and war, and endangering our very survival as a species. This side of the continuum gives us a partial view of reality built upon separation.

The other side of the continuum, directed by a *unitive consciousness*, upholds universal human rights, gender equality, economic equity, and social justice, leading to unity-in-diversity—all interconnected preconditions to peace.

This side of the continuum offers a wholistic view of reality built upon wholeness and unity that culminates in peace. As our consciousness moves along the continuum toward the unitive side, and shifts to seeing the whole first, reality does not change, we do. As we change, we see the same reality differently. Carl Jung explained this process: "The personality desires to evolve out of its unconscious conditions and to experience itself as a whole."

Consciousness is a gift designed to help us see beyond what is evident, delve into the hidden meanings of the obvious, and extract the essence of what we are pondering. We develop a second sight—the power of insight, intuition, and illumination—by using the gift of consciousness to its fullest. Life is a process of moving from an underdeveloped, localized, fragmented consciousness toward a fully developed, universal, boundless, unitive consciousness. The consciousness we live with is our window into reality.

The Consciousness Principle states: *Consciousness is an innate potentiality guiding us toward an awareness of the unitive nature of all things.* The power of our own consciousness, reflecting upon itself, reveals how connected we all are.

Evelyn Underhill captures its universality: "The germ of the transcendent life, the spring of the amazing energy which enables the great mystic to arise to freedom, is latent in all of us, an integral part of our humanity." Our consciousness within is like a magnet attracting us to an all-embracing, all-inclusive unity.

Putting these three primary components of reality together, we have a central organizing principle ensuring the inevitability of the eventual reality of peace on Earth: *Consciousness evolves toward unity and wholeness.* This understanding offers us an abiding hope for the future.

PART 2

Unity Is the Remedy for a Divided Humanity

CHAPTER 4

The Emerging Unitive Age

A ll the leaps in consciousness that have occurred throughout humanity's ongoing spiritual evolution have been leading to this time when the interconnectedness and interdependence of all parts of the whole are becoming evident.

A more widespread unitive worldview has been gradually emerging since the mid-19th century when divisions, discord, and inequities reached an unsustainable level. Those darkest of times yielded a renewal of spiritual verities designed to do something no other sacred tradition had been tasked with doing: bringing the peoples of the world together as one family.

In the Bahá'í teachings lie the antidote to the deep disunity that has long prevailed. It took over a century, after World War II, for the relevance of a wholistic worldview to even be seen as remotely meaningful or possible. Now, eighty years beyond that, a vision of world unity is becoming acknowledged by many as a necessity for humanity's survival. and a potential we are witnessing glimpses of now.

The tumult of the present moment, rather than a cause for despair, is but the earliest sign of our collective coming of age. The impending arrival of a natural phase in an organic process leading irresistibly to the unity of humanity in a single social order embracing the whole Earth gives us a greater reason for hope and optimism than ever before.

This wholistic perspective bestows upon us the daunting yet welcome responsibility of taking on our part in building a peaceful world. The Bahá'í writings assure us that supportive spiritual forces are assisting us in this process, not only giving us the confidence that such an enterprise is possible, but also that the accompanying unifying social structures will be built out.

This assurance lies precisely in a deep understanding of the nature of reality and the purpose of creation. A wholistic, unitive view of evolution includes the expansion of unity beyond existing circles of unity to create new, larger, and more inclusive circles of unity until all eventually merge into one. This view of social evolution as an expansive and unifying process was first seen in the mid-to-late 19th century by both science and spirituality.

Beginning in 1852, the writings of Bahá'u'lláh signaled a leap in humanity's consciousness that moved beyond the prevailing nationalistic perspective to introduce the primary principle of the unity of the human family. He said:

> "The earth is but one country and mankind its citizens... Ye are
> the fruits of one tree, and the leaves of one branch... So powerful is
> the light of unity that it can illuminate the whole earth."

This spiritual perspective was confirmed by science just a couple decades later with Charles Darwin's view of social evolution expressing the principle of collective altruism, or the universal Golden Rule writ large. Although many scientists have emphasized Darwin's theories as supporting a "survival of the fittest" approach in an entirely competitive world, they do so at the risk of missing Darwin's even more significant studies related to "survival of the species" from a social evolution perspective.

Darwin took the natural law of cooperation from the individual level to the collective level, clarifying not only the evolutionary trajectory but also the unitive nature of evolution itself. The underlying harmony of science and spirituality illustrates how cooperation and unity are destined to prevail on greater and greater levels, culminating in world unity. A full-bodied understanding of Darwin's social evolution theory, coupled with the most recent spiritual teachings, serve as important indicators that we are on the threshold of a Unitive Age.

WAYS OF UNDERSTANDING THE CHANGELESS AND THE CHANGING

A look at humanity's spiritual heritage shows that each sacred tradition has provided an important and necessary step along humanity's challenging journey toward maturity. Each tradition has had its unique contribution in this process that is culminating now in the realization of world unity, bringing us within reach of peace on Earth.

As we irresistibly move toward greater and greater levels of cooperation, collaboration, and unity, we are also moving closer to the fullest expression of our innate Wholeness. This is exactly what the Catholic monk and Hindu sanyasi Brother Wayne Teasdale recognized at the turn of this millennium. Brother Wayne identified a new set of historical circumstances making possible a shift in consciousness that is bringing about:

- an interrelatedness of all spiritual traditions
- a new interconnected, universal civilization
- an ecological awareness and sensibility to the natural, organic world
- an emerging unitive consciousness available to all

This shift draws its inspiration from perennial wisdom and moral insights that come from "the heart of all mysticisms." It confirms, at the deepest level, that all things are one. As Brother Wayne put it, "The unitive level of consciousness is both integration with the divine and nondual awareness or perception." With nondual awareness, or a consciousness of the inherent wholeness of all things, there is no separation between any part of that which exists in either divine or secular realms.

This view of the reality of our common heritage is what led Teasdale toward "finding what unites us." He concluded that this interconnectedness is "an inescapable fact of our contemporary world," and "a value that promotes stable global peace."

Teasdale's understanding did not appear out of nowhere. After a century and three-quarters of continually expanding circles of unity, beginning with the end of the transatlantic slave trade, when this phenomenon was first noticeable, an awareness that all of creation is grounded in unitive consciousness has been evolving gradually, unfolding in stages over a few millennia.

An overview of the evolution of humanity's spiritual heritage reveals collective leaps of consciousness throughout our history. As all sacred traditions are within this single evolutionary flow, its trajectory is guided by a divinely inspired force impelling humanity toward its destiny.

In the study of comparative religions, there are two quite different models used to illustrate humanity's collective spiritual evolution and the essence of each tradition, one from Andrew Harvey and the other from Stephen Prothero. Similar to the parable of the blind men and the elephant, because they are looking at the "elephant" of religion from different perspectives, they end up seeing very different things.

The first model approaches the sacred traditions from an esoteric perspective, looking primarily at their Changeless, eternal, or mystic aspects, while the second model takes an exoteric perspective, looking primarily at the changing, social conditions that make up the times that tradition came into. In both models, each sacred tradition has contributed a unique quality, or *way of* approaching the sacred, in this unfolding process.

In the first model, sacred activist Andrew Harvey, notes "a relatedness at the deepest level," and identifies these interrelated "*ways* of approaching the unfathomable mystery" as:

- from the First Peoples traditions, *the way of reverent intimacy with nature*, being humble before the majesty of the Universe
- from ancient Greek mysticism, *the way of beauty*, sensing deeply the splendor of the world
- from Hinduism, *the way of presence*, being in pure awareness of the indivisibility of all things
- from Judaism, *the way of holiness*, seeing the divine as pervading human life
- from Taoism, *the way of the Tao*, living in unimpeded harmony with all things
- from Buddhism, *the way of clarity*, waking up to the pure freedom of unconditional compassion in the world
- from Christianity, *the way of love in action*, becoming transformed to reflect the Creator's unwavering love for the entire creation; and,
- from Islam, *the way of passion*, knowing the peace that comes in surrendering one's entire being to the Unknowable

Continuing this thread of the essence of the world's spiritual traditions into the present, I would add *the way of unity*, to represent the approach and purpose of the Bahá'í tradition, emerging out of the division, discord, and inequality pervading Persia in the mid-19th century.

Bahá'u'lláh renewed and updated the spiritual teachings that have guided people all over the world throughout the ages with a comprehensive revelation focusing on the essence of the nature of Creation itself and on precisely what will heal the ills of a divided humanity:

> "*The tabernacle of unity hath been raised; regard ye not one another as strangers. Ye are the fruits of one tree, and the leaves of one branch.*"

Addressing further the long-standing division between the human family, he adds:

"Turn your faces from the darkness of estrangement to the effulgent light of the daystar of unity."

The ongoing evolutionary flow of spiritual cycles ensures the forward movement of progress while bringing about periodic leaps of consciousness. The evolving thread of different *ways* of approaching the unfathomable mystery had reached a formidable block in the mid-19th century, and a renewal of spiritual verities was needed.

The way of unity is preparing the world for a universal spirituality. In this culminating stage of a long evolutionary process, the greatest challenge of our time is to fully reflect the wholeness-in-motion around us and the unity-in-diversity amongst us in our everyday interactions and relationships. Unity in all realms of being and doing is the overarching, all-encompassing principle that all progress in the world depends upon. Unity is the natural outcome of an organic process of restoring seemingly opposing forces to their inherent wholeness. This is what will result in a global spiritual interdependence and the healing of an ailing humanity.

As made clear by 'Abdu'l-Bahá:

"Unity is necessary to existence. Love is the very cause of life; on the other hand, separation brings death. In the world of material creation, all things owe their actual life to unity."

Following this spiritual regeneration in the mid-19th century, advances in all realms of human rights have occurred toward unifying the human family. Humanity is now approaching a time promised by the sacred traditions, when the world will be restored to wholeness, bringing about a complete renewal on a global scale.

The second model, from religious scholar Stephen Prothero, conceptualizes the contributions of each tradition to humanity's spiritual heritage from a social, or exoteric, viewpoint, while framing them in the context of a "problem" to be addressed and its "solution."

Prothero's model responds to the prevailing "human predicament," with each tradition offering a resolution to the social problem of its time through their teachings and practices. The traditions he covers, with their problem/solution dynamic, are:

- for Hinduism, *the way of devotion*, the problem is the perpetual cycle of birth, death, and rebirth, and the solution is liberation
- for Judaism, *the way of exile and return*, the problem is exile, and the solution is return to God
- for Confucianism, *the way of propriety*, the problem is chaos, and the solution is social order
- for Daoism, *the way of flourishing*, the problem is lifelessness, and the solution is flourishing
- for Buddhism, *the way of awakening*, the problem is suffering, and the solution is awakening
- for Christianity, *the way of salvation*, the problem is sin, and the solution is salvation
- for Islam, *the way of submission*, the problem is pride, and the solution is submission.

Again, I'd like to augment this model by adding *the way of unity* to capture the clarity of the Bahá'í writings on the pre-eminent problem of our time: the separation, disunity, and estrangement of the human family, with the solution being unity.

Bahá'u'lláh applied and expanded an illness/cure, or problem/solution, model by clarifying that needs do change with the times as well as the remedy needed:

> "*The All-Knowing Physician has His finger on the pulse*" of humankind. "*He perceives the disease, and prescribes, in His unerring wisdom, the remedy. Every age hath its own problem, and every soul its particular aspiration. The remedy the world needs in its present-day afflictions can never be the same as that*

which a subsequent age may require. Be anxiously concerned with the needs of the age ye live in, and center your deliberations on its exigencies and requirements."

The foremost concern of our time is healing the divide between the peoples of the world. *"The distinguishing feature"* of *the way of unity* in this context, in offering a remedy *and* a technique or teachings, precepts, and practices, is that it provides the means for removing *"the cause of strife, of malice and mischief"* by laying down *"the essential prerequisites of concord, of understanding, of complete and enduring unity."*

The disease of disunity creates and exacerbates symptoms ranging from family disfunction to community conflict to racism to national strife and international warfare. It is only the light of unity that can dispel the darkness of its despair. Whatever perspective we look at the world's sacred traditions from, whether it's the esoteric or exoteric view, the mystical or the social, in both cases it is *the way of unity* that best captures the essence of the Changeless and the changing needs of our time.

THE UNITIVE NATURE OF HUMANITY'S SPIRITUAL EVOLUTION

Wholeness, and its inherent unity, is the underlying principle defining reality and what we are evolving toward. Humanity's age of maturity will be characterized by cooperation, harmony, and unity. This represents a distinct and long-awaited epoch in humanity's history. We are already beginning to get glimpses of this shift toward more collaborative ways.

The *way of unity* is ushering in the Unitive Age. All great "ages" have taken centuries to play out through a transformative cyclical process that defines evolution and human history. It is through these cycles that the fullest expression of their potential is reached.

When philosopher Karl Jaspers coined the term "Axial Age" in 1948 to refer to the broad universal changes in religious and philosophical thought from the 8ᵗʰ to 3ʳᵈ centuries BCE, he saw it not only as the time when the spiritual foundations of humanity were laid, but also as "a base for the unity of humankind." This promised time is now approaching.

We are at a time now when we can begin to visualize the dawning of this unity. We are in the longed-for position, with all the tools and unitive principles at hand, to manifest this unity-in-diversity in the world. For us, the realization of the unity of the human family is a necessity for our very survival *as well as* for sustainable peace in the world.

While each "age" takes in a centuries-long process to reach its fulfillment, we are now witnessing the necessary full and complete yet gradual breakdown of the conditions of the previous age while at the same time seeing new conditions being put in place for the emergence of the Unitive Age.

This is happening even as there is still widespread disunity in the world. Our emerging Unitive Age will not achieve or maintain harmony and unity until this wholeness is the basis for all our endeavors. Unity on a global scale – in all social, cultural, and economic spheres – means living by common values and principles that bring about the oneness of humanity.

What still needs to be acknowledged is that there is but one origin and direction of humanity's spiritual heritage. This would be a compelling, evolving story showing not only a deep interconnectedness among all the sacred traditions but also a common source and purpose to them all that has brought us to this propitious moment, approaching peace on Earth.

A consciousness of this interconnectedness has been evident in a continuous line of spiritual teachers throughout our long evolution. The release of spiritual energies, essential in our past and future alike, is always needed to transform human hearts, shape new social institutions, and expand circles of unity.

The search for transcendent meaning most characterizes us as *Homo sapiens*. Our quest for understanding ultimate concerns is a process by which the truth we seek is revealed little by little, progressively and gradually over time, all the while coming from the same Source. It is in this context that we can best understand our evolving spiritual heritage.

A unitive view of spirituality requires re-visioning the way we've understood our collective relationship to the Sacred. Historically, humanity has viewed religion through the lens of multiple, separate, and independent knowledge systems. However, if reality is one, and evolution is a unitive process of all things unfolding according to one force, then, through this unitive lens, we could also envision religion as one evolving knowledge system, though with many branches.

This would resolve the long-standing paradox in the study of religion of having one Creator with so many religions. It is a view that can be found to be verified in many scriptures of sacred wisdom, as many Prophets have accepted those before them and acknowledged that there would be others to follow.

The continuing nature of divine Revelation has been expressed by Krishna, a principal deity of Hinduism, as:

"*Whenever dharma declines and the purpose of life is forgotten,
I manifest myself on earth. I am born in every age to protect the
good, to destroy evil, and to reestablish dharma.*"

In the Hebrew Bible is written:

"*And thou shalt be called by a new name, which the mouth of the
Lord shall name.*"

And Buddha taught that Brahman is continually manifested in the world:

"*I am not the first Buddha who came upon earth, nor shall I be the
last. In due time another Buddha will arise in the world, a Holy
One, a supremely enlightened One... He will reveal to you the same
eternal truths... such as I now proclaim.*"

Jesus of Nazareth also took an eternal perspective on the progressive nature of revelation:

"I have many things to tell you, but ye cannot bear them now...
when the Spirit of truth is come, he will guide you into all truth...
and he will show you things to come."

Muhammad also looked ahead to the *"day unto which mankind shall be gathered together"* as *"a time appointed,"* adding, *"To each age its Book."*

To this interconnected line can be added Bahá'u'lláh, who in this age reaffirmed the progressive nature of religion. He acknowledged and told the story of the prophets from Abraham, the *"Friend of God,"* to Moses, *"He Who held converse with God,"* to *"the Manifestation of Jesus,"* and to *"the Day-star of Muhammad,"* all *"Manifestations of Holiness,"* as *"the Prophets and chosen Ones of God."*

They, and the other major prophets (including Krishna, Zoroaster, and Buddha), are all *"Treasuries of divine knowledge,"* each a clearly polished mirror reflecting the light of one sun, each central to the Creator's promise to never leave humanity alone.

Wholistically, we no longer need to separate the world's religions from each other; they can be seen as joined in purpose and origin. The story of the prophets is the story of the Creator providing a never-ending book of guidance to humanity, chapter by chapter.

Humanity's spiritual evolution can be re-envisioned as built upon a dynamic, interconnected sequence of divine messengers who manifest the attributes of an inaccessible Divinity and convey divinely inspired Revelations that guide and educate humanity from age to age. As 'Abdu'l-Bahá has put it, *"Religion is the outer expression of divine reality. Therefore, it must be living, vitalized, moving, and progressive."*

With this perspective, we can see that Indigenous spiritual leaders and the founders of the world's major religions (including Abraham, Krishna, Zoroaster, Buddha, Jesus, Muhammad, and Bahá'u'lláh) each brought messages representing a stage in the limitless unfolding of a single reality which has gradually yet purposively awakened humanity to its innate transcendent nature, empowering us to serve the evolutionary process itself, and guiding us toward a unitive consciousness. As one universal law governs the entire creation and its evolution, the same law would govern the evolution of religion.

After the late-19th century work of Darwin, when evolution entered popular discourse, we now understand that everything evolves: life, society, cultures, civilization, and especially science and technology. We can also add to this list our sacred knowledge systems that guide our relationship to the Creator. How different would our sense of meaning and purpose in life be if we saw religion as part of evolution?

Re-visioning religion for our time would mean recognizing religion as one. Rather than religions having popped up here and there, now and then, at the deepest level religion has taught us how to love on greater and greater levels over time. The evolution of religion rests upon the progressive unfolding of a single reality, toward a common destiny.

Referring to his own revelation and all those preceding and following, Bahá'u'lláh said:

> "This is the changeless faith of God, eternal in the past, eternal in the future."

This concept, crucial to understanding the evolution of religion, is eloquently, yet mysteriously, expressed in the Gospel of John (1:1-10):

> "In the beginning was the Word… and the Word was God… There was a man sent from God… He was not that Light, but he was sent to bear witness of that Light. He was in the world, and the world was made by him."

In these trying times, we cannot afford to lose sight of the many individual and social benefits humanity has reaped from religion. Within the world's religious and spiritual traditions lie the seeds for rebuilding a tired and worn world.

The Universal House of Justice asserts in *The Promise of World Peace* that "No serious attempt to set human affairs aright, to achieve world peace, can ignore religion." This is because humanity's most profound achievements have all been made possible by what we might call the spiritual impulse, or the endowments in what is known as the human spirit that have enabled humanity to build civilizations and to prosper.

The purpose of humanity's transcendent nature, and the heights this can lead to, is to create bonds of unity among all peoples and establish the foundations of love and fellowship necessary to build peace in the world.

Peacebuilding depends upon the unifying nature of humanity's innate tendency toward cooperation, harmony, and goodwill being expressed in its fullest. The moral and ethic foundation of the universal Golden Rule, of acting toward others as we would like to be acted toward, is the primary impetus for building peace in the world.

According to Samuel P. Harrington, the author of *The Clash of Civilizations and the Remaking of World Order*, "Whatever the degree to which they divided humankind, the world's major religions… share key values in common. If humans are ever to develop a universal civilization, it will emerge gradually through the exploration and expansion of these commonalities."

The Parliament of the World's Religions 1993 declaration "Towards a Global Ethic" states that this "already exists within the religious teachings of the world," and that a "new consciousness of ethical responsibility" is evident in many areas of life. They note that the special task of religions is to pass these timelss, universal values on to future generations.

This global ethic is essential to achieve a peaceful, unified world. All the human, social, and natural sciences confirm today that we are but one human species, albeit infinitely varied in the secondary aspects of life.

Leading thinkers today recognize unity as the fundamental principle of the global age. Ervin Laszlo states that humankind "needs a star to follow," or "standards by which we can direct our steps." These come from "the great ideals of the world religions," he says, from the Christian vision of universal brotherhood/sisterhood, Judaism's vision of all the families of the Earth being blessed, Islam's universal vision of an ultimate community of God, man, and nature, the Hindu vision of matter as the outward manifestation of spirit attuned to cosmic harmony, the Buddhist vision of all reality as interdependent, and the Confucian vision of supreme harmony in ordered human relationships.

Laszlo continues, "The essential goal of the Bahá'í Faith is to achieve a vision that is world-embracing and could lead to the unity of humankind and the establishment of a world civilization based on peace and justice." These "are perennial ideals based on universally human values," and need to be rediscovered to guide our steps.

This leads us to hypothesize that the direction of humanity's spiritual evolution is toward a *unitive spirituality*, or a spirituality that brings about unity. A unitive spirituality no longer sees religion as separate, discrete systems but rather as interconnected strands of the spiritual evolution of humanity. Though each tradition has developed in different times and places, all are branches of one tree, with a common trunk and root system that supports the entire tree throughout its seasons of renewal.

A unitive spirituality also sees the variety of religious expression in the world as having the same source and sharing a unity of purpose. A continually unfolding message is one and the same; timeless spiritual teachings and social teachings appropriate to their time, all facets of one truth illuminating one reality.

By exploring this understanding, interreligious dialogue could benefit considerably from whatever insights emerge from such a collective and open sharing. This effort would certainly enrich the search for peace. The contribution that spirituality has made toward peacebuilding and providing an ethical and moral framework for humanity to live in harmony and unity cannot be overstated.

The universal values and principles found in many of the world's spiritual traditions have been catalysts for bringing humanity together in wider and wider circles of unity. Though religious fanaticism still fuels conflicts, spiritual-based traditions embody a peace-inducing potential to play a positive role in the quest for peace. This potential must be tapped in working to bring about unity and peace. Interreligious dialogue toward peace is fundamental to the process of reconciliation and returning to wholeness upon which humanity must embark for its collective good.

Humanity's spiritual heritage is unitive beyond perceived boundaries. Its perennial wisdom aligns with the latest findings of quantum physics. This convergence signals our imminent entrance into the Unitive Age. Yet a great deal of hard work is needed to achieve the basic human rights and universal social justice required to manifest this unity in the world.

UNITIVE CONSCIOUSNESS WILL BE THE NORM IN THE UNITIVE AGE

The Unitive Age is the culmination of humanity's long evolution. Its coming of age will be characterized by a unitive consciousness, or a consciousness that brings about unity, being the norm, the standard by which all things are seen and responded to in all personal, social, and global relationships.

This Age will lead to a time of the fulfillment of sacred prophesies of a time when peace on Earth will prevail. Unity of thought and action will be the basis of all interactions and endeavors. Though a divided consciousness currently determines how the world runs and carries out its affairs, having for too long led to conflict, prejudice, oppression, racism, and all wars, in the future, when the Unitive Age is in its fullest bloom, these will all be aberrations of an immature humanity trying to make its way beyond the limited knowledge available.

Up until five centuries ago, in the secular Western world, it was believed that there was nothing beyond the boundary of the known world at the time.

This was represented by the motto "*non plus ultra*," or nothing further beyond. But after Christopher Columbus ventured beyond the Strait of Gibraltar to find the so-called "New World," that motto was transformed to "*plus ultra*" (further beyond) and became a metaphor suggesting striving for excellence.

The relevance of this for us today is that striving for excellence is just as much about striving beyond whatever limits us. There certainly is something beyond the known consciousness of division, separation, and finiteness. And that is a unitive consciousness in which all of existence is an undivided wholeness.

Humanity is at that transformative moment when we are ready to replace our worn-out motto. Striving for a higher, unitive consciousness is the "*plus ultra*" of our time. Living into a unitive consciousness, and merging with the greater wholeness all around us, is the quest of our time. This requires a conscious, open-minded independent investigation of reality, or a search for truth that takes us into the embrace of wholeness.

A unitive consciousness, or a consciousness that brings about unity, has been available since the earliest times, when many First Peoples lived in harmony with the natural world around them and created unitive narratives (narratives that bring about unity) to sustain this living worldview.

With the symbolic fall from wholeness in the Garden of Eden, when humanity metaphorically became comfortable with the illusion of separation, a divided consciousness gradually became the norm, while a unitive consciousness was lived by only within the world's mystic traditions, ritual processes, core patterns of myths, and sporadically through individual experiences of wholeness.

Today, we understand better that unitive consciousness derives from ancient wisdom and that leading edge science is now recognizing this as well. We see this understanding as well in Ralph Waldo Emerson's Oversoul, in Richard Bucke's *Cosmic Consciousness*, in Aldous Huxley's *The Perennial Philosophy*, and in David Bohm's Implicate Order, or undivided wholeness.

It succinctly describes a consciousness that emerges from unity, maintains unity, and seeks only to bring about unity on all levels and realms throughout the entire creation.

Direct experience of this wholeness in our own lives brings us to this unitive consciousness. This experiential understanding brings with it a recognition that all things are deeply interconnected, and that our inherent potential cannot be fully realized without the experience of this wholeness-in-motion. Its resultant *unity-in-belonging* is what we will most want to pass on to others.

As more and more people discover the wholeness all around us, and live into a unitive consciousness, this will replace a long domineering divided consciousness as the social norm in all cultures and societies; it will become the basis for the common way of seeing all things and living in right relationship with all things.

CHAPTER 5

Peace Is the Natural Outcome of the Way of Unity

There is a special potency latent in this dawning Unitive Age. This is the promised day yearned for since ancient times, the day unlike any other. What pulls most at *our* heartstrings is the peace and tranquility of all beings.

It is the day of vision. Blazing this new path requires meaningful conversations that put unity as the focus, the way, and the goal in building out a social infrastructure that can support and sustain the flourishing of the complete expression of unity-in-diversity.

It is the time of realizing the Golden Rule writ large. This ethic is at the heart of all secular and spiritually based peacebuilding approaches. This deeper feeling of respect for and compassion between people makes it clear that peace has been the universal goal of all:

- From the Hindu tradition, "*The noble minded dedicate themselves to the promotion of peace and happiness of others – even those who injure them.*"

- From the Jewish tradition, "*Seek peace and pursue it... to the counsellors of peace is joy.*"

- From the Buddhist tradition, "*He heals divisions, and cements friendships; seeking peace, and ensuring it, for in peace is his delight, and his words are ever the words of a peacemaker.*"
- From the Christian tradition, "*Blessed are the peacemakers, for they shall be called the children of God.*"
- And from the Muslim tradition, "*Shall I tell you what acts are better than fasting, charity, and prayers? Making peace between enemies are such acts; for enmity and malice tear up the heavenly rewards by the roots.*"

As H.H. the 14th Dalai Lama has said:

"Today's world requires us to accept the oneness of humanity. In the past, isolated communities could afford to think of one another as fundamentally separate. Some could even exist in total isolation. But nowadays, whatever happens in one region eventually affects many other areas… Peaceful living is about trusting those on whom we depend and caring for those who depend on us… The more we care for the happiness of others, the greater is our own sense of well-being."

In our time, when the entire planet is but one home, one intertwined community, the missing conditions for uniting the human family are clear. The way of unity is a laborious process of adopting a universal global orientation that addresses all the current social, political, cultural, economic, moral, and spiritual problems as one interconnected, interdependent challenge facing humanity.

The way of unity builds wider, deeper, and stronger ever-expanding circles of unity by breaking down the barriers that keep the human family separate from one another. Many practical, on-the-ground embodiments of unitive consciousness-in-action are needed to make an impactful difference in everyday lives and relationships of all people everywhere.

An early form capturing such unitive action and acknowledging humanity's progression through the stages of unity of family, of tribe, of city-state, and nation, and its preparation for world unity, is seen in the image of *Candles of Unity* used by 'Abdu'l-Bahá at the beginning of the 20th century. Expounding upon the teachings of Bahá'u'lláh, his seven *Candles of Unity* illustrate the power of unity as it advances all forms of human endeavor, while transforming the world:

- Unity of Thought, in world undertakings of vast programs for development, aid, human rights, and the environment
- Unity in the Political Realm, sovereign states collaborating through international organizations, such as the United Nations
- Unity in Freedom, the end of colonialism and the rise of movements around the world for equality and self-determination
- Unity in Religion, uniting all people in the recognition of humanity's common spiritual heritage
- Unity of Nations, uniting all people in the acceptance that, however wide the differences and dire the challenges, all are inhabitants of one planetary home
- Unity of Races, uniting all in the foundational principle of the oneness of humanity
- Unity of Language, uniting all in the choice of a common auxiliary language, enabling all people to converse freely

These seven *Candles of Unity* are variations on the nine unitive principles described below and began to be implemented in the world during the 20th century. As barriers to their light illumining the whole world continue to fade, their influence will become more evident.

NINE UNITIVE PRINCIPLES AS PRECONDITIONS FOR PEACE

As the Unitive Age further unfolds, and the interconnectedness of our global village becomes more apparent, we'll see the unity of the human family as a looming reality. Although the 24-hour news feed may seem to indicate otherwise, never in the history of the planet has this been more possible.

Previously, harmony and unity have only been established on smaller scales, at family, community, city, and national levels, when natural (geographic) as well as man-made (restrictive boundary) divisions kept humanity apart. In our time, means of instant communication and ease of travel have merged the continents of the Earth into one, making the unity of the entire human family much more reasonable to envision.

But this central theme – the oneness of humanity – is only going to be made possible when humanity embraces a set of unitive principles that will support and sustain such a new level of unity-in-diversity in our time. These nine unitive principles make up the foundation of a new paradigm that is already guiding us toward a consciousness of wholeness. They are inspired by the late 19th century teachings of the Bahá'í Faith, which are inherently scalable to bring about unity locally, regionally, and globally, culminating in world peace.

1. Unitive Consciousness
2. Unitive Education
3. Unitive Relationships
4. Unitive Justice
5. Unitive Economics
6. Unitive Global Development
7. Unitive Language
8. Unitive Narratives
9. Unitive Global Governance

We'll explore each of these principles briefly and add a few necessary developments that will make the Unitive Age a global reality.

1. Unitive Consciousness

In unitive consciousness, reality is one, and all things in the entire Universe are viewed in their wholeness and unity through their common source. As a universal consciousness that brings about unity, unitive consciousness is a precondition for the realization of the unity of the human family and of world peace.

Utilizing our innate capacities, we can arrive at a unitive consciousness by independently investigating reality. Through this process of the unfettered search for truth, limited, divisive, and exclusive forms of consciousness are encountered, transcended, and let go of, in favor of the consciousness that brings about unity.

Unitive consciousness is a potentiality in all people waiting to be drawn out and activated, wholly dependent upon our initiative to act and reflect upon all that we engage with. Only when we see beyond the seen do we understand beyond the understood. Becoming complacent with what we know can be a deterrent to fully developing all that we are inherently capable of. Always knowing there is more to know will keep us on the trajectory toward a unitive consciousness.

Consciousness expands as greater and greater levels of awareness and comprehension of self, society, the mysteries of life, and the wonders of the Universe are explored to their fullest, giving us a greater sense of their place in the greater whole. Unitive consciousness is the end goal of the consciousness continuum. Anyone open to something new, to the unknown, or to whatever can lead us toward the truth we seek, will make their way through challenge after challenge, typically responding to what comes along first from a divided consciousness, until, at some point, we are able to shift to see all things as they are intended to be seen, whole and complete. This is when we know we are approaching what we have been seeking, that this is where we belong, and that this is the knowing we want to pass on to others.

Multiple paths lay out the ways to a unitive consciousness. From the mystic way to the ritual process to the monomyth and more, a unitive pattern exists illustrating the process of transformation that brings about a unitive understanding. These are explained in my 2022 book, *A New Story of Wholeness*. At each step of the way, guidance becomes available to assist us in the direction we are headed.

Even for those who feel held in place by oppression, persecution, or some other injustice, all that is really needed to turn wherever we are into an opportunity, and begin this process of transformation, is an openness to the unknown, a curiosity for the mysteries of life, and detachment from those things, and views, we think we need to hold on to. This is why we are a planet of immigrants. The ability to pursue truth on our own, no longer following others blindly or uncritically, leads us to unexpected jewels of insight into the nature of reality.

And even though this may involve an outer quest, it is mostly an inner quest that can eliminate one of the main sources of conflict in the world today – the inability or unwillingness to distinguish truth from falsehood, right from wrong. We have an inherent urge to understand reality. A fundamental obligation of our humanity, of our sacred nature, is to seek to fulfill the capacity of consciousness within us and the responsibility to others this brings with it.

The prevalence of fake news in our time makes seeking a unitive consciousness one of the only things that can save us from being gaslighted into a make-believe realm of concoction. Our pursuit of truth leads us to the understanding that truth is one, as many perennial wisdom traditions confirm.

Both chosen and chance life experiences are meant to lead us from an undeveloped, localized, fragmented consciousness toward a fully developed universal consciousness that unites us with the sacred unity of all creation. But only when our actions and effort become conscious can the potential of unitive consciousness be realized.

Unitive consciousness makes possible unity of thought in the world, also understood as a "unity of conscience," all three being intricately tied to how a process of peace will unfold involving a series of local and global interrelated initiatives that are necessary to create sustainable universal peace.

In the early 1900s, 'Abdu'l-Bahá noted that world leaders have mostly conceived of peace in purely political terms, which has proven temporary at best. He identified the essential missing ingredient to achieving a lasting peace, clarifying that it needs to be built on a broader consensus of values and principles: "*At present universal peace is a matter of great importance, but unity of conscience is essential, so that the foundation of this matter may become secure.*"

This use of "unity of conscience" on the collective level depends upon two interrelated dimensions involving knowledge, moral social responsibility, or will, and action. First, "unity of conscience" requires the acquisition of knowledge needed to understand "the complex, multifaceted organic nature of the present world" condition "that bind together the elements of human society and the barriers that stand in the way of peace." Second, "unity of conscience" also includes "the development of ethics and moral purpose that relate to motivation and the will to engage in action that creates an environment conducive to peace." What is required, then, in the pursuit of peace, "is unity of thought and action around a set of principles."

Peacebuilding consists of a sense of duty accompanied by a moral responsibility to work to promote both peace and the common good at the same time, all guided by a unitive consciousness founded upon unitive principles, all with the aim to heal a divided humanity by bringing about a deep and lasting unity-in-diversity of the human family.

World peace requires a global unity of thought in which all of humanity agrees upon the unitive principles that define the preconditions for peace, foremost being the principle of the oneness of humankind. These principles must be addressed at the level of moral principle as the foundation for bringing about unity in the world.

A consciousness of the oneness of humanity is the natural by-product of a unitive consciousness. Understanding that reality is one is understanding that humanity is one. This becomes the foundation and framework for all relational endeavors, which would simultaneously require abandoning all notions of prejudice, superiority, and entitlement of any one person over another.

When unitive consciousness becomes the norm, humanity will have reached its developmental age of maturity. With a unitive consciousness, all seeming differences and distinctions are imaginary. Unitive consciousness is consciousness that brings about unity.

If we have a unitive consciousness, all the other unitive principles will naturally follow, as they are all the resulting outcomes of the former. A unitive consciousness can also be developed by unitive education.

2. Unitive Education

Unitive education is a universal system of education designed to bridge the gaps in our knowledge of reality so we can more fully understand the unified nature of the world and the Universe we live in.

Unitive education denotes at its core the classic sense of education, from the Latin *educere*, to draw out what is within. Unitive education focuses on nourishing spiritual attributes and qualities that support the early childhood shaping of values, beliefs, and a wholistic worldview.

Unitive education incorporates *unitive learning*, a philosophy of learning that actively seeks unity. This shifts the primary process of education from one of "training" or "molding" to one of "drawing out." It nurtures a process that is internally coherent by encouraging exploration, investigation, and searching on one's own for what is ultimately accepted as true, while at the same time providing guidance along the way.

Unitive education as an approach to learning needs to be freely available to all, especially the young, the most precious treasure a community can possess, to help them achieve their highest potential, and also to women and girls, whose education is crucial in a balanced, harmonious community. The responsibility for carrying out a system of unitive education in any community lies equally upon all its members. Such a universal system of education would centralize the teaching of the concept of world citizenship as part of the standard education of every child.

Unitive education aims for children to grow up free from all forms of prejudice, appreciating the innate dignity and nobility of every human being. With these as its goals, unitive education is a precondition for the realization of the unity of the human family and of world peace.

Because ignorance is the principal reason for the perpetuation of prejudice, unitive education also serves the spiritual domain of our human nature by nurturing and guiding our necessary discovery of reality on our own while also verifying that the reality we seek to understand is indeed an indivisible wholeness. It is directed toward the realization of the full and complete unity-in-diversity of the richness of the entire human family.

This parallels a Bahá'í-inspired model called "Education for Unity," which upholds the world's cultural mosaic by promoting "the individual's loyalties to family, tribe, country, and nation, while at the same time generating a wider loyalty to all humanity. It teaches a consciousness of the interconnectedness, interdependence, and basic unity of all human beings."

This model would add a new domain to the curriculum – an education of the heart, which is needed as much as that of the intellect. The heart is where the necessary lasting transformation takes place. The deepest learning is that which touches the heart.

Education for Unity strives to create a global identity, an awareness of world issues, a balance of knowledge that unfolds the mysteries of nature and the sciences, and a virtue-centered ethical approach that transforms from within. The result is the development of the whole being in service to the needs of humanity in this momentous age.

Underpinning unitive education is the principle of *unitive knowledge*, or knowledge that brings about unity. This is built upon the understanding that all ways of knowing, all disciplines, are overlapping, interconnecting, interdependent, and complementary means for discovering the realities of the Universe. Each knowledge system adds a needed piece to fully grasp the whole of reality in its entirety.

Founded upon a unitive worldview of reality as one and guided by a unitive consciousness in which all things are understood to have a common source, unitive education sees all knowledge as a reflection of a greater wholeness. It seeks to identify the underlying harmony and unity of all knowledge systems by breaking down the boundaries between our ways of knowing this reality.

The primary example of mutually reinforcing unitive knowledge systems is science and spirituality, long thought to represent competing and conflicting views of reality. Yet, both are complementary paths to understanding the same reality, both sources of truth, and both unveiling the mysteries of the Universe.

Both science and spirituality advance our understanding of an ever-evolving civilization. Both are facets of one truth that is progressively discovered and revealed. Science evolves under the guidance of great teachers who create a natural progression of each one figuratively standing on the shoulders of those who came before, thereby seeing farther. Similarly, spirituality evolves sequentially under the guidance of great prophets, teachers, and souls on their individual journeys.

Albert Einstein, one of the leading scientists who wanted to remove the pseudo-boundaries between these knowledge systems, stated: "Science without religion is lame, religion without science is blind." This unified perspective has spawned many books that blend, merge, or integrate science and spirituality and seem to understand well what Paul Davies said, "By means of science we see into the mind of God."

Both science and spirituality recognize a common force guiding evolutionary progress toward a consciousness of wholeness. Both emphasize the interconnected nature of all things as part of the same reality. All ways of knowing are paths to understanding the same whole, each supporting the other, the boundaries between them becoming less identifiable, with more overlap in their realms than previously thought possible by mainstream thinkers.

Unitive education is essential to peacebuilding. It has been thought by many for over a century that peace is a matter of education, of *learning* to deal charitably, justly, and openly with one another, as nations. And so, many peace organizations have peace education programs at the core of their mission to assist in the process of acquiring values, knowledge, attitudes, skills and behaviors to live in harmony with oneself, others, and the natural environment. These initiatives prioritize truth telling through safe, supported dialogue, reflection, and building systems that promote right relationships.

In 1999, the United Nations adopted the Declaration and Program of Action on a Culture of Peace that has since become a multi-organizational global effort using dialogue and peacebuilding to embrace humanity's interconnectedness and oneness by adopting the universal values of respect for life, liberty, justice, solidarity, human rights, and gender equity.

These and so many more initiatives to build a Culture of Peace begin with efforts to educate for peace, which must start in the family to develop a spirit of peace in the community. This would become an integral part of school curricula, other school activities, and would extend to society as a whole, deepening a desire for peace and unity.

Unitive education would teach peace by illustrating how consciousness evolves toward unity, which is a necessary precondition to peace. Educational systems would release the intellectual and moral capacity of students by equipping them to recognize and overcome injustice, to identify, address, and eliminate root causes of inequality, and by preparing them to build societies that foster compassion, kindness, and respect. As citizens of a rapidly changing world, it would reorient all to view learning as a lifelong endeavor.

The purpose of unitive education is to expand the knowledge, qualities, skills, attitudes, and capacities that enable individuals to become conscious agents of their own growth, as well as active, responsible contributors in a systematic process of building world unity. Unitive education is education that brings about unity. When education is approached from a unitive perspective, the groundwork for unitive relationships will be in place.

3. Unitive Relationships

Unitive relationships hold the world together. The many ways human beings relate to each other and all other life on the planet determines the fate of existence. Unitive relationships are designed to express and maintain the inherent harmony, balance, and unity of all life and between all beings in all settings from family to community to national and global interactions.

Unitive relationships include those that recognize and express gender equality, those that nurture the innate potential of children and youth, those that honor and respect the inherent diversity of the human family, and, just as importantly, humanity's harmonious relationship with nature and all living things.

For civilization to advance and keep up with the maturation of humanity, we need to implement a new understanding of the interdependent relationships between the individual, the community, and the institutions of society. Any old paradigm conflicts between these levels of relationships must be replaced by a recognition of the complementary roles played by each in building a unified world.

The harmonious relationship between all the layers of society opens opportunities for all of humanity to experience the hidden powers of cooperation, love, and unity in action. Unitive relationships are a precondition for the realization of the unity of the human family and of world peace.

Relationships Building Gender Equality

Gender prejudice perpetuates inequities, which maintains disunity among all. Gender-based injustice promotes harmful attitudes and habits in those perpetrating the injustice. These are passed on through the family to all community settings, impacting economic and social life all the way to international affairs.

The fulfillment of humanity's potential cannot be realized until its development is balanced and coordinated. Because of the already long and arduous path through suffrage and equality, this is especially true in all relationships between women and men, as 'Abdu'l-Bahá makes clear:

> "The world of humanity has two wings—one is women and the other men. Not until both wings are equally developed can the bird fly... Not until the world of women becomes equal to the world of men in the acquisition of virtues and perfections, can success and prosperity be attained."

In everyday life, this would mean all people, regardless of gender, would have equal access to decision-making positions in all spheres of life. Gender equality is a basic human right. The Universal House of Justice has stated in *The Promise of World Peace*, "The emancipation of women, the achievement of full equality between the sexes, is one of the most important, though less acknowledged prerequisites of peace."

With huge gaps still to be overcome for women in realizing full partnership in all fields of endeavor, and essential for the ethical climate to be right for international peace to emerge, full gender equality is as natural as all people being equal in the sight of their Creator.

Understood as a spiritual reality, all people share the same divinely bestowed soul. At this depth, there is no gender. No distinction is evident in this universal spiritual condition. Equality is innately established, only needing to be recognized and embraced, rather than being a social aspiration to be pursued. Our consciousness and our social structures need to be reshaped and renewed to reflect this reality by removing the obstacles that have hindered the full realization of the equality intrinsic to all of humanity.

In reimagining the role of institutions in building gender-equal societies, one example of this already being implemented in the world comes from the Katuyola village of Zambia. In their 2024 statement to UN Commission on the Status of Women, the Bahá'í International Community (BIC) reported that in an ongoing process of consultation and collaboration among traditional leaders, faith actors, parents, youth, and children, the governing institution of a local faith community, elected by its members, organized a two-day gathering of some 120 local women of various faith backgrounds to explore questions related to the role of women in society. The men of the institution handled logistical arrangements such as cooking and serving food so the women could more fully participate in the gathering. This level of support was described by many as a remarkable shift within the historical context of their society.

This gathering resulted in literacy classes for women in the village, assistance with backyard gardens, a local savings bank to help them generate income for the establishment of a local center of learning, and, just as importantly, adjustments to the functioning of the village institutional structures to more fully embody the principle of gender equality.

This example gives a glimpse of the influence that institutions can have on the roles and opportunities for women and girls in a community, especially when constructive social change based on belief, attitude, and values emerge from and are put into practice at the grassroots level. It also illustrates that men can have an important role in supporting the efforts of women coming together to benefit all.

The values and qualities the world needs most – compassion, nurturance, cooperation, and empathy – are not just the domain of the feminine but are essential human qualities available to all. These vitally necessary qualities, in loosening the intransience of attitudes, must be brought to the forefront of everyone's consciousness and actions to create the social milieu supportive of change.

The establishment of the full equality of all people in all affairs of life and state has critical implications in the political realm as well, particularly in relation to the abolition of warfare. As one example, women are statistically less likely to sanction war, allowing their sons and daughters to be sacrifices on the battlefield, after lovingly devoting two decades of their life rearing them.

In a wholistic context, gender equality is both a virtue and a right, as this principle emerges from a divine source and provides an unambiguous assurance which transcends social barriers and has a profound effect on the individual identity of all people.

Relationships Nurturing the Innate Potential of Children and Youth

Children need to be raised knowing they are born as noble beings, with an innate potential to fulfill through their own conscious and independent initiative. This will ensure that their perception of what leads to their own advancement or degradation is clear and unclouded.

It is through education and the moral and spiritual understanding and actions of the parents that the integrity of the family is established, maintained, and strengthened. The education of young children, prior to any public or private schooling, should focus on and foster an appreciation of the spiritual character of all human beings and its implications for the moral well-being of society.

This first, in-the-home education should seek to develop in the child the desire and capacity to be a responsible and caring member of the family and society at large. This would require the transmission of values conducive to cooperation, harmony, and unity among all.

If children are raised from a young age knowing that that are valued members of a larger human family, and that all people, women and men, have equal rights in all their endeavors, the implications of this knowledge will be profound in domestic and social life. Values, attitudes, and behaviors learned within the family are carried over to the wider society, to the workplace, and into the political realm. Children should therefore be given the strong foundation early to best prepare them to contribute wisely and effectively as they enter the unknowns of the greater community.

The United Nations Summit of the Future in September 2024 placed children and youth at the forefront, recognizing that they are the ones who will bring about more impactful outcomes through their increasing engagement in social action across the globe. "The Pact for the Future," adopted by this summit, specifically identified four "Actions" that will a) invest in the social and economic development of children and young people so they can reach their full potential, b) promote, protect, and respect the human rights of all young people, c) strengthen meaningful youth participation at the national level, and d) strengthen meaningful youth participation at the international level.

They also adopted an "Annex," called the Declaration on Future Generations, with its own set of Guiding Principles, Commitments, and

Actions that focus on safeguarding the needs and interests of children, youth, and future generations, covering all the human rights areas. Young people have a significant role to play in transforming society. When youth are turned to and given the opportunity to channel their energies toward efforts that raise their capacity while making them meaningful contributors to the advancement of society, the results will always be remarkable.

Throughout the ages, seeking an identity of their own, young people have been characterized by the qualities of being curious, questioning and probing the world around them, and being adaptable and open to change, with an acute sense of justice. The current generation of young people can contribute these qualities that are central to transforming the foundations of community life.

There is a reservoir of young people ready to serve humanity. Their voices need to be raised through meaningful engagement in the decision-making processes of renewing society to ensure the most impactful outcomes.

Relationships Honoring Humanity's Inherent Diversity

Humanity is not composed of separate and distinct races or castes that supposedly possess varying capacities or potential. This is a misconception at the root of all forms of discrimination, prejudice, and racism. These perceived distinctions originate in the mind. The scientific and spiritual reality, now clarifying and resolving millennia-old illusions that gave rise to false notions of superiority and inferiority, is that there is only one human race, a single people inhabiting the planet Earth, bound together in a common destiny.

Unitive relationships are founded upon this reality, that all people are members of one human family. This underlying core principle of human oneness means transcending and eliminating all forms of racial and ethnic prejudice – as well as notions of tolerance that tend to restrict full and meaningful relationships with each other. This is an essential, precondition to be realized for humanity's long-sought goal of building a peaceful, just, and unified world.

This reality is, for the first time in human history, becoming more visible, and is brought into sharper focus, because it is now possible for all the peoples of the world to directly perceive their interdependence and intended wholeness.

Humanity's Harmonious Relationship with Nature and All Living Things

The intended unity of all relationships goes well beyond our own kind to embrace all living things and the planet. This is also a necessary precondition of world peace.

Nature is the embodiment of the Divine. The whole Earth is sacred; its vast resources are a common heritage *and* a trust for all humanity to safeguard and protect now and into the farthest future. An intricate web of interdependent relationships sustains our planet. Our collective survival depends upon our caring for the natural environment – all plant and animal life, land, and sea. Environmental vandalism is caused by the corruption of the moral fabric that guides and disciplines human life; indeed, climate change is an ethical issue.

We must become more conscious of our attitudes and actions towards the source of our sustenance; we must extend our compassion to all living things. With a firm and binding set of environmental ethics, we must answer the call to environmental stewardship of the planet. Ecological health is inextricably tied to spiritual health.

All that the wealth and wonders of the Earth offer are common to all people. For too long have we failed to protect the environment from ruinous damage. Society's attachment to expansion, acquisition, and the constant creation and gratification of wants has created unsustainable goals. As we have gradually, and now out of necessity, come to recognize humanity's interconnection with and dependence on the environment, we have also come to realize that our unique impact carries with it the inescapable duty to nurture and protect the natural world.

Humanity's relationship with the natural world needs refashioning; notions of progress and development need to be redefined. A process of learning how to achieve and sustain unitive relationships with all life on the planet is needed to support the growing numbers of world citizens who are laboring to realize the vision of a flourishing global civilization in harmony with the natural environment. Unitive relationships are relationships that bring about unity. When unitive relationships are achieved, the groundwork for unitive justice will be in place.

4. Unitive Justice

Unitive justice is a system of justice designed to maintain coherence on all social levels, from the local to regional to global, protecting all communities from schism or separation due to any act of injustice. It heals and reconciles all relationships, ensures community solidarity, and maintains the balance of life.

As a universal system of global justice, unitive justice is a precondition for the realization of the unity of the human family and of world peace. Unitive Justice replaces all forms of prejudice, discrimination, oppression, and racism with the implementation of the principle of the oneness and equality of all peoples.

Prejudice toward any group causes all of society to suffer; it is a false perception that blinds us to the fact that every person comes from the same Creator, is endowed with the same innate potential, spiritual qualities, attributes, and capacities, and is therefore entitled to the same equal and just treatment by others.

Unitive justice is required to bring about unity-in-diversity, which requires the unity of the so-called "races." This is the role, purpose, and function of unitive justice in society and the world today, in this time of increased polarization and unforeseen rapid change, as the Universal House of Justice addresses in *The Promise of World Peace*:

"Racism, one of the most baneful and persistent evils, is a major barrier to peace. Its practice… retards the unfoldment of the boundless potentialities of its victims, corrupts its perpetrators, and blights human progress." They add that if this problem is to be overcome, the recognition of the oneness of humanity must be implemented and upheld by appropriate legal measures.

Only a deeper respect for the intrinsic value of each culture *and* individual will help us see that diversity is a means for fulfilling humanity's potential and an expression of our species' wholeness. All assaults on diversity must be countered by the power of unity and love, to release the greatest inherent potential to heal the ills and divisions afflicting humanity.

The elimination of all forms of prejudice requires a universal system of global justice built upon a standard of equity and fairness for the entire human family. The world's sacred traditions understand justice as the embodiment of divine order on Earth. Justice finds its fulfillment in a standard of unconditional love; it prepares the way for unity, leads to the well-being of humanity, and carries a power that can transform society. Justice is the unifying force expressed in every dimension of reality.

Bahá'u'lláh makes its role in society very clear: "*Justice is a powerful force. It is… the standard-bearer of love and bounty*." He further identifies its goal: "*The purpose of justice is the appearance of unity…*"

This is the promise of justice: to bring about unity among the peoples of the world. Though our understanding of justice, and our capacity to carry it out, has expanded with every social advance we've taken with wider and wider circles of unity, the punitive system of justice humanity has lived by for many centuries has not allowed us to experience the fullest effects of our growing circles of unity.

The "eye for an eye" and a "life for a life" system of justice has led to the extremes of unbridled genocide and war, which have created the need for restorative justice, another step adding on generations to the process of achieving true justice. This is where the Indigenous cultures that apply a system of unitive justice could serve as a model. The world community desperately needs a model of justice with a built-in system of restorative justice that simultaneously offers meaningful support to victims *and* helps perpetrators restore community harmony.

Indigenous communities living by unitive justice express the heart and soul of the way of unity. When a transgression occurs, rather than separate or isolate the perpetrator, they were integrated back into the whole through a process of restoring wholeness and maintaining coherence, by applying the principle of compassion along with the practice of consultation. As humanity's collective consciousness evolves toward a level of maturity, we desperately need a global system of unitive justice with the ability to restore harmony built in.

Love *and* justice combined results in unity right away, rather than needing more energy later to restore other injustices. Unitive justice is needed for world unity. The fate of humanity depends upon the twin forces of love and justice bringing about equitable relationships on all levels.

A global system of unitive justice would acknowledge the hidden wholeness of all existence. As the declaration of the 1993 Parliament of the World's Religions made clear, "We must strive for a just social and economic order... Let no one be deceived, there is no global justice without truthfulness and humanness." To this, we must add: there can be no global justice without the recognition of the oneness of humanity. Carrying out global justice today based on oneness and interdependence is the only thing that will ensure the achievement of the purpose of justice *and* the most practical need of our time: establishing unity-in-diversity.

This unity-in-diversity of the human family cannot be realized without global *unitive healing*, or healing that brings about unity. Though healing typically focuses on ailing parts, unitive healing accomplishes what all healing is intended to do: make whole again, by addressing and maintaining the harmony and balance of the whole.

Unitive healing is a holistic approach toward seeking coherence across mind, body, heart, and soul of the individual as well as the same across the collective body of humanity on all levels of society. This needs to occur on both individual and collective levels, from all the injustices accrued across the generations and over many centuries.

Unitive justice will help bring about unitive healing, individually and collectively, from all the injustices accrued across the centuries. The process of carrying out unitive justice real-time, with each infraction that occurs, would contribute toward eliminating the need for restorative justice later, while also addressing and incorporating the healing of past cultural trauma and soul wounds carried across generations.

The complete transformation of the world depends upon this balanced and inclusive formulation of justice in the world. Only a fully functioning global system of unitive justice can reshape and prepare communities worldwide for effective global security. This would be an expression of the purest reflection of absolute unity that is possible on this Earth.

Unitive justice is justice that brings about unity. When unitive justice is achieved, the groundwork for unitive economics will be in place.

5. Unitive Economics

Unitive economics is a system of economic exchange founded upon a just, moral, and equitable framework of universal human rights. It is designed to ensure and maintain the well-being of all through the balanced distribution of all resources, both natural and human-made, as well as services from local to global levels, that would foster prosperity for all.

As a universal system of equitable economic exchange to bring about unity, unitive economics is a precondition for the realization of the unity of the human family, for achieving world peace, and for a harmonious relationship with our living planetary home and Universe.

Unitive economics would help bring about world unity by eliminating the extremes of poverty and wealth on a global scale. These ever-expanding extremes should not be allowed to widen. A 2021 Oxfam report showed that the 10 richest men in the world combined owned more than the combined wealth of almost half the entire world population. Their combined wealth doubled during the pandemic. To achieve balanced global prosperity, all available human and material resources, rather than being used only for the short-term advantage of a few, must be used for the long-term good of all.

There is a spiritual solution to the world's economic problems. This lies in the moral dimension to the generation, distribution, and utilization of wealth and resources, which reflects not only the universal Golden Rule and the principle of the common good, but also the oneness of humanity.

The material and spiritual dimensions of civilization must advance in harmony for prosperity to be more equitably experienced by all. This requires building out more balanced economic structures to encourage and support voluntary change in individual behavior toward the accumulation of wealth which will allow new patterns of equity to emerge, uplifting all.

This is particularly relevant in understanding that the welfare of any segment of humanity is intricately connected with the welfare of the whole. Humanity's collective life suffers when any one group thinks of its own well-being in isolation from that of its neighbors. Collective potential is reached through individual potential being achieved.

The best use of wealth is in service to humanity, and in accordance with unitive spiritual principles. New systems needed to enable this must be created in this light. Achieving such a vision requires individual and collective transformation, based on learning over time and through experience how to put spiritual principles into practice.

Addressing this egregious barrier to peace, the Universal House of Justice has said in *The Promise of World Peace*: "The inordinate disparity between rich and poor, a source of acute suffering, keeps the world in a state of instability, virtually on the brink of war... The solution calls for the combined application of spiritual, moral and practical approaches... involving the people directly affected in the decisions that must urgently be made."

The world today no longer has just local or national economies to balance, we also have a global economy where it is just as, if not more, critical to maintain a balance between wealth and poverty. With a wide range of economic crises pending in the world, and multiple challenges, from climate change and environmental threats to the displacement of refugees from war-torn countries, dire humanitarian *and* economic needs must be addressed wholistically.

This means both understanding and acting upon the incompatibility of poverty with what it means to be a compassionate human being. The world's spiritual traditions highlight care for the hungry and destitute. The social protection of all members of society means addressing the true causes of the inequities that plague humanity by building relationships of mutual support and assistance.

Adopting the principle of the oneness of humanity is the starting point for resolving these challenging issues of a global economy. This expression of human unity in the widest of circles may be the only solution for humanity's long-term peace and prosperity.

The notion of prosperity itself must be re-examined in order for civilization to advance in harmony. Unitive economics is founded upon universal human values that ensure all people have equal access to global resources, rather than just a few who accumulate all the wealth. The inherent moral dimension to the generation, distribution, and utilization of wealth means that the prosperity of the whole ensures the well-being of all.

The economic, moral, and spiritual welfare of any village, city, or nation is bound up with welfare of the whole. If any segment of the whole is held back in any way from its share of prosperity, the whole suffers, whether evident or not. True prosperity is not attainable until the interests of all peoples are served. When local to global economic systems are functioning to bring about unity, the groundwork for unitive global development will be in place.

6. Unitive Global Development

Unitive global development is a coordinated worldwide enterprise to build capacity on larger and larger scales by establishing harmony and balance across all levels of society while working shoulder to shoulder to contribute to the well-being of the whole.

Unitive global development is an effort to involve people of all walks of life to work together to reconstruct a social order built upon justice, reciprocity, and collective prosperity. It is founded upon equity and reflects the reality that humanity is one family. As a universal system of social development, reflecting both the material and spiritual dimensions of the individual and community, unitive global development contributes to the betterment of society while being a precondition for the realization of world peace.

Well into the new millennium, the drive toward world unity is a dominant feature characterizing life on the planet now. A global consciousness is emerging, convincing increasing numbers of people that constructing a peaceful and just planetary society is essential to humanity's survival. This has formed the foundation for much work in the social development sphere that provides the inspiration for unprecedented social progress.

The underlying responsibility of unitive development is to foster the well-being of all the peoples of the Earth. This can only be achieved by implementing the principle of the oneness of humanity – and its corollary of unity-in-diversity – in all social development plans. This is the practical and essential standard for re-ordering humanity's collective life on the planet. It identifies the longing of people everywhere for a world infused with a spirit of community, fellowship, and compassion at all levels, from local to global. In this new world, peace, social and economic justice, prosperity, and liberty will be the resulting outcome.

Universally embracing the central organizing principle of the oneness of humanity may be the only thing that will ensure the development of a sense of confidence about the future, a willingness to sacrifice for the common good, and a commitment to play an active, constructive role in building a viable and thriving world community. Such a capacity to think globally is becoming increasingly recognized as a guiding principle for social and economic development in nearly every region of the world. A rapidly integrating world depends upon such a global consciousness.

The purpose of unitive global development is to transcend and eliminate systems that privilege some while impoverishing others, and to learn how to create new systems that empower and give equal opportunity to all. Humanity's inherent unity-in-diversity will not be realized until those who benefit the most from the current system allow those whose voices have not been heard or heeded to become decision-makers and implementors of development action plans.

This creates a direct path to the ultimate objective of development – human lives and societies increasingly characterized by peace, well-being and happiness. This end result of a deep and thorough transformative change and renewal is initiated by a unitive consciousness that guides an action-oriented approach to an international unitive development agenda.

A universal unitive social development paradigm for the 21st century and beyond would include the integration of the essential elements of all the unitive principles identified so far here with a balance of the material and spiritual needs and aspirations of all peoples met and satisfied. This wholistic approach translates into the most complete global prosperity possible.

One way to ensure and accelerate the development process toward peace, well-being, and happiness for all is to adopt the concept and goal of world citizenship as the ethical foundation for unitive social development. A wider loyalty, a love of humanity as a whole, is needed now. Vast financial, technical, and human resources could be freed up as the peoples of the world commit to a profound sense of responsibility for the fate of the planet and the well-being of the entire human family. This sense of responsibility naturally flows from the recognition of the oneness of humanity, which also inspires a unifying vision of a peaceful, prosperous world society.

This vision would have to be preceded by the full integration of a complete curriculum on world citizenship at all levels of education and accompanied by wide ranging public awareness campaigns. Such a curriculum would be framed by a global ethic embracing all peoples in a vision of unity and wholeness. This call for unitive values – "our common humanity," "world citizenship," and "unity in diversity" – anchoring a universal curriculum has been heard in UN and NGO circles and beyond since the early 1990s. The world community is poised to come to accord on the need for a global ethic and unitive development initiatives that will solidify world citizenship as a rallying cry for the good of humanity and the good of Earth, our home.

World citizenship directly results from the contraction of the world into a single neighborhood. Scientific and technological advances have created an indisputable interdependence of nations. Love of all the world's peoples does not exclude love of one's country. Any part of a world society is best served by promoting the good of the whole. Current international activities in fields that nurture mutual affection and a sense of solidarity among peoples need to be greatly increased.

When social development initiatives collaboratively assist in bringing about global balance, equity, and unity, the groundwork for unitive language will be in place.

7. Unitive Language

Unitive Language is language designed to sustain harmony and unity within diverse communities and the entire world by conveying an underlying truth of the reality all around us. It is language that connects, rather than divides, by expressing our commonalities and wholeness.

As a universal way of communicating across boundaries and across differences, unitive language, and a unity of language, is a precondition for the realization of the unity of the human family and of world peace.

Unity of language will unite all peoples of the world in the choice of a common auxiliary language, or a common second language, to be used locally and globally, enabling all people to converse freely, as we are beginning to see the early signs of now with online apps that instantaneously translate one language to another.

The world has become a neighborhood, with multiple languages being spoken right next to each other even when the native language of that neighborhood might be missing from the conversations going on around one. This is a sign of global unity. Yet, it also points out that a common second language could easily be a solution for making any conversation anywhere all inclusive.

If we could all – the entire 8 billion of us – understand each other, regardless of our native language, we'd all feel less "foreign" to each other when we wanted to communicate something important, especially when it comes to peacebuilding in some way, or even in building cohesive multilingual communities, which there are more and more of now everywhere.

A universal auxiliary language would serve as a means of international communication, reduce and eventually eliminate misunderstandings due to language, become the cause of unity, and the greatest instrument for promoting harmony and advancing civilization.

In the early 1850s, Bahá'u'lláh recommended to the kings and rulers of various nations that a world language, either invented or chosen from the existing languages, be "adopted by all governments." This would be taught in the schools of all nations as an auxiliary to their mother tongue. This is a key principle, and why a world language is an essential precondition to world peace. It is well known that a national language promotes national unity. It needs to be equally understood that a world language would promote world unity.

Language may be the most critical component of how we interact with and relate to each other. Language is our original, innate tool for communicating who we are, what matters most to us, and what we care most about. The more carefully we choose the words we use, the more connected we become with each other. Socrates said, "The misuse of language induces evil in the soul." He was most likely referring to our choice of words, whether they unite or divide us, and what the speaker's intention is in choosing certain words.

Language is being misused more often these days by greedy profiteers or deceitful politicians to get something they want by trying to take advantage of others. When language is proactively used to gain power by distorting or, even worse, turning reality into its opposite, Socrates was right on target about how damaging to one and all the misuse of language can be.

The language we use comes with a responsibility to honor what the words are intended to mean and the truth they are intended to convey.

Our language needs to reflect the reality that humanity is one family. In this regard, language is a crucial component of social transformation. Language has long been used to separate groups and classes of people who otherwise share a common cause. In these divisive times, using language to help bring about unity is critically important. Language is the basis for the stories we tell and live by and can therefore be a primary catalyst for the evolution of consciousness. The use of unitive language in describing various parts of the unified nature of reality is now in its early stages of being understood and applied.

When language is used to bring about unity, the groundwork for unitive narratives will be in place.

8. Unitive Narratives

Unitive narratives are grounded in unitive consciousness, form the basis for a wholistic, unitive worldview, and represent a tradition in storytelling we need to reclaim. Before conflict and warfare kept tribal communities apart, the First Peoples lived by unitive narratives, narratives that brought about and maintained their unity, as guiding stories embodying the values and principles of the harmony, unity, and wholeness of Creation they observed all around them.

Over time, as communities grew, expanded, spread out, and became more focused on differences, divisive narratives emerged that supported separation. After many millennia of conflict and chaos, as we approach a consciousness of global integration, we are again in dire need of narratives that bring about unity.

As the storytelling species, we think in story form, speak in story form, and find meaning and purpose through our stories. Telling our stories in a recognizable narrative form, structure, and pattern is central to who we are, to our core identity. When meaning, purpose, and direction are missing from our stories, personally and collectively we are lost, without a rudder to guide us. We need to expand, deepen, and reframe our identity based on the demands of our time.

A unitive narrative inspires, reflects, validates, supports, and guides the reality of the inherent unity-in-diversity of the human family and all life as we experience and come to know this in everyday life. In describing the parallel functions of a living mythology, Joseph Campbell noted, "If they are successful, you get the sense of everything – yourself, your society, the universe, and the mystery beyond – as one great unit."

A unitive narrative invites us into the mystery of what seems unknowable, renders the impossible possible, catalyzes the potentialities within us and creation, identifies the ascent of individual and collective consciousness as central to the processes of the Universe, and expands the expression of love and goodwill among all peoples, as in the story of the Good Samaritan.

A unitive narrative for our time, meant to guide and inspire us all, will be alive, in harmony with the evolutionary impulse, upholding the latest scientific discoveries and spiritual revelations, bridging interpersonal and social divides, contributing to unity-in-diversity, and integrating all things in the Universe; it will return us to wholeness.

Expressing and representing the unified nature of reality, unitive narratives facilitate the process of transformation. Beyond the basic story pattern of beginning, middle, and end, unitive narratives take us to a hidden deeper level where the formula for transformation plays out on both the individual and collective level, through the pattern of *beginning, muddle, and resolution*. The muddles, or challenges, we face represent the core of the pattern that brings the process of transformation to its completion, or resolution, and to an understanding of the inherent unity of all things, as discussed in *A New Story of Wholeness*.

In this context, a unitive narrative keeps us on the track of truth-telling, of following the way of unity. A unitive narrative is a truthful personal or collective story of living into the wholeness of the unified field of existence all around us.

The stories we live by carry the possibilities we collectively envision as the fulfillment of our dreams. As a narrative that brings about unity, unitive narratives are a precondition for the realization of the unity of the human family and of world peace.

Our challenge today is creating an inclusive narrative that answers the questions of our common history and shared destiny: Where have we been? Where are we now? Where do we want to be? How do we resolve the crises we're in to get to where we want to be?

In finding answers to these questions of our time, we strengthen social coherence while collectively identifying and forging pathways for action that will bring about unity. Identifying and sharing our unitive narratives is a necessary part of the process that will move us closer to where we want to be. We need narratives that will guide us through times of change and transition, illustrating the power of the human spirit to overcome injustice and myriad crises, which has shaped our enduring sense of hope for the future.

We need narratives that acknowledge the reality of our inherent unity as a human family, in unitive relationship with each other and all life, of our collective appreciation of each other's contributions to the whole. These unitive narratives of social coherence and harmony need to be reflected in our media, our boardrooms, our social institutions, and every limb of government at all levels.

We live for – and can't live without – narratives that explain reality as it is, life as it is, and our place and role within reality as a unified whole. We need truth-telling narratives to get to the essence of who we are, how we got here, and how we're going to get to where we want to go. And we need open, receptive, respectful audiences who welcome these narratives.

For our narratives to reach this deeply, to become unitive, for us to become truly harmonized, we need to recognize that we are one people, one human family, sharing a common planetary homeland, that societies exist for the well-being of everyone involved. This is the only way we will all flourish and thrive.

Unitive narratives create pathways for action by building resilient communities. The sharing of our common, universal human experiences brings us all closer together, making unity a reality that we feel and want to act upon, which can lead to new social networks and infrastructure that further advances social coherence and capacity.

In this emerging Unitive Age, it is vital that we shift our entire approach to storytelling toward sharing unitive narratives with each other. A unitive narrative is founded on the convergence of the latest scientific breakthroughs and the earliest universal spiritual wisdom. We now understand that evolution is not driven by randomness and chance. It exists instead to evolve from simplicity to complexity toward ever greater levels of interdependence.

Unity-in-diversity characterizes the flow of evolution at each expanding level. Evolution's path is never a straight line. Its movement is spiral, like the cycles of nature, always in the direction of the good of the whole. Acknowledgment of the whole enables us to look deeper and probe fundamental truths of essential relationships throughout the Universe. There we see that the physical realm we exist in did not create itself. The Universe, at all levels of existence, arose from deeper non-physical causes.

The underlying message of a unitive narrative gives us a felt sense of unity with all life, and unity with the ineffable source of all being. It unites us with the evolutionary flow of all things. A unitive narrative invites us to embrace the wisdom of the complementarity and wholeness of seemingly opposing forces, such as feminine and masculine attributes, enabling us to honor and achieve unity in the diversity of expressions on our way to a consciousness of wholeness through which we carry out our actions in the world.

A unitive narrative recognizes our fundamental interbeing, interconnectedness, and interdependence with the whole community of our planetary home, Gaia, and with the entire Universe. In addition, this empowers us to envision and co-create a love-based rather than separation-based future in which regenerative and sustainable development, unitive justice, and peace are natural outcomes of a world that works for all beings and our planetary home.

Unitive narratives are needed now more than ever to lead us through a process of shifting the focus from individual well-being to collective well-being. In our time, the part no longer takes precedence over the whole. As a result, both are completely interdependent. Exclusive emphasis on any one part endangers the whole. Built upon a unitive consciousness, a unitive narrative gives us a deeper commitment to ensuring Earth's well-being, as a living organism, as we understand more clearly that this depends upon collaborative relationships and dynamic coevolutionary partnerships on a planetary scale.

Indeed, our planet's continuing emergence and evolutionary progress is so interdependently tied together with humanity's evolving consciousness that the fate of one is inextricably bound up with the other.

When narratives are used to bring about unity, and all other unitive principles are in place, the groundwork for unitive global governance will be in place.

9. Unitive Global Governance

Unitive global governance is a multi-level system of governance interconnecting all strata of society, from community to regional to national and global, by the same set of organizing unitive principles designed to create, sustain, and deepen the harmony and unity of civic and political interactions of the human family. As a universal system of governing the whole world, unitive global governance is a precondition for the realization of the unity of the human family and of world peace.

The primary purpose of unitive global governance is to bring the people, communities, and nations of the world into closer cooperation by reflecting and implementing the principle of the oneness of humanity.

Unitive global governance is an advanced form of Unity in the Political Realm and Unity of Nations as referred to earlier in the *Seven Candles of Unity*. It is designed to facilitate and carry out the effective and full collaboration of sovereign states through an international commonwealth, expanding and strengthening the bounds of the United Nations, as well as providing the multi-level infrastructure for uniting all peoples of the world.

Many who are in international affairs and aware of a growing global consciousness consider the time we are living in to be an incubation period for the coming of a system of unitive global governance. Only as an era of unbridled nationalism runs its course will we have a sane and legitimate patriotism that also includes a wider loyalty, a love of humanity as a whole, as in Bahá'u'lláh's statement, *"The earth is but one country, and mankind its citizens."*

The outdated predominant system of nationalism, with its lingering discord and disunity, requires the antidote of unity on all levels of society, and needs to be replaced by a fully equitable and balanced system of unitive global governance that places the whole Earth and all its peoples as its highest priority. Unitive global governance, discussed in more detail in chapter 9, is governance that brings about and sustains world unity.

Integrating All Nine Unitive Principles into One Whole System

The way of unity, with its nine unitive principles guiding each step, offers a powerful process leading humanity out of its current crises – from strained family relations to the multiple conflicts and wars characterizing international relations – and into their resolution of once and for all healing the many ills of a divided humanity.

These nine unitive principles incorporate, integrate, and predate the United Nations 17 Sustainable Development Goals (SDGs) emerging from *Our Common Agenda* and the *2030 Agenda*. Each of the 17 SDGs can be aligned with one or more of the nine unitive principles.

An important distinction between how the 17 SDGs are being approached through the UN related efforts compared to a unitive worldview, or through a wholistic model, is that typically each goal is being addressed separately, while from the unitive perspective, all SDGs are seen as interdependent and interconnected, all interrelated preconditions to peace, rather than as separate goals to be met. Each are dependent upon the other, and none on their own will be fully accomplished without and until the successful implementation simultaneously of all the others.

While the SDGs are comprehensive for achieving external sustainability, a set of Inner Development Goals (IDGs) would balance them out and better assist their achievement. These are already being implemented as transformational tools and values to support, direct, and maintain all initiatives toward overall sustainability. Inner and outer efforts need to complement each other for lasting, wholistic development. Material development needs the support of our inner capacities for spiritual development to sustain it.

The unitive principles outlined here form a balanced whole that fully integrates all inner and outer component parts. Like the human body, with cells and organs each intricately tied together and essential for the well-being and optimal functioning of the entire body, humanity cannot solve its current crises separately, but only by seeing them as a deeply interconnected, interdependent whole.

Implementing these unitive principles would be manifesting the inner meaning of peacebuilding – a long-term commitment to a conscious process of bringing about unity personally, socially, and globally.

THE UNITY OF THE HUMAN FAMILY IS THE CULMINATING CONDITION FOR WORLD PEACE

These nine unitive principles represent an all-embracing vision of what is needed to ensure humanity's promised future. These will lead us from a consciousness of duality to a consciousness of oneness and wholeness, from a divided human family to a fully unified whole, supporting and inspiring each other.

So interdependently tied together are these principles that the realization of one depends upon the realization of all the others. They are each a component, a necessary precondition, of the over-arching principle of the oneness of humanity, which is the undeniable spirit of this age, just as the Ten Commandments were when first codified.

As these unitive principles are put into practice, as were earlier scriptural injunctions against idolatry, theft, and false witness in their time, these will be clearly recognized as catalysts to an ever-advancing civilization, and preconditions to world unity and lasting peace. They are principles founded upon universal moral and spiritual values. There is not a problem in the world today for which one or more of these unitive principles does not provide a clear and lasting solution.

These unitive principles represent a spiritual basis for harmonizing and resolving practical, everyday problems with solutions that are reflected in the cycles of nature and that inspire a will to implement the necessary measures to achieve the desired solution. If leaders at all levels of society and government sought first to identify the principles needed to be applied in solving the problem at hand, and were then guided by them, the world's problems would be solved much more easily.

One central organizing principle – *humanity is one family sharing the entire planet with all life* – determines the essential context and framework for envisioning a set of interdependent unitive principles that guide the dynamic process of the way of unity toward creating the conditions for the realization of peace on Earth.

By starting with the central organizing principle that *humanity is one* and then finding the supporting unitive principle that will contribute to that all-encompassing vision in the most direct way in each setting and circumstance, that vision will surely be realized. Accepting the oneness of humanity as a biological fact, a social necessity, and a spiritual reality may well be the only thing that will lead to the destination of our millennia long journey toward peace on Earth.

This is the culmination of an evolutionary process set in motion at the beginning of time. Having passed through the stage of childhood, humanity is now struggling to leave behind its adolescent ways while taking on new patterns of thought and action as it approaches its age of maturity.

In 1931, Shoghi Effendi elaborated on the implications of this pivotal principle being achieved through a deeply complex process of adjusting national political attitudes, and much more, taking many stages over much time. He said it would involve a process "to remold institutions to the needs of an ever-changing world," that would "not ignore, nor suppress, the diversity of ethnic origins, of climate, of history, of language and tradition, of thought and habit, that differentiate the peoples and nations of the world."

This principle, he affirmed, represents "the consummation of human evolution," which "carries with it no more and no less than a solemn assertion that attainment to this final stage in this stupendous evolution is not only necessary but inevitable."

The result of this unfolding evolutionary process will be a degree of social coherence on all levels of society never witnessed. When we carry out our lives based on the acceptance of our primary identity as belonging to a single human family, this all-inclusive identity solidifies our place and role in our local, national, and international community. It expands the more restrictive and potentially destructive identities we would otherwise have. When our over-arching identity leads us toward bringing about the unity-in-diversity of the entire human family, we protect distinctive expressions of culture that enrich and strengthen the whole, which in turn ensures the coherence of society's many layers.

We have in hand the guiding principles that will bring about world unity, with the oneness of humanity in the forefront, the realization and implementation of which will finally clear the way for an effective and fully sustainable unitive global governance that will usher in an age of global prosperity and peace.

ADDITIONAL EXPRESSIONS
OF THE UNITIVE AGE

The way of unity is all-encompassing. Every aspect of our lives in relationship with others and our planetary home calls for us to be unified, to be in harmony, and to act in cooperation with all others in every way and in everything we do.

To achieve the promise of our time, many on-the-ground, practical expressions of unitive consciousness are needed. A select few of these further expressions of the Unitive Age are considered here. The unitive principle of reality as one, and its corollary of evolution as purposeful, guides us from simplicity to complexity, toward ever greater levels of interdependence and interconnectedness.

As we enter further into humanity's Unitive Age, we will see more of the desire, the deep commitment, to carry out our lives in service to the whole. Shifting our focus from the part to the whole, we become convinced that what is best for all is best for one. Most importantly, we see a moving away from means that begin and end in disunity toward means that bring about unity in everything we do.

The use of "unitive" in describing various parts of the unified nature of reality is just now beginning to be understood and applied in a range of settings, from leading edge to mainstream thinkers. As this unfolds further, it will be more common to approach all forms of relationships and interactions as ways to bring about unity. The following examples relating to change, technology, media, leadership, and others, reflect the unitive expressions that will emerge as we move closer toward unitive consciousness becoming the norm in the Unitive Age, which will transform every aspect of our lives.

Unitive Change

The Unitive Age needs a theory of change that not only brings about deep change but in doing so, also brings about unity. Such a theory of unitive change would be supported by efforts and initiatives that start out with the goal to realize the preconditions that will result in group, community, organizational, and larger scale unity. Many theories of change appear to fall short of the end goal of unity, as well as on identifying how and why there is an inherent scalability to a design that would result in world unity.

Social change 1.0 models were designed for slow-moving, incremental change. This might not be a bad thing if the change is deep and lasting – and results in unity. Social change 2.0 models focus on change that transforms and reorganizes a system to a higher level of performance. This addresses complex change, requires people to change, and requires the cooperation of the entire system.

Social change innovator David Gershon calls this process of bringing the whole system into collaboration building a "unitive field." He acknowledges no pretensions, though, in believing that social change 2.0 design principles and practices are the solution for "any of these enormous challenges facing us as a human community."

What would enable a full and deep change – or transformation – of the entire system of the humanity community? Could setting out to build a unitive field not only for changing the human community but also, at the same time, for bringing about its unity be what we're looking for?

What if we started out with an approach to change that was designed to bring about a higher level of performance as well as the preconditions necessary to support unity on all levels within the system of the human community? This would mean approaching change not only on the level of principles, but with principles specifically designed to bring about unity.

Large scale change happens through the repetition of small scale change that has applied unitive principles in its thinking and actions. This focused, purposeful small scale change is scalable. Unity achieved in a community, through the application of principles that bring about unity, can be repeated in other communities, and that can be repeated in surrounding regions, and those then repeated in larger communities and regions.

All this change generated on those various scales eventually and systematically can connect small scale change to large scale change, making both possible through the same set of unitive principles, while illustrating how interconnected all parts of the whole really are. Having a clear, commonly accepted, and universally applicable set of unitive principles will bring about unity on all scales, *because* the same set of principles that bring about unity at one scale will do the same on all scales. Unity is what empowers all people in the same way at the same time at all scales of society.

Unitive change is inherently scalable because it happens through the application of unitive principles that are universal. Unitive, human rights-based principles when applied locally, regionally, nationally, and globally, will achieve the intended outcome of unity on all those levels.

Applying unitive principles for unitive change is unity-in-action. Striving to achieve change that brings about greater unity by acting upon unitive principles that bring about deeper unity in the setting it is applied in is how unitive change becomes inherently scalable to other similar settings and larger contexts at the same time. Unitive change starts with the common goal of building greater and deeper unity around the common good.

Unitive Technology

Technology is usually advanced and adopted simultaneously as discoveries or creations emerge, without much, if any, consideration for how it will impact the individuals and societies utilizing it, or those left without its use, as we've seen with the advent and advance of Artificial Intelligence (AI).

A unitive view toward new technologies is urgently needed in this pivotal moment. We are still at the frontiers of technological development.

Decades ago, social development projects carried out around the world had few universally held guiding principles to direct those projects. Today, we are beginning to recognize the crucial importance of approaching those projects from a unitive global development perspective.

New technologies must also be approached from a unitive perspective. The development of new technologies must be seen as a global enterprise that all individuals in all societies have access to and that contributes to the advancement of their communities and the world by helping to bring about justice, equity, reciprocity, collective prosperity, and unity.

There is both great interest in and concern for new technologies, like AI in their many forms and platforms now becoming available, as evidenced in the many global summits on AI. The question of human nature in relation to AI needs to be fully explored by regional, national, and global institutions and organizations.

Since our conception of human nature inevitably shapes the design of new technology, we must examine whether human nature is both material and spiritual, where we derive our greatest meaning from, and what our greatest source of hope and inspiration is. Only then will we be able to answer whether AI technologies are conducive to the flourishing and advancement of individual and social potential.

With these parameters as preliminary considerations, we can better conclude how AI needs to be designed to help individuals contribute meaningfully to their communities and to society at large by becoming active participants in positive change. Ensuring that AI driven data is bias-free is another matter that requires social discourse to shape social structures and educational systems to reflect the reality of unity-in-diversity.

The world's technology entrepreneurs, social leaders, civic planners, government representatives, and other thought leaders would do well to convene and consult on the best approach and practices to follow to ensure that AI and other new technologies are indeed designed and utilized with the best interests of the common good as the priority in its advancement.

The constructive use of modern technology for the collective good is essential in ensuring our harmony, equity, and unity as a human family. It is also vital to ensure that our own innate qualities, sensitivities, and creativity are not ignored by relying too much on AI to assist in things our own intuition, creativity, or insights can accomplish more authentically.

There are spiritual energies released into the world, ready to infuse new life into every sphere of human endeavor, inaugurating a new stage in the social evolution of the planet toward its unity and wholeness. It would be anti-climactic to become dependent upon an intelligence that is artificial, while we ourselves have access to sources yet unknown that will lead to further discoveries and insights, through a greater intelligence, just as scientists and artists always have had access to in making the greatest advances the world has seen. Unitive technology is technology that will bring about unity.

Unitive Media

Media typically serves a full range of functions, delivering whatever message comes along. Media often shapes and influences the way the message is received and understood, and can either enhance or detract from a message, having a profound effect on the way it is perceived. Unitive media would seek to convey messages that bring about unity, build harmony, serve the good of the whole, and contribute to making unitive consciousness the norm in all media communications.

Unitive journalism is a key component of unitive media. In *Activating the Common Good,* Peter Block refers to journalism giving "first priority to what is working and end the obsession with what is not..." Rather than perpetuating divisive narratives, storylines that continue to separate us, journalists, as well as media platforms, could instead shift to covering those stories that connect and unite us.

Unitive Leadership

To move away from leadership that is only concerned with advancing one's own group or agenda, regardless of what that requires to accomplish, we need leaders whose primary intent it is to break down barriers between groups to work for the good of the whole and the betterment of the world. This would be primarily a leadership style designed to foster connection and cooperation, thus empowering others toward unity in action.

Unitive leadership would be built upon our shared responsibility of implementing the transformation of words and ideas into deeds, or action steps that bring about unity. The instability in the world calls for leaders who will overcome the prevailing paralysis of will and lead in a movement from words to deeds.

Unitive leadership is leadership that first and foremost strives to bring about and maintain unity. Critically important in these times is for groups and organizations of all sizes to consciously attempt to achieve the most effective outcomes for the greatest good in all their endeavors. Further exploration and development of unitive leadership styles and models are greatly needed.

Unitive Pattern

Though patterns are typically seen as separate from each other, there is an invisible thread linking all patterns into a greater wholeness. A unitive pattern reveals connections in apparent randomness and hidden power in a common source that, when consciously understood, lead to significant advances. One example of this is the traditional story model of beginning, middle, and end, or, taken to a deeper level, the mythic pattern of beginning, *muddle*, and *resolution*, which represents a universal pattern defining the process of transformation, as made popular by Joseph Campbell's hero/heroine journey, consisting of separation, initiation, and return. This is ultimately a pattern that brings about unity.

Applied in a different, proactive way, a unitive pattern can also be consciously built out by systematically discovering unifying, inclusive approaches to community building and social action and then replicating these to solve social problems in other settings. This method has been carried out by the communities referred to in the next chapter utilizing a collaborative learning process to achieve unity in their communities.

Unitive Politics

We must also emphasize and prioritize the art and practice in public affairs, government, and affairs of state the need to undertake activities and make agreements between people for the purpose of bringing about unity. Decision making and relations among individuals in civic affairs must be equity-based, seeking outcomes and a course of action for the good of the whole, rather than power-based and seeking what would benefit the few.

The Unitive Age will invite and inspire many more such unitive ways of being, becoming, and doing in the world. The way of unity is at the forefront in designing and building the greater fullness of unity-in-diversity needed for world peace.

This great new era that will unfold over the coming decades and centuries is the time foretold by many of the world's sacred traditions when a unitive consciousness will become the norm. This is the time when all our relationships and initiatives from local to global levels will be carried out for the express purpose of bringing about and maintaining unity. Our evolutionary flow is toward one unified circle of Wholeness, from which no one will be excluded.

Our emerging unitive age depends upon achieving and maintaining harmony and unity in all endeavors. Unity is what will most characterize the spirit of the age. Unity cannot be achieved without wholeness. Achieving this wider unity on a global scale in the social, cultural, and economic spheres means living by the common values and principles that bring us together in unity, as one human family sharing the planet with all other life.

CHAPTER 6

Unity-in-Action for the Betterment of the World

The way of unity is integral to humanity realizing the undivided wholeness that is the nature of the Universe. The reason we exist, the goal toward which we evolve, is the realization of our unity. Becoming the living, embodied reflection of the sacred unity around us is humanity's purpose to carry out in the world.

This is achieved by living with a unitive consciousness, where unity is all there is. In this consciousness, we are connected on a deep level with all living things. This is the way of unity built upon a love that is universal and selfless.

There is no greater, more sacred, purpose than to become the cause of peace and well-being in the world. As spiritual traditions affirm, love is a universal, timeless elixir, the supreme force through which we can achieve wholeness and coherence on Earth.

A unitive process in its fullness and completion ensures the long-desired outcome of peace. It begins with the *knowledge* of the relevant principles buoyed by the will, or *volition*, to do something with this knowledge and culminates in the well-thought out *action* to bring the vision inspired by the principles into reality.

As each set of circumstances requiring action presents its own challenges, there can be no rigid formula for action in all settings. Insights gleaned from effort exerted informs a general process of growth and development toward unity. Commitment to the guiding unitive principles and a contribution of all involved are what most enrich the whole.

One example of such unity-in-action is found within the Bahá'í world community that has been building an infrastructure of local, regional, and national and international administrative bodies for over a century. Currently, an estimated community of eight million, who constitute quite possibly the most diverse organized body of people on the planet, Bahá'í communities at each of these social levels have diligently striven to apply unitive principles in their daily lives and activities by working together to achieve a common goal and purpose to create conditions for peace within the community and throughout the world.

The Bahá'í international community shares a deep commitment to these unitive principles that guide their personal and community endeavors toward fully realizing a long-standing vision of peace on Earth. For over a century, Bahá'ís around the world have been carrying out the vision and plan established by Bahá'u'lláh for creating a world based on justice and the unity of all peoples. With representation in more than 100,000 localities in virtually every country and territory worldwide, including over 1600 ethnic groups, its members seek by constructive means, within the national structures under which they live, to advance society toward that world consciousness which must underlie eventual peace and a world civilization.

In 1985, the Universal House of Justice suggested that the experience of this global community can serve as a living example of the expanding unity in the world. And, as "a single social organism, representative of the diversity of the human family, conducting its affairs through a system of commonly accepted consultative principles, and cherishing equally all the great outpourings of divine guidance in human history," it also offered it as "a model for study" for "reinforcing hope in the unity of the human family."

This effort toward global transformation currently occurring in every corner of the globe is the latest stage of an ongoing process to create the nucleus of an enterprise of infinite complexity and scale, one in which there are no shortcuts, and no formulas, only much learning to take place as every effort is made to draw on insights from the spiritual guidance applied, to consult on the questions that arise from local concerns and to reflect on the social action taken.

Because this "long-term process of community building seeks to develop patterns of life and social structures founded on the oneness of humanity," the Bahá'í community "recognizes the many challenges it faces as it strives to live up to its own lofty ideals. It is work that will take generations" of exertion by all of humanity to bring to fruition. Nevertheless, this "monumental task is approached with a humble attitude of learning," starting with small efforts in local neighborhoods. "The main thrust of Bahá'í efforts toward social change is to build vibrant communities characterized by unity in diversity, mutual support, and collective well-being."

The overall, long-range goal of reaching a global consensus about how we want to achieve world unity may feel like an impossible task. Yet, the Bahá'ís are pursuing this immense undertaking, first on a community level, knowing the overall goal will require the greatest of efforts and that it will be achieved in the fullness of time.

A UNITIVE APPROACH TO SOCIAL CHANGE

In his 2024 book, *Activating the Common Good*, Peter Block states:

"All of us, one way or another, are drawn to what is considered good for the Earth, for the community, for the general well-being of all individuals. This can go under the idea called *the common good...* The intention is to reach the point where the common good is the organizing principle and paradigm for our culture."

Applying the unitive principles highlighted in the last chapter, Bahá'í communities around the world, through what Block refers to as "relational activism," have had the common good as their organizing principle for over a century.

What enables the common good to be an organizing principle is the adoption of the overarching principle of the unity of the human family. This is what characterizes the distinct Bahá'í approach to social and economic development, what I refer to as the way of unity, which prioritizes the capacity building, empowerment, and flourishing of all communities and individuals within them to ensure the intended outcome of the social action undertaken – the equitable, balanced, harmonious, and unified functioning of all social levels of civilization.

Flourishing also rests upon the freedom to choose one's own destiny, which is required to reach one's inner potential. This is needed on a global level, ensuring that all who are impacted have a voice in the process. Social development has been at the forefront of activities in the Bahá'í community since the beginnings of the Faith in Iran during the nineteenth century. The earliest forms were a network of Bahá'í schools established across the country, among them the nationally renowned Tarbiyat school for girls started in the early 1900s.

The nascent Bahá'í community in Iran, while under persecution from state authorities, grew largely from individuals without an ability to read and write to, by 1973, a community whose members had achieved a 100% literacy rate among women under the age 40, while the national literacy rate among women was less than 20% at that time.

As the Bahá'í community grew and expanded beyond Iran, similar efforts to offer service to humanity continued to take shape across Africa, Latin America, Asia, and the Pacific on a modest scale informally integrating the principle of the unity of humankind and its corollary principle of balanced social and economic development into its community building efforts in hundreds of languages worldwide.

In 1983, this focus on the unity of humankind was incorporated into the Bahá'í community's regular pursuits, with the establishment of the Office of Social and Economic Development (OSED) at the Bahá'í World Centre in Haifa, Israel. Over time, this has evolved to facilitate a global collaborative learning process involving not only Bahá'ís but also the wider community. Meaningful conversations have addressed a range of current concerns such as the advancement of women, education, health, mass communication, agriculture, economic activity, and the environment in response to specific problems and challenges faced in those localities.

What stands out about the Bahá'í-inspired development process is that, first and foremost, it is based upon the implementation of the primary principle of the unity of the human family, and because of that:

- both development and social change are seen not as a process carried out by one people on behalf of another, but rather one in which people themselves, wherever they reside, are the protagonists of their own internally oriented process of development;

- the world is not seen as divided into categories of developed and underdeveloped regions, because the entire world is in need of a process of social and economic transformation that will manifest itself in an underlying coherence of the material and spiritual dimensions of life;

- what is seen as most needed in this unifying process of change and development is to create an environment that provides the spiritual, social, and material conditions necessary to ensure the security and flourishing of all; and,

- throughout all steps of the process, the overriding intention is seen as bringing about unity in all interactions, relationships, and activities.

By 2018, the extensive spread and increasing complexity of Bahá'í development efforts had yielded these lessons from placing the way of unity at the center of all their undertakings and applying them globally. This became the framework of a new institution, the Bahá'í International Development Organization, that assumed and extended the functions previously carried out by the OSED.

This new office reinforces the efforts for social action and change by individuals, communities, institutions, and agencies everywhere. Its primary purpose is to facilitate the global collaborative learning process that is unfolding in the world by fostering and supporting action and reflection as well as the gathering and systematization of experience, conceptualization, and outcomes.

The unitive approach to development and social change, founded upon the unitive principles described previously, emerges from the primary intention to maintain all relationships at the level of spiritual interactions. This is the natural outcome when the agreed upon operating principle is that the peoples of the world constitute a single human family living in a common global homeland.

With this primary unitive principle as the starting point to all social action initiatives, it is understood, because agreements reached in far off capitals impact the lives of multitudes around the world, that the welfare of any part of the human family is tied to the welfare of the whole. The foundation for progress and lasting development is the prosperity of the whole.

Progress toward this vision is already noticeable in the consensus the international community has achieved around the form of the UN Sustainable Development Goals and their various targets. However, the recognition of the interconnected nature of humanity is a precondition to translating those goals into lived reality.

For these goals to be achieved, the BIC has stated these ideals will require the practice of unity-in-action, or wholistic collaboration, inclusive processes, and mutual respect across every race, class, nationality, and religion. This includes decision-making, planning, execution and assessment to reflect the conviction that all people have a unique and vital role to play in the advancement of civilization and that more unified patterns of interaction can become an essential part of Agenda 2030's transformational vision.

Agenda 2030 is a vision involving a long-term process of billions of people worldwide arising together to release the universal capacity for transformative social change. But, because there is still much social upheaval based in assumptions of difference, there is much to be done before this can be realized. At the level of principle, there needs to be widespread agreement that humanity indeed constitutes a single people, although significantly diverse in language, history, and cultural expression.

Consciousness of this central organizing principle, though not fully practiced, is at the foundation and the heart of the United Nations system itself. This is a vision that requires a commitment on all levels, from grassroots community efforts to policies and tools provided by the UN to bring about the conditions worthy of the highest aspirations of the people.

The BIC's statement addresses the need to avoid the inequalities of the donor/recipient relationship, as well, by establishing new patterns of relationship between local communities, individual citizens, and social institutions through thoughtful consultation on their shared future and incorporating meaningful decision-making that seeks to set in motion a process to draw on the talents and perspectives of all involved.

This is a process most concerned with expanding prosperity by strengthening the bonds of unity. The UN is uniquely positioned to play a leading role in facilitating such processes of learning at the global level that result not only in more balanced global development but also in greater global solidarity, and in world unity.

There are clear signs of integration accelerating on all sides. This is not only marked by the decline and decay of existing structures that is occurring, but at the same time a worldwide process of transition and transformation, with new forms of collaboration and cooperation emerging, ultimately requiring global solutions that address inequality and social fragmentation, that in turn call for an expansion of consciousness and identity where thinking of oneself as a global citizen will become the norm.

This unitive vision would be built upon universal systems that cannot be undermined by picking and choosing between a patchwork of independent national policies. This is why it is essential that the United Nations truly functions as one body for the good of the whole Earth. Building societies of equality and inclusion that work together as one global agency to release universal capacity is a process of societies refashioning themselves during times of transition and transformation while inspired by a shared vision of the future and committed to a common course of action. This is how the vast potential of an increasingly united and purposeful humanity will be unleashed.

The complete unity-in-action required for this to happen means increasing international cooperation to a level that ensures a collective commitment to a deeper deliberation of the time horizon within which the results of such unitive action need to be evident. The need for such action is urgent and the parallel need for shifts in consciousness, thinking, and behavior are dramatic. Finding a balance between these tensions, and also between a social order built upon state sovereignty with the practical needs of our global interdependence is a great challenge.

A fully effective international commitment to collective social change may seem like a long way off. Yet, the only way to realize the completion of the transformation already in progress is to begin to center our wider deliberations, in this moment, on finding, agreeing to, and committing to carry out a shared and long-term vision. The current dichotomies need not slow us down.

The opportunity for meaningful dialogue is ever-present. The approach chosen can be both urgent and thoughtful, innovative and efficient, at the same time, acknowledging the breadth of cooperation and collaboration necessary, from individual concerned citizens to all reaches of civil society and all emerging structures of global institutions.

We are entering new territory, a new chapter in human evolution that is largely uncharted, except in the vision we carry of its promise. We are engaged in a gradual but deliberate process that depends upon learning as we go from our guiding principles and from the direct experience we gain from their implementation. Balanced and unitive development is best discovered and refined as it is practiced. This is a learning process that enhances peaceful interaction, solidifies our common identity as a human family, and reaffirms our interdependence with our one shared planet.

CAPACITY BUILDING, EMPOWERMENT, AND COHERENCE FOR DEEPER IMPACT

Capacity building results in the realization of innate potential. When initiatives are undertaken to release this inner potential on a community or collective level, and a framework for collaborative learning is followed, the results are empowering.

These possibilities provide great hope; yet there is much to be overcome before we see their full and complete realization. Inequity, discrimination, economic and every other kind of exploitation, deep seated structural defects in society, and political schemes of every sort stand in the way of this greater coherence in the world.

Historically determined conditions do not define the future. As humanity continually evolves, and cyclical processes continue, what might have sufficed for its adolescent phase of development will no longer serve its dawning age of maturity. Unitive relationships are built upon trust. Humanity is being called to rethink its approaches to solving global problems. Each crisis thrown its way exposes the precarious nature of relationships within communities as well as between nations. All these relationships are foundational to a stable global order.

As Principal Representative of the Bahá'í International Community to the UN Bani Dugal puts it, "There are certain prerequisites for success in any collective endeavor and paramount among them is trust... Without both trust and trustworthiness, the stability of every endeavor is compromised." Trust at all levels of society must be earned. As trust is built and nurtured through honoring commitments, a genuine will to work becomes evident, and as actions correspond to those most valued commitments, capacity is also built.

Trustworthy relationships create a framework for collective learning that contributes to growing, vibrant communities that in turn heighten social consciousness, which, through focused meaningful conversations on the community's most challenging issues, lead to increased social action undertaken by individuals, small groups, and communities.

This commitment to building vibrant, peaceful communities already goes beyond the Bahá'í community itself to its friends, neighbors, and colleagues. It includes implementing a regularly occurring series of core activities that bring the wider community together to accomplish a range of outcomes under one focus. These gatherings are both collaborative learning processes and the foundation for social action initiatives that merge to bring about personal and social transformation.

Author and president of the International Environment Forum Arthur Dahl explains the deep and wide impact the collaborative learning process can have.

> "If a community or neighborhood has developed children's classes to teach basic virtues and moral values, accompanies its junior youth in adopting their own framework of values and discovering the satisfaction of acts of service to the community,

and holds devotional meetings and study circles on spiritual themes to help people find shared spiritual perspectives in all their diversity, it will have the capacity to consult together about any challenges it may face and to find local solutions and ways forward. An organic process of governance at the grassroots will empower people for change to everyone's benefit."

Such collective learning can only occur through the long-term, world-wide, inclusive and cooperative efforts of all to apply spiritual principles, coupled with the latest knowledge and methods of the sciences, to achieve the fullest possible material and social progress. This collective process of learning in diverse contexts, exploring the meaning and implications of development in all its dimensions, is essential in assisting humanity's movement toward its collective maturity.

Effective social action can only operate on the principle of universal participation. This must transcend tools such as surveys and focus groups to actively involve growing numbers of diverse peoples of all beliefs in a collect-ive process of learning throughout neighborhoods and villages worldwide. Endeavors of social and economic development that are intended to serve all people in a community must strive to elicit the widest possible participation as a service to humanity. They are often undertaken in collaboration with government agencies and organizations of civil society that share similar aims.

Inspired by principles promoting unity-in-diversity, these projects avoid and move beyond divisions prevalent in society today. Bonds of collaboration extend across ethnicities and national boundaries to show the practicality of the oneness of humanity. This global endeavor must be founded upon the context of an emerging world civilization existing to ensure the flourishing of all its citizens, as expressed in the BIC's *For the Betterment of the World*:

"The barriers raised by the thoughts, attitudes, and habits of the childhood of humankind are gradually being uprooted, and the structures of a new civilization that reflect the powers of adulthood are taking shape. This conception of history endows every instance of social action with a particular purpose: to foster true prosperity, with its spiritual and material dimensions, among the diverse inhabitants of the planet."

The experience of this "true prosperity" requires that the hallmark principle of the oneness of humanity be fully recognized and integrated into the patterns of life at all levels of society, which in turn requires the essential diversity of humanity to be honored and preserved through a fully functioning system of justice that brings about unity in all circumstances.

This ultimate goal necessitates the full development of the spiritual and material aspects of society and the coherence and balance between them to enable all to enjoy the fruits of a prosperous global society. Only the achievement of such a dynamic coherence will enable the reform of social structures on all levels to sustain harmonious relationships that foster vibrant communities contributing to a flourishing civilization.

The full spectrum of tools, capabilities, and perspectives, from scientific ways of observing and rigorously testing ideas to the deep awareness of faith and spiritual convictions that contribute to virtue, good character, and cooperation must be incorporated in the process of social development.

Understanding, adopting, and implementing the unitive principles underlying this collective learning is essential to the capacity building process also under way. Beyond the provision of goods and services, which can create its own problems, it is even more essential in development and social action endeavors to expand the capacity of participants, and therefore communities, to contribute directly to the process they are benefitting from.

Building capacity includes developing interrelated capabilities. Both individuals and communities will flourish as they develop the capacities – intellectual, social, technical, and moral – to make informed decisions about how their grassroots actions can best be exerted in ways that make coordination and cooperation possible on a global scale.

Organic growth is the goal in all development and social action endeavors. Progress depends largely on the natural stirrings that arise where there is a unity of purpose. A strong sense of community results from unified engagement. Out of this emerges a growing group consciousness resulting in the collective will to carry out unified action toward a common goal.

A cycle of success is seen in this process as relatively simple sets of actions managed locally gain in complexity naturally and in an organic fashion as the participants gain experience and increase their capacity to make and implement decisions about their spiritual and material progress.

This gives rise to projects of a more sustained nature with more ambitious goals, and this cycle is repeated on larger and larger scales as new organizational structures are created along the way to support the advances made. Well-conceived methods and approaches that emerge in one country or region are then shared with others to channel the flow of knowledge and add to the cycle of successes.

The wise application of the unitive principles to bring about social transformation is learned through such experience. These principles not only define and delineate *the way of unity* as leading to practical solutions to challenging issues but also, with each repeated cycle, reaffirms their inherent wisdom and truth as operating principles for bringing about unity.

As the BIC points out, development as a collaborative learning process for bringing about unity "can best be described as one of study (reading society and formulating a vision), consultation, action, and reflection on action – all carried out in the light of the guidance inherent in religious teachings and knowledge drawn from science."

This involves an ongoing cooperative effort through which "visions and strategies are re-examined time and again. As tasks are accomplished, obstacles removed, resources multiplied, and lessons learned, modifications are made in goals and methods… The learning process… unfolds in a way that resembles the growth and differentiation of a living organism." Rather than being a "top-down" *or* a "bottom-up" approach to development and social transformation, this is one of reciprocity and interconnectedness, with both operating at the same time toward a common goal and meeting in the middle.

To facilitate this ever-expanding cyclical collaborative learning process of study, consultation, action, and reflection on action even further, women, youth, and other people traditionally marginalized need to be fully involved in every step. Without their unique and extremely valuable perspective, the narrative of the process is incomplete.

The future belongs to today's youth, and they have a vital role to play in helping to build a compelling vision of the future they hope to inherit and pass on to future generations. While humanity navigates its turbulent yet promising period of collective transformation to a new stage of maturity, youth are in the throes of their own adolescent transition. Their direct experience of what is needed to complete this transition to a new world is vital to the process.

Youth have always been at the forefront of movements for social change. Young people possess a strength of imagination, a depth of belief in transformation, and a direct understanding of the need for thorough change. They are not only less attached to the systems that need to be replaced, but they can also better conceptualize alternatives and have more energy and freedom to put them into practice. This is not to romanticize young people. Some may well need to escape attachment to conditions of privilege and the like, but this is all part of their own process of forming an identity they will be comfortable living with.

Just as important is how the community, or society, views their own youth. As BIC youth representative to the UN Liliane Nkunzimana put it:

"Any society's vision of itself and its future is inextricably tied to its attitudes toward youth... The way that a population views the qualities and characteristics of youth themselves is connected to its own sense of identity and collective purpose."

The spiritual truth of gender equality also needs to be raised to the level of an operating principle in the affairs of a world that is struggling through a deep and fundamental transformation toward unity-in-diversity. The role of women especially in building a flourishing world civilization cannot be ignored or denied any longer.

Throughout most of history, imbalanced systems and infrastructures have favored men's progress and participation over women's. Crisis after crisis, women's potential continues to be suppressed by systemic and structural injustice. The educational opportunity of women should be given emphasis in all communities as they are most often the first educators of the next generation. The distinct qualities that women can bring to the workforce, and to every sphere of life, have long been undervalued.

As the BIC has put it, "Humanity can be likened to a bird with two wings, the male and the female, that has struggled to take flight because the female wing has been suppressed for so long. Who can fully envision the great heights to which humanity will soar when both wings are coordinated and strong?"

The full participation of youth and women in the building of a new world will enable and ensure the collective empowerment of all. Empowerment is a means of improving quality of life and expanding the basis of human well-being. It serves as a leading mechanism for effecting deep and broad-based social transformation.

The impact of social action resulting from an organic process built upon increased capacity and empowerment is more noticeable and longer lasting. This approach is targeted toward renewing and strengthening just and equitable social structures that at the same time are enabling and supporting individual and collective transformation.

The collaborative learning process, as a method of empowerment and a mechanism for social transformation, assists three levels of society at the same time: *individuals*, to manifest constructive capacities in creative and disciplined ways; *institutions*, to exercise authority that leads to the progress and upliftment of all; and, *communities*, to provide an environment in which culture is enriched and individual wills and capacities combine in collective action.

In the collaborative learning process, all perspectives, all points of view, listen to each other to identify their common ground, to become one, and to realize the whole they already are. Collaborative learning is the way to unity and harmony. This process further requires a reset on certain limiting notions of human nature, such as "us" and "them," to rectify existing social inequalities, making the approach a truly universal and shared enterprise, not something the "haves" bestow on the "have nots," where all have the capacity and the honor to advance the welfare of the whole, and where "power" is spread out equally among all.

In seeking to promote the well-being of people of all backgrounds and beliefs, all social action is placed within the broader context of the advancement of civilization. This is laying the foundation for the next stage of a centuries-long process of social evolution that will achieve a dynamic coherence between all the various dimensions and requirements of life when the very patterns of life – social structures, interpersonal relationships, economic practices, and models of governance – will all be aligned for the same common purpose.

All such social action intended to transform toward unity is dependent upon – and framed by – the application of unitive principles. This not only ensures consistency of the values underpinning every initiative, but it also provides a clear method to be employed for attaining the end goal that is sought.

Maintaining consistency and coherence between belief and practice, principle and action, is essential – even necessary – in preventing disharmony or disruption of the process and achieving the desired outcome of every social action initiative. Placing this on the policy level for carrying out initiatives ensures the ethical, focused behavior needed to succeed. It also validates the proposition that humanity thrives most when we all cooperate.

MODELS OF SOCIAL ACTION FOR BUILDING COMMUNITIES OF PEACE

Bahá'ís around the world are working at the community level, building capacity on larger and larger scales, enabling people everywhere to take the lead in their own development, with everyone involved unified around the principle that humanity is one people, all contributing to the well-being of the whole, carrying out a common enterprise of deep renewal.

Within the last decade, as local populations have built the capacities and qualities needed to sustain long-term progress, including the creation of consultative spaces in their villages and neighborhoods that invite all members to participate, Bahá'í communities have increased their social action initiatives from 400 to 200,000 in over 180 nations and territories, preparing millions around the world to support and encourage global transformative change.

The infrastructure enabling this progress is the emergence over the last couple decades of a global network of some 330 national and regional training institutes functioning in virtually every country in more than 100,000 localities. These institutes offer courses to assist individuals in strengthening their moral and spiritual capacities, as well as drawing insights from spiritual writings that identify their projects' guiding principles and inform the social action process.

People from all walks of life engage in a participatory process of study, action, and reflection that contributes to the betterment of their communities, multiplies community-based initiatives, and contributes to greater collaboration among a broader range of participants. This global network represents the diversity of the entire human family. In a spirit of cooperative and collaborative learning, Bahá'í families and friends of all religious backgrounds, social standing, gender, and ethnicity strive to cultivate hope not only for their own community but also for the future of humanity, by promoting unity and the upliftment of all.

Their activities range from small informal group efforts of limited duration to sustained more complex and sophisticated initiatives carried out by development organizations, each one commensurate with the capacities of the people in the community carrying it forward to apply the appropriate principles to improve their quality of life.

Social Action Projects of Fixed Duration

Of the more than 100,000 grassroots initiatives of a limited duration annually following this framework of study, consultation, harmonizing points of view with collective decision-making, and strengthening the bonds of trust, leading to well-informed and purposeful action as service to humanity to transform the world around them, here are a few to serve as models.

In the densely populated neighborhood of Mtandire, in Lilongwe, Malawi, several grassroots initiatives in an area of about 500 homes have been underway after a group of youth who had participated in Bahá'í educational programs offered their own spiritual education classes to children and junior youth around their homes. The number of participants in these activities increased as parents readily encouraged the efforts to contribute to the academic and moral development of their children.

Over time, a pattern of community life bringing together spiritual study and service to others took root and expanded further. The spirit of mutual support and concern for the well-being of their community led to additional endeavors focused on service projects, including visits to the sick and elderly, helping establish a shared vegetable garden, peer academic and creative tutoring, and supporting mothers with adult literacy programs who then work together to start small income-generating activities to improve their economic circumstances.

This has also led to collaborating with local professionals and organizations to help resolve challenges, such as promoting the education of girls by having an organization offer assistance, as well as managing more complex undertakings like having a community preschool sustained by local resources which they envision will gradually grow into offering all grades of primary education with the assistance of nearby Bahá'í-inspired organizations.

A group of youth, in Sao Sebastao, Brazil, consulting about the local environment, decided to clean a river littered with trash. They created a newsletter to raise awareness of protecting the environment and shared other uplifting news. Over time, a municipal office became aware of the clean-up effort and provided resources to reinforce the initiative.

In Makeni, Sierra Leone, a group of youth, inspired by the important role that young people play in serving society, created a film to convey information on effective health measures at the start of the COVID-19 pandemic. The initiative assisted doctors, village leaders, and the broader community during a time of great need.

A family in Stockholm, Sweden, arranged for an artistic workshop in a public space for a few volunteers and local artists to create a mural together on the theme of spiritual and material transformation. This workshop was open to all and provided a space for meaningful conversations in the community to continue.

In Durham, North Carolina, as an example of similar initiatives across the United States, community gatherings were held to consult about how groups of families can share resources and support each other. This resulted in several initiatives including a pop-up clinic for vaccinations and language classes for parents new to the country.

A group of youth in Battambang, Cambodia, planted trees alongside a road to beautify the village and provide shelter from the heat. One year later, the trees protected that section of the road from severe erosion at the onset of flooding.

These modest activities represent responses to challenges in a variety of locales that sprung from the application of spiritual principles, such as oneness, generosity, and trustworthiness. They illustrate the universality of the transformative power of a unity-in-action approach in a diversity of social settings and realities.

Sustained Social Action Projects

Over 2000 ongoing larger scope sustained development projects are also being carried out by Bahá'ís worldwide. They are built upon the same spiritual principles and follow the same process as the short-term projects but involve more complex circumstances.

Ownership of sustained social action endeavors is with the community itself, as building capacity is even more vital here, and learning in action is still the mode of operation. But wider support also becomes important as co-sponsoring or facilitating institutions become involved as partners in the endeavor offering a voice of moral authority or coherence in relation to other processes of community life. Here are a few examples.

In India, a group of high school students, after having been in a Bahá'í educational program that builds capacity for service, were challenged with finding access to suitable study environments for after school hours. With the closest library three kilometers away, they explored the idea of collectively creating a library and discussed the importance of involving their parents and others in the community. The parents lent their support to the idea, and this led to identifying an extra room in a village temple that could be used as a study space.

The village leader pledged the needed funds for magazine and newspaper subscriptions. The youth collected and contributed books, with more added over time, including high school textbooks, storybooks, and scriptures from various religions, while items for furnishing were donated. The youth decided to elect annually, through secret ballet, a chairperson who would voluntarily facilitate the needs of the library in consultation with others.

Over the following years, more than 100 youth became members of the library study space. This influenced and changed community life by helping to nurture a culture of collective study and mutual support among young people, who learned to create an uplifting, inclusive environment, build unitive relationships, and tutor younger students, enhancing the standard of education in their village.

They further met the challenges and temporary setbacks inherent in development initiatives by reflecting on the importance of applying spiritual principles to new situations, consulting with local institutions, and when the facility no longer became available, expanded their vision to eventually shift the library to a larger hall at the center of the village, which was more accessible to all ages and boys and girls alike, and became the Samudaaya Shiksha Kendra (Community Education Center).

When the country went into lockdowns resulting from the COVID-19 pandemic, the closure of schools meant increasing numbers of tutorial activities in and around the center, which necessitated formalizing a five-member education team, who drew on the technical support of a Bahá'í-inspired development organization operating in the region. This led to a broader, deeper analysis of the existing education system, resulting in the center strengthening its bonds of collaboration in the village to foster a spirit of mutual collaboration and support in service to the common good. They plan to continue to evolve activities in the coming years by reflecting the aspirations of the community to promote environments of unity-in-diversity.

For over a century, the central African nation of the Democratic Republic of the Congo has experienced a series of violent struggles, the most recent being a war from 1998-2002 that claimed over 5.4 million lives, the world's deadliest crisis since World War II. During 2016-18 it had the highest number of people displaced by conflict, over 1.5 million according to the UN. Yet, there are communities throughout the country that are learning to transcend the traditional barriers that divide people.

In the remote village of Ditalala, connected to the closest town by a 25 kilometer path, a morning tradition of drinking the coffee they grow themselves before heading out to work on their farms has been transformed into a community-building experience. For the past few years, many families have been inviting their neighbors to join them for coffee and prayers before starting the day.

As a visitor to village described it, "Friends from the neighboring houses would gather while the coffee was being made, say prayers together, then share the coffee while laughing and discussing the issues of the community. There was a sense of true unity."

Where there used to be distinct divisions in the community, this tradition was not only transformative but also expanded to other related and more formal gatherings. These included moral and spiritual education classes for people of all ages, community consultation for decision-making supported by the Ditalala chief, and social well-being projects involving agriculture, maternal healthcare, clean water, and establishing a community school.

All of these changes impacting the entire village are inspired by the local Baha'i community applying unitive principles, including the oneness of humanity and the elimination of prejudice, to find ways to address deep-rooted problems while also giving youth a particular voice to be a force for positive change in their communities. The village name, Ditalala, means "peace" in the local language, and the village itself has been transformed by the vision of peace.

In other Congolese villages, regular conferences bringing together members of the community and special gatherings convening local chiefs have been taking place. One example is a three-day meeting of 60 village and tribal chiefs, many of whom were on opposing sides of armed conflict in the past, coming together to discuss social progress and decide on practical action to transform a tense coexistence into constructive and peaceful collaboration among the various ethnic groups and religious communities. This resulted in many chiefs calling regular meetings of all the women in their villages to discuss taking steps toward this goal, understanding that their participation was essential for successful reconciliation.

In Papua, New Guinea, a three-day community gathering with over 600 participants, arranged by the local Bahá'í institutions in collaboration with local government officials, resulted in an exploration of social, economic, and cultural barriers impeding spiritual and material progress, ways to strengthen cooperation among various entities central to community life, and establishing a committee to engage in more systematic collaboration with the local government.

In Myanmar, a microfinance project was started under the auspices of a local Bahá'í institution to provide material support to local farmers and vendors in the aftermath of a cyclone. A three-member task force oversees the project with the assistance of local institutions and was later extended to individuals in surrounding villages.

In Panama, a Bahá'í radio station was established in the 1980s to give voice to and serve as an educational and cultural channel for indigenous peoples, creating content in the form of original songs, stories, and interviews inspired by concepts such as service to society, coherence, love, and generosity.

A group of individuals in Iceland having conversations about the moral dimensions of tree planting through the Skogar reforestation project, first initiated in 1990, and bringing the Bahá'í community into contact with the wider society and other religious organizations, unfolded around the spiritual objectives of tree planting as part of the United Nations Environment Program's Faith for Earth initiative, which aims to "lay the foundation for inter-faith collaboration for sustainable and regenerative development to achieve Sustainable Development Goals."

And in neighborhoods throughout the United States, Bahá'ís and their friends are learning to put into practice the unitive principles of our time, engaging in community building following a collaborative learning process leading to unity-in-action.

Development Organizations

Bahá'í endeavors to contribute to social action toward the betterment of the world have also led to many formal development organizations that have grown organically in scale and complexity, gaining in capacity to work at all levels of society with many agencies of government and civil society, and ensuring their long-term viability.

Some are agencies of Bahá'í governing councils and others are initiatives undertaken by groups of individual Bahá'ís as nonprofit, nongovernmental organizations operating under local civil law. Both types of organizations aim to apply spiritual principles to one or more areas of social concern. Here is a glimpse of a few of the over 170 such organizations.

FUNDAEC (Fundacion para la Aplicacion y Ensenanza de las Ciencias), established in 1974, engages in research and action to address the needs of young people in Colombia through education, social action, community leadership, and youth programs to help develop a strong sense of purpose in contributing to the transformation of society. Their Preparation for Social Action program leads to becoming a "Promoter of Community Well-Being" and has inspired many participants to initiate similar programs around the world.

Yayasan Bhinneka Tunggal Ika Universal (Unity in Diversity Foundation), was established in 1996 in Indonesia to contribute to the advancement of remote communities in the country by improving educational opportunities for children. It now supports over 30 early childhood development centers and offers ongoing training for over 40 teachers.

Breakwell Institute was formed after a group of youth and young professionals in the Netherlands reflected on the systemic forms of injustice and unequal access to education in their neighborhood. Over several years, the group collaborated with local agencies, community centers, and a mosque to develop educational materials and ways the youth could channel their talents toward the betterment of their societies and their own career aspirations.

Emergence Foundation for Education and Development, established in 2003 in Cameroon to contribute to the moral empowerment of young people in the country, focuses its efforts on implementing action research and programs in the area of agriculture.

Four Bahá'í inspired organizations in Canada and the United States – **Center for Studies in Community Progress, Coherent Development Research Institute, Colibri Learning Foundation,** and **Wordswell Association for Community Learning** – have initiated a process of collaborative action research around shared areas of endeavor to release the potential of youth by assisting them in developing certain capacities, skills, and attitudes that can help them meet their noble aspirations.

Foundation for the Advancement of Science, based in Uttar Pradesh, India, has been engaged since 1996 in training teachers from schools in rural communities, and more recently has been focusing on promoting health through the training of young mothers by creating awareness-raising materials on the subject.

Ootan Marawa Educational Institute began in the 1990s to support teachers in Kiribati to build capacity in their students for service to society.

Extending its educational efforts over time, it now has around 900 youth participating in the program and has provided technical support to 17 kindergartens serving over 200 students.

Kimanya-Ngeyo Foundation for Science and Education in Uganda established an agricultural research farm for participants in the Preparation for Social Action program to apply the knowledge and capacities they gain from their study toward sustainable agricultural approaches that serve the community's needs more effectively.

These are just a few of the thousands of examples of Bahá'í inspired unity-in-action projects for the betterment of the world to assist and facilitate efforts toward social transformation and peacebuilding. They demonstrate that there is much that can be done worldwide to resolve the myriad social concerns of our communities.

The conditions of the world are being shaped by the actions each person takes each day. These initiatives to build a culture of peace in our own neighborhoods, over time, contribute to building a world at peace. The ongoing progress toward this end goal could well take centuries. Yet, this process is what every generation has longed to be part of.

The approach to social action and transformation set forth in the previously identified unitive principles and implemented in these examples are effective remedies for removing the root causes of the ills afflicting society and preventing us from realizing the long-held vision of a peaceful world.

In carrying out the way of unity in their everyday lives, these communities model and move toward fulfillment of the vision and principles of Bahá'u'lláh and 'Abdu'l-Bahá, for whom peace is the essence and goal of all humanitarian work in the world.

As Hoda Mahmoudi and Janet Khan put it in *A World Without War*, "The objective of the Bahá'í Faith as laid out in the teachings of its founder, Bahá'u'lláh, is the attainment of universal peace." Indeed, "There was no separating peace from the Bahá'í Faith, nor was there any separation between the Faith and peace. Peace was both medium and message, and the Bahá'í Faith itself was the vehicle for establishing peace."

The Bahá'í Faith, with its worldwide social action initiatives, transcends and transforms the prevailing definitions of both traditional and modern religion. Sometimes described as the world's newest religion, beyond that, it is:

- a way to cultivate a unitive consciousness;
- a way of building equitable and unitive relationships at all levels of society;
- a way to the flourishing and prospering of all humanity;
- a global model of coherence for unity-in-action;
- a system for bringing about the deep transformation of the individual, the community, and the world; and,
- an initiative for world peace that has already been carried out in 1000s of communities worldwide.

And, ultimately, it is:

- a way to inner peace,
- a way to interpersonal peace, and
- a way to world peace.

PART 3

Unity in All Spheres Is the Only Way to Peace

CHAPTER 7

The Way of Unity to Inner Peace

A committed spiritual practice, such as prayer and meditation, is the surest way to cultivate inner peace. Any way you choose to accomplish this is a way toward not just inner peace but also toward world peace at the same time.

We can easily become burdened by inner conflict and turmoil going on within us due to so many things in this complex, divided world we live in. The injustices going on all over the world cause great suffering beyond their point of origin. They also threaten and disrupt our own inner peace. That's all the more reason to commit to practices that will help maintain a quality of balance that can withstand these tumultuous times. It's not a once and for all effort to achieve unwavering inner peace, but rather an ongoing process that is aided and assisted by the regular practice that suits each of us best.

The goal is to achieve alignment of all parts of ourselves to each other and to our whole self, harmonizing the various elements of our mind, heart, body, and spirit to the greater whole they all make up.

True inner peace is all our component parts functioning as a smoothly run unit, as a unified organism, in which all work together for the benefit of the whole. If we are not united within ourselves, or at peace as an individual, we will be ill prepared to contribute to the wider peace around us.

One of our first, most important, tasks is to resolve any inner incoherence to ensure that we are aligned with our higher being and our higher purpose. This is how we'll know clearly what is most important to us and how we can best accomplish our personal goal of contributing to the greater goal of unity and peace around us and in the world. But this takes inner work and regular practice to make the changes that might be needed in our outlook and approach to the whole. At the same time, it is by working on our whole self all at once that leads us toward inner peace and wholeness, ultimately enabling us to contribute to the greater unity of which we are always part.

As Vietnamese Buddhist monk Thich Nhat Hanh said, "Peace is the practice of mindfulness, the practice of being aware of our thoughts, our actions, and the consequences of our actions." This means bringing "awareness into each moment of our lives," which is the way that "peace will bloom during your daily activities."

The peace that begins to bloom through the practice of being aware is the peace that cements our connection with all other things. As Lakota holy man Black Elk said: "The first peace, which is the most important, is that which comes within the souls of men when they realize their relationship, their oneness, with the Universe and all its powers... There can never be peace between nations until there is first known that true peace, which is within the souls of men."

This hidden inner peace is latent within us all, inhabiting and animating our soul. It is always aligned with the Greater Unity. As historian Arnold Toynbee noted, "The quest for ultimate spiritual reality is inborn in human nature... We are now moving into an age in which it will be more difficult to ignore this truth."

NURTURING PEACE IN OUR HEARTS

The location of inner peace is the spiritual center of our being, most often identified as our heart. This must be discovered, nurtured, and harvested, as systems thinker Ervin Laszlo said, "Attaining peace in people's hearts is a precondition of attaining peace in the world. Inner peace depends very much on creating more equitable conditions in the global village."

The reciprocal interdependence of inner and outer peace may seem obvious to some, but it is also backed up by significant research. The HeartMath Institute has shown that the optimal state of heart coherence benefits the entire body, generates a magnetic field that can be detected outside the body, affects the mental and emotional state of others around us, and connects every living organism on the planet, all of which all contribute to global coherence and world peace.

Personal coherence begins in the heart and is experienced as inner peace. This is the state that harmoniously unites our mind, body, and spirit in cooperation and flow, to assist each other in manifesting their innate unity and wholeness. In this state we not only desire peace in the world, but also have begun the process of bringing it about by planting peace in our own hearts. HeartMath has undertaken the research and provided the findings for what spirituality has said for centuries.

Humanity has been endowed with the treasury of love everlasting. This is to be cherished as is every other endowment we have been gifted. Our every thought, utterance, and action is intended to be an expression of this love. This is the fruition of our spiritual nature, which has very different powers than our material nature. In the former, we approach the divine, and in the latter we live *"for the world alone."* The attributes of our spiritual nature *"are shown forth in love, mercy, kindness, truth and justice,"* while the *"material aspect expresses untruth, cruelty, and injustice."* As Abdu'l-Bahá explains: *"Every good habit, every noble quality belongs to man's spiritual nature, whereas all his imperfections and sinful actions are born of his material nature. If a man's Divine nature dominates his human nature, we have a saint."*

Because we have been endowed with an innate spiritual nature, the expression of which in the everyday world creates the necessary conditions for peace, we are like the glass of the lamp which reflects the divine light within it as we express our spiritual virtues in all our actions. These spiritual virtues are humanity's crowning endowment, assisting and guiding us toward both inner peace and world peace. They arise from the human spirit, guiding humanity toward transcendence and enabling us to advance both materially and spiritually.

To truly satisfy this inner endowment of the human spirit, which is the primary link between humanity and that ultimate reality, would be for us to fulfill our capacity to achieve spiritual success and social progress, both of which are essential to realizing world peace. The unitive principles outlined in chapter 5 show that there are some very significant preconditions that need to be established in the world for the complete and full realization of world peace. These preconditions stem directly from the flowering of the love in our hearts.

The coherence of the heart enhances and hones "the power of thought." When this finds "its manifestation in action," the greatest of results are achieved. Heart coherence turned into "the power of implementation," by taking the unitive principles leading to peace and shaping them into a practical strategy for pursuing peace, generates the coherence and energy within and beyond the human heart that finds its expression and fulfillment in the everyday world. This depends exclusively upon the love-in-action we bring into the world.

The coherent heart is very much needed to take real world action by applying its inner peace directly in practical ways toward building cultures of peace throughout the planet, as seen in chapter 6, founded upon the unitive principles that bring about and maintain unity on all levels of society. This requires a great deal of focused, conscious effort, but it may not be as difficult as it sounds. Humanity has more innate assets at our beck and call than we might think. As many spiritual traditions agree, human beings are not driven by self-interest alone, and possibly even more by altruistic means.

The soul, which is the part of us that connects us to all others, endows us with innate noble aspirations to foster the harmony, cooperation, and unity needed to build a peaceful world. This is the real, eternal self that inspires the mind to utilize its powers of thought, language, and action to refine the character with which we relate to all others and by which we contribute to the betterment of the world. The expressions of the soul are love, compassion, faith, courage, and all the other human qualities that cannot be fully explained by considering only our material or lower nature yet are essential in building peaceful relationships and a peaceful world.

All these expressions of our spiritual nature leading us toward peaceful actions in the world are developed and maintained through the practice of meditation and prayer, which in turn infuse the development of society.

The sacred unity at the root of humanity's essence is always available to us, but can only be fully realized by understanding our true nature as spiritual beings. The spiritual law of unity is the hallmark of our time. Its manifestation is inherent within us as a reflection of the greater unity all around us. Humanity is the channel of the appearance of unity in the world by bringing into being the expression of unity through living by unitive principles.

This essential, universal unity also provides an understanding of our true identity as a human being. The paramount need in the world now is the attainment of unity, uniting the diverse elements of a greater whole. Our task is to act on the awareness of our true reality, as spiritual beings, and express this unity in the world through such means as a spirit of service to others that will manifest our individual and collective unity and that build peace throughout the world.

In a Statement to the United Nations, the BIC identified the dual obligation to be met by each person: "First, the responsibility to establish unity within self, and among ourselves; then, to build a world society and bring about world order and a world civilization."

Humanity's essential identity as an expression of sacred unity provides the means for us to create a loving, harmonious, cooperative global civilization. Recognizing our innate unity, we can also see humanity's innate unity, with each of us being an essential component of that whole, knowing that if suffering afflicts one, it results in suffering for all. This means our individual inner peace depends upon our considering the welfare of the entire human community as our own. With every person being a cell in the body of humanity, and every nation a vital organ in the body of humanity, this is true for all of us.

As psychotherapist and Buddhist meditation teacher Tara Brach has said, "The hope for inner and world peace lies in our evolutionary capacity to shift from Fight-Flight-Freeze reactivity to responding to aggravation with Attend-Befriend." This depends on "three elements on the path of awakening that support us in this transformation: remembering our true aspiration; taking full responsibility (for whatever arises in our experience); and, widening the circles of our caring to include all beings."

DEVELOPING INNER CAPACITIES

Unitive consciousness is a precondition for the realization of the unity of the human family and of world peace. This is an inherent potentiality waiting to be drawn out and activated. But because we have an interconnected dual nature that is both spiritual and material, we are susceptible to the variations in the external environment and its influences. And so, each of us must pursue an earnest, committed quest to fulfill our spiritual nature.

This quest consists of utilizing our free will vigilantly and independently to investigate reality through a process of the unfettered search for truth.

English poet John Keats describes this quest as a process of "soul-making" since we are "sparks of divinity" who need to undergo all that "a World of Pains and troubles" gives us in order "to school an Intelligence and make it a soul."

This world is the anvil upon which the heart and the soul are shaped and formed, tested in the fire of difficulty, that they may become stronger. Soul-making happens when light merges with the dark, when joy and sorrow intermingle, and when the eternal breaks through from the temporal realm. Without developing our inner capacities on the anvil of outer challenges, we would never discover that which we inherently possess, and never become the strong beings we are created to be, to know the sheltering and soothing power of unity.

Spiritual inquiry develops spiritual perception. It only takes a little of one thing providing us with a taste of joy and contentment to create the desire to continue with that no matter what else might call to us. One such easily established habit leading to spiritual insight and understanding is regularly reading the sacred writings of the tradition or philosophy you are called to. The purpose of such a practice is not to read too much of the sacred verses and "*be overcome by languor and despondency*," or even carry out "*a multitude of pious acts*," but rather to read the verses with "*joy and radiance*," to be uplifted by them.

Meditation, too, can have a similar effect, beyond centering, focusing, and calming oneself, toward bringing about inner and outer peace, as Bahá'u'lláh makes clear, "*One hour's reflection is preferable to seventy years of pious worship.*" Through the practice of meditation we receive "*divine inspiration*," as the Bahá'í writings affirm. It is "*the key for opening the doors of mysteries*" and the way we immerse ourselves "*in the ocean of spiritual life*" to "*unfold the secrets of things-in-themselves.*"

The power of meditation depends upon the direction toward which we turn our efforts. The meditative faculty is like a mirror. If we turn it toward earthly subjects, we will be informed of those. But, if we turn the mirror of our spirits *"heavenwards, the heavenly constellations and the rays of the Sun of Reality will be reflected in your hearts."*

Through meditation, we *"may discover the secrets of the Kingdom, and comprehend the allegories of the Bible and the mysteries of the spirit."* This is the way we may *"become mirrors reflecting the heavenly realities,"* and *"become so pure as to reflect the stars of heaven."* Meditation can be the means for retrieving all the spiritual qualities and characteristics latent within that lead to actions that implement the structures and conditions for peace in the world. Similarly, *"prayer need not be in words, but rather in thought and attitude,"* as 'Abdu'l-Bahá noted. Turning a prayerful thought or attitude into a deed conveying love-in-action is a way of building peace in the world.

Through this practice we acquire inner and outer perfections which result in possessing a good character. This endows us with as much tenderness and joy for others as we have for ourselves, contributing all that is needed for a peaceful world, as 'Abdu'l-Bahá noted:

> *"Care for the stranger as for one of your own; show to all souls the same loving kindness ye bestow upon your faithful friends... Should any taunt and mock at you, meet him with love... Perchance such ways and words from you will make this darksome world turn bright at last; will make this dusty earth turn heavenly... so that war and strife will pass and be no more, and love and trust will pitch their tents on the summits of the world."*

STRIVING FOR SPIRITUAL DISTINCTION

The human soul is a mirror for the reflection of the divine. If our hearts are to be aligned with the divinity of the soul, and both be our connection to this source of supreme love, we are called to sanctify our hearts so we can fully express our deepest nature in the world. If we were to appreciate the greatness of our station and the loftiness of our destiny, we would, as

Bahá'u'lláh says, "*manifest naught save goodly character, pure deeds, and a seemly and praiseworthy conduct.*" He adds to this our other sacred task. "*Great also must be [our] endeavors for the rehabilitation of the world and the well-being of nations.*"

Good words are sorely needed, but even more so are good deeds. Bahá'u'lláh proclaimed in the mid-19th century:

> "*Guidance hath ever been given by words, and now it is given by deeds. Everyone must show forth deeds that are pure and holy, for words are the property of all alike... Strive then with heart and soul to distinguish yourselves by your deeds.*"

Standing out as distinguished can mean being as a "*lamp of divine guidance shining amongst the kindreds of the earth, with the light of love and concord.*" 'Abdu'l-Bahá gave an example of how this might be noticed in an everyday situation: "*Should any one of you enter a city, he should become a center of attraction by reason of his sincerity, his faithfulness and love, his honesty and fidelity, his truthfulness and loving-kindness towards all the peoples of the world.*"

This is spiritual distinction in its fullest expression, what 'Abdu'l-Bahá gives further example of, showing how this distinction is not dependent upon wealth or other material or intellectual means:

> "*You must become eminent and distinguished in morals... You must become distinguished for loving humanity, for unity and accord, for love and justice... you must become distinguished in all the virtues of the human world... for service to the human world, for love toward every human being, for unity and accord with all people, for removing prejudices and promoting international peace.*"

This is a recipe for bringing about deep and lasting inner peace in our daily lives. Though this is a lofty standard and high code to conform to, how else are we to build the foundation for peace on Earth?

By turning inward to ensure that all our relations with others are helping to bring about unity, and by standing with confidence against those forces attempting to sway society, we can offer acts of service to promote the welfare and common good of all.

The "honor and distinction" of a person is in benefiting society. The noblest deed is service to the common good, and the greatest blessing for any human being is to "become the cause of the education, the development, the prosperity and honor of one's fellow-creatures."

Striving for spiritual distinction first requires that we are committed to a spiritual path. That doesn't mean being religious, necessarily. But it does mean that we acknowledge that we have a spiritual nature. And when we believe we have a spiritual nature, that is also true for all human beings who have come from the same Creator.

Being spiritual, and attaining spiritual distinction, is first knowing that "everyone is connected," as Deepak Chopra says in his book *Peace is the Way*. Through the consciousness our soul gives us access to, we know that in every moment of our life, we "also affect every moment in everyone else's life." Acting on this knowledge of connectedness "creates a new kind of power" for us: power in unity, as in "a simple social act like casting a ballot," because "the way of peace says that no action is more powerful than action from the soul." This means that what is true for you – having the inner capability to know peace and desire peace for all – is true for everyone.

This was affirmed by Bahá'u'lláh through the interdependent twin principles of the oneness of humanity and universal peace. There will not be peace "*unless and until*" humanity's unity is firmly established. If we realize that this inherent unity already exists on the soul level, attaining world peace will come much more quickly.

Humanity was created to exist in a state of cooperation, unity, and peace. As 'Abdu'l-Bahá has put it, "*Bahá'u'lláh has drawn the circle of unity. He has made a design for the uniting of all the peoples, and for the gathering of them all under the shelter of the tent of universal unity... we must all strive with heart and soul until we have the reality of unity in our midst, and as we work, so will strength be given unto us."* To make this very clear, he adds: *"The divine religions were founded for the purpose of unifying humanity and establishing universal peace."*

Spiritual distinction is the way to inner peace which is the way to interpersonal and world peace. Coming into a world divided and torn apart, achieving any peace at all depends upon us remembering we come from wholeness and are on a journey of returning to wholeness. To know inner peace is to have a calm mind, which goes forth into the world as a calm voice and calm deeds. This is the state of tranquility and joy, the state of inner peace that passes all understanding, that is within our reach.

CHAPTER 8

The Way of Unity to Interpersonal Peace

Interpersonal interactions and relationships are the testing ground for world peace. If we can't be cooperative, harmonious, and peaceful in our everyday relationships, peace in the world will be impossible to achieve.

In *Activating the Common Good*, Peter Block says, "What is needed is local, relationship-based activism that endures over time and is less dependent on the transformation of people in traditional leadership positions." The change needed to assist humanity toward world peace is building natural, everyday relationships where people show up because they know they can trust each other, and because they understand that through the unity created by this trust, together they can make a difference.

These organic relationships are important because they are built for relational activism. The main intent of these already naturally existing relationships, Block says, is to create social capital. This is a counterapproach to strategies calling for better management or leadership. Organically created relationships produce something compelling, immediate, and critical to work on together, through their shared concerns and predicaments.

Dynamically emerging relational activists discover and learn together what is most needed in their local setting to transform their community.

Whether their common concerns are related to racism, access to a quality education, a just economic system, or the local environment, they soon recognize the power in their unity.

Thich Nhat Hanh, in *Creating True Peace*, looks at relational peacebuilding as well, from couples to families to communities. His "Peace Treaty for Couples" is a promise to practice living peacefully and happily together by addressing anger and respecting commitments. The generational importance of healthy relationships within families cannot be overstated. Practicing peace with our children influences them in positive ways for their entire lives. This may be the most significant contribution to peace we can offer as parents and educators.

BECOMING A SOURCE OF SOCIAL GOOD

The greatest personal fulfillment is not in solely serving our own needs, whether they be material or spiritual, but rather in striving to achieve our own moral and spiritual heights while simultaneously contributing to the advancement of the welfare of others. This is confirmed by 'Abdu'l-Bahá who said that when we look within ourselves and find that we have "*become the cause of peace and well-being, of happiness and advantage*" to others, "*there is no greater bliss, no more complete delight.*"

This describes a twofold moral purpose in which the real completion of this mutually beneficial process is only found when we take our practice – and our peace – into the world, as Thich Nhat Hanh has suggested. Once we've found our own peace, the only true refuge is practicing peace with others.

With this as our mindset, we are most comfortable, even more greatly rewarded, when our focus is on others, not ourselves. As Bahá'u'lláh taught, "*Let your thoughts be fixed upon that which will rehabilitate the fortunes of mankind and sanctify the hearts and souls of men.*" This is achieved "*through a virtuous life and a goodly behavior.*"

The goal is to get to a point where our every action can be an act of worship. In the words of 'Abdu'l-Bahá:

"Strive that your actions day by day may be beautiful prayers... seek always to do that which is right and noble. Enrich the poor, raise the fallen, comfort the sorrowful, bring healing to the sick, reassure the fearful, rescue the oppressed, bring hope to the hopeless, shelter to the destitute."

The way of unity as manifested in the behavior within relationships of all kinds thus becomes the conveyance of compassion, kindness, and caring to others. But it's not easy to arrive at and remain in these lofty realms. Having our interactions with others become as *"beautiful prayers"* is only possible after much tempering of our thoughts, desires, and will.

This world is made up of trials, tribulations, hardships and sufferings. By facing them, remembering their purpose for us, and persevering, we overcome them and grow. Our difficulties are the source of our moral and spiritual development, often what provides us with the opportunity to try again, gain a deeper consciousness of our inner potential, and continue to strive toward our true purpose.

Even as our individual hardships and sufferings are reflected in the collective conditions and circumstances of humanity, with the darkness of prejudice and ill-will enough to chill the warmest of hearts, and time-honored institutions, cherished ideals, and sacred traditions being assailed, the perennial voice of peace must resound unsubdued with immovable resolve for the good of all.

Humanity's organic oneness will prevail over all assaults because its inherent nature consists of essential relationships that bind not only families and communities but also states and nations as members of one family. This is not merely an ideal, but a reality clearly and definitively demonstrated in our own biology.

From an understanding of DNA, as well as simple genealogy, comes the revelation of the interrelatedness of all human beings. We all share common ancestors. All eight billion of us, no matter what our so-called "race," can be, in fact, no less closely related to any other human than fiftieth cousin, and most of us are a lot closer.

The movement toward the greater realization of this inner, spiritual and biological, reality of humanity's oneness will continue to propel the unfolding transformation of society to its fulfillment by individuals, institutions, and communities worldwide to reshape, with new conceptions of each emerging, appropriate for a humanity that is coming of age.

New, unitive relationships at all these levels are bringing into existence civilization-building powers. They are being released by increased cooperation and reciprocity, the very reflections of the interconnectedness that governs the Universe.

Our deepest connection is our shared identity as members of one human family and our common purpose as stewards of one planetary home. In this Unitive Age, no longer is it viable to think of "us and them." It is only "we" who are on a common journey to oneness, realized through the goodness and kindness we give to each other every step of the way.

This awareness is exactly what heightens social consciousness and coherence as the interrelatedness of all aspects of a community – parents, children, youth, and inter-community groups – become more closely involved with each other through meaningful conversations and service projects that make their commonality and connection unmistakable.

Care and compassion toward each other feeds a deeper reflection on the nature of the contributions their growing, increasingly vibrant community can make to the progress of the wider society. Raised to the surface then are the interconnected two-fold mutually reinforcing areas our being a source of social good is accomplishing: involvement in social action and participation in the needed discourses of society.

A spectrum of social action also becomes evident through the range of social good that is undertaken. However modest, from one-time informal efforts by individuals or small groups of friends to more well-planned sustained social and economic development programs, all such endeavors built upon applying unitive principles to a social need seek to improve the collective life of all involved.

This all contributes enormously to a world civilization in dire need of achieving a dynamic coherence between all aspects of social life. Just, equitable, unified, and vibrant communities, regions, and nations lead to a world in harmonious and interdependent relationship with itself. Most important to remember is that both our inner potential and greater purpose are fulfilled by the service we devote to the common good of others. It is in this field of service that knowledge is tested, questions arise, learning unfolds, and new levels of understanding are achieved, all while humbly forgetting ourselves and delighting in the progress of others.

The source of this evolutionary impulse of contributing to the social good comes from the love received in our relationship with the divine. There is a love emanating among every member of a community, without restriction, that undertake together intimate conversations to open their hearts in meeting the requirements of humanity's age of maturity.

This collective maturation depends upon the loving action we take now to usher in a gentle, peaceful path to peace on Earth. Love is the sacred activism of our time, binding all hearts together. Peace in the world is the outcome of the love shared between all members of the human family.

COMPASSIONATE CONSULTATION AND COLLABORATION

Many forms of consultation have been utilized since groups and communities first came together to address and resolve common concerns. Over centuries, the techniques of consultation have become refined and focused on fair and effective decision-making leading to mutually beneficial action.

Various dialogue and conversation techniques have been successfully developed and applied as a means to reach a new and deeper understanding in small scale settings. One perspective commonly accepted in such efforts is the intent to experience everyone's point of view equally and nonjudgmentally. All groups have some degree of a diversity of views and thoughts that come into play and need to be considered and integrated.

One example of a dialogue method that brings this into focus, emphasizing diversity's strength, is "Bohmian Dialogue" created by quantum physicist David Bohm. He was clear on how to deal with the inevitable diversity in interpersonal or social settings:

> "People have to make a cooperative effort to have a dialogue in which we not merely exchange opinions, but actually listen deeply to the views of others, without resistance. We cannot do this if we hold on to our own opinion and resist the other. We have to be able to look at all the opinions as suspended in front of us without suppressing them."

This openness to inclusion and equity of all views in any process of dialogue is essential. It may be the only way to ensure the full participation of all voices that are needed for the full representation of the whole. But if the dialogue "has no predefined purpose, no agenda," and "the group agrees that no group-level decisions will be made," it will not be able to address the need to achieve unity, or carry out a plan intended to bring about unity.

Central to the functioning of Bahá'í communities, the ultimate purpose of consultation is to create spiritual unity. This is initiated by being conducted in an atmosphere of respect, trust, openness, and learning from others. Here, the practice of the art of consultation is expressly utilized as a primary all-purpose tool for fostering unity, strengthening social coherence, and peacebuilding at all levels, from small groups to national and international gatherings. Consultation is specifically used to arrive at unity of thought, which is needed to result in unity of action.

Consultation is a process that invites and respects the full range of human diversity and the inherent differences of thought and opinion. Different views, rather than being a source of dissension or conflict, can be an asset, a challenge creating both a deeper understanding and the opportunity to unify previously unvoiced or divergent thoughts. It's not a format for the struggle for power, assertiveness, or dominating with one's views. Rather it is a selfless seeking of the truth in collaboration with others. The truth being sought is that which would most benefit the whole of humanity.

Consultation is a way to achieve spiritual unity, a way of consciously and collaboratively working toward group or collective coherence. It can be a way of arriving at a state of unity that reflects in human affairs the greater wholeness of Creation. Acknowledging and accepting all the diverse—even opposing—views within the whole enables the whole to function in its entirety. Yet to experience the inherent potential of our collective unity, we must be able to resolve differences within the whole so it can function as one, while maintaining its inherent diversity. Diversity is not an inherent problem for organic wholeness. In fact, it is needed on all levels. Diverse opinions are openly welcomed, taken in, and weighed for their contribution to the truth being sought.

The art of consultation is a consensus-based approach to arrive at collective decision-making. It is a process and an art consisting of distinct elements that offers a unique power in bringing people, groups, and organizations of differing viewpoints and backgrounds together to explore, read, and find unity around an existing reality.

Consultation is a way to gain unexpected insights from a range of perspectives and seemingly irreconcilable views that end up being trans-cended upon new common ground that is more readily found. Consultation is designed to unlock the capacity of each individual and group to contribute most effectively to constructive social change.

Ideas contributed in the spirit of service to the whole belong not to the individual who articulates them, but to the group. Others are invited to build on previously offered ideas, and all are challenged to be open to learning and to transcend their original points of view rather than insisting upon them. It is up to the group to find consensus around what it feels best represents the truth being sought and how to determine the best course of unified action.

In this process, everyone expresses with absolute freedom their own opinion without feeling hurt if another has an opposing view. 'Abdu'l-Bahá confirmed that only when matters are fully discussed can the right way be revealed: *"The shinning spark of truth comes forth only after the clash of differing opinions... the purpose of consultation is to show that the views of several are preferable to one..."*

The prime requisites for consultation are purity of motive, radiance of spirit, detachment, humility, and patience, since the object is *"the investigation of truth."* Individual opinions from all involved are expected and encouraged, not *"as correct and right"* but rather as *"a contribution to the consensus of opinion"* because *"the light of reality becomes apparent when two opinions coincide."* Each should *"carefully consider the views already advanced by others"* and *"not willfully hold to an opinion of his own,"* as this is how we arrive at *"unity and truth."*

Consultation is a cordial method to achieve unanimity in decision-making. It starts with identifying the spiritual principles within which reside solutions to every social problem that are relevant to the specific problem being addressed. This is because spiritual principles induce an attitude, a dynamic, a will, and an aspiration which facilitates the discovery and application of practical measures. It thus ends with unity-in-action.

Effective consultation is a process consisting of the following qualities and conditions:

- Consultation is a collaborative means by which a common understanding can be reached and a collective course of action defined.
- Consultation is a free, respectful, dignified, and fair-minded effort on the part of a group of people to exchange views and seek truth, even though an initial difference of opinion may be the starting point for examining an issue, with the goal being to reach greater understanding and consensus.
- Individual opinions and views are sought from all and are offered freely, without passion and attachment, while hearing and respecting the views of others, without contention, is also essential to consultation.
- All opinions and views are offered in a manner of dignity, courtesy, and care toward others, and are free of a domineering attitude.
- Differing opinions are not to be avoided, as their clash may reveal an underlying truth.

The primary steps in the process of consultation are:

- Overall, attempt to ascertain the truth concerning the problem or issue at hand.
- Identify the spiritual principle(s) directly related to the problem or issue being consulted upon.
- Seek and discuss all views, perspectives, and proposals on the issue by all in the group, discuss and resolve any concerns about a possible course of action.
- Allow a clear consensus to emerge organically, or, if needed, by a majority vote, that seems to lead to the best course of action.

- Devise plans for the decision to be carried out, including plans for a future consultation on a process for review, reflection, and learning from the course of action taken.

These steps in the process of consultation represent a cycle to be repeated as often as needed to achieve the unity that is essential for releasing the power required for social change.

Consultation, consensus, action, reflection, and learning is followed by the same process with a deeper understanding and a firmer commitment to the goal each time.

Consultation, or the collective investigation of reality following these procedures, is a means of harmonizing points of view, promoting unity, and strengthening bonds of trust and love that also serves to foster systematic action. This is an under-utilized tool, at all levels of society, from in-house, grassroots gatherings to national and international forums, for social coherence, social change, and peacebuilding.

A current challenge for the emerging global community seeking to live in peace is to recognize that the art and practice of consultation is naturally adaptable *and* scalable to the international stage for addressing and resolving issues that require collectively seeking truth and putting the findings into unified action. The size of the group and the scope of representation involved need not matter, as long as the conditions and steps of the process of the art and practice of consultation are followed.

All that is needed is for the participants to enter a consultative space first as human beings, and second as representatives of their organization, nation, or constituency, not bound to a particular position, and without attachment to a desired outcome. With this openness to the process, they can genuinely pursue solutions founded upon truth and create an opportunity for a search for common ground. This approach of adopting a posture of learning, while following the respectful conditions underlying the process, ensures that participants see themselves as active agents in a collaborative endeavor to achieve a commonly arrived at solution while becoming more committed to its success.

What is sought, and arrived at, through consultation, when drawing upon all viewpoints, is the power of unified thought carried into action. The very attempt to achieve peace through consultative action can release such a spirit among the peoples of the Earth that no power could resist its unified outcome.

SOCIAL JUSTICE TO BRING ABOUT UNITY

Social coherence, brought about and supported by social justice, is an absolute necessity for world unity and world peace. Both are the result of social action, which by its very nature is designed to bring about the advancement of civilization and the prosperity of all.

A balanced, harmonious, and peaceful global civilization begins within each community. Achieving a dynamic coherence between the practical and spiritual aspects of life as well as ensuring the just and equitable needs of society is the goal. Community building, through empowerment and realized capacity, accomplishes personal growth and social transformation at the same time. It strengthens relationships beyond the supposed barriers of race and class while weakening prejudice. It inspires neighbors to be more considerate of each other's needs and see them as shared challenges.

Building communities that cross boundaries and build bridges cultivates love and translates that into action. This is the way to ease tensions and erase divisions caused by lingering prejudice of all kinds and the injustices resulting from this that are set deeply in the fabric of society. Reshaping society, our communities, organizations, and networks, around principles that bring about unity is a way to cultivate love and reciprocity, expand inclusivity, and reach common goals that benefit the whole.

The way of unity necessitates the abandonment of prejudice of every kind – race, class, color, gender, creed, nationality, age, economic status, mental health – anything that people have used to place themselves above others and deny others any kind of human resource.

Prejudice is built upon a false assumption that blinds us to the reality that every person is not only a human being with the same universal human rights, but also a spiritual being with unique and vital inherent qualities, capacities, and potential. While prejudice is anti-social, altruism and service to others is its prosocial antidote. This is the direction an organic change in the nature and structure of present-day society is headed. As the Bahá'í writings indicate, this change calls for a "world organically unified in all the essential aspects of its life," while also infinite in its diversity. Such a growing, universal commitment to selfless service to our fellow human beings would transform the world. A society free from all forms of prejudice appears when we consciously choose to move from otherness to oneness.

A new model of community life is emerging and being built out globally where concern for and service to others is paramount. This is being achieved by forming and nurturing relationships with a wide range of diverse people, collaborating on commonly beneficial projects, and engaging in challenging dialogue that results in a shared purpose. Relationships not built upon equity and equality limit the potentialities of those being restricted while unfairly advantaging and corrupting those who create the unjust relationships.

Our communities need more open and frank conversation around common identities, shared purpose, the nature of social transformation, truth telling and reconciliation, what it would look like to become communities and nations free from racial prejudice, without racism to debilitate our humanness.

All work toward social justice will ultimately be more effective if it begins with a consciousness of the oneness of humanity. This helps shatter the distorting looking glass in which tests, difficulties, setbacks, and misunderstandings can seem insurmountable. This principle must be the central organizing principle that guides our efforts to overcome racism, along with every other form of injustice and oppression that stalls human progress. As an interdependent social body, the well-being of every member and every group depends on the well-being of the entire body.

It is one thing to acknowledge something in principle, but quite another to embrace it with all of one's heart and to carry it out in practice to reshape one's society in ways that give full collective expression to it. Groups and communities carrying out unity of thought in action are always in the best and most vital position to make this difference. In communities across America and the world, Bahá'ís and their friends and neighbors from all walks of life are learning to apply unitive spiritual principles to gain personal insight and to take collective action to address social problems encountered in everyday life.

Primary among these principles is justice. It is necessary to have justice to bring about unity-in-diversity, just as it is necessary to apply unifying approaches to bring about justice. This is a process of applying a spiritual framework for social change. This is always a process of study, consultation, action, and reflection on the changes taking place within and around them, in themselves and their neighborhoods, as the ongoing cycle of learning more and sharing what is being learned with others is repeated, ensuring a growing and effective collective body of knowledge.

This is a unique moment in history. In this time of turbulence and transition, community-building efforts are more needed now than ever. As society rapidly changes, and feels increasingly polarized, it is essential to find empowering and unifying solutions towards building a more harmonious, all-inclusive society.

Members of the Bahá'í community are fully aware of the many challenges they face in living up to and carrying out these lofty ideals. They recognize that this work will take generations, but they are committed to the long-term process of learning through action by applying unitive principles that will transform society. The main thrust of Bahá'í efforts toward social change is building vibrant communities characterized by unity-in-diversity, mutual support, and collective well-being. Each community of peace is an essential link in the chain leading to world peace. This process is freely and humbly offered to the world as a model to explore for achieving lasting, positive change through a profound process of personal and social transformation that is consciously designed to lead to peace on Earth.

The time has come when we are being called upon to work for the healing and betterment of our communities, nations, and the world. Society-building powers are being released in ever-greater measures. The power of unity, of love, and humble service will spread more quickly than any other power on Earth. Everyone has a part to play in this next stage of the fundamental reconstruction of human society. All have unique gifts to contribute.

Our personal and group peacebuilding represents the bedrock upon which the Great Peace rests. As 'Abdu'l-Bahá has noted, *"peace must first be established among individuals,"* as this will create *"genuine love, spiritual communion, and durable bonds"* in all relationships and communities. Then, this can lead *"in the end to peace among nations."*

CHAPTER 9

The Way of Unity to World Peace

This final, all-inclusive sphere of peacebuilding is the most elusive. The need for a global infrastructure that will support and maintain world peace is far overshadowed by the requirements and sacrifices it demands on the level of national sovereignty and the complexities involved in syncing all levels of society, to achieve the global unity and solidarity necessary for universal peace.

The universal leap of consciousness required for this to transpire will not be an easy one. Humanity must recognize and implement our collective unity and wholeness in the face of millennia of division and separateness. This leap of consciousness to unity and wholeness will require knowing beyond any doubt that all things in the entire Creation are one, and that consciousness evolves toward wholeness.

World unity has many preconditions that need to be established in this journey to wholeness and true interdependence. A global society must be built upon a foundation of unifying principles designed to bring about and maintain unity on all levels of relational interactions, from family, to community, to city, to region, to nation, and the entire planet.

The implementation of unitive principles are indispensable to an unfolding process of building unity from one sphere of life to another, until all spheres are harmonized forming one fully synergized whole. All spheres of personal and social life on the planet radiate like spokes of one wheel supportive of the one hub of unitive life that extends outward holding all life on the entire planet together in harmony and cooperation. Yet, there is still a long way to go in getting each of these unifying interconnected components firmly in place for lasting harmony, unity, and peace.

Just beginning to glimpse the dawn of this Unitive Age, we may not yet fully appreciate that we live in a time that will become known as an early stage in the development of an inclusive, effectively functioning commonwealth of all the world's nations, when humanity lives as one with a common purpose ensuring our collective destiny. This promised time cannot be fully realized until a unitive, all-inclusive approach to building out the infrastructure of our wholeness, is consciously taken up and followed as the way to lasting world peace.

AN EVER-ADVANCING CIVILIZATION

The Bahá'í writings state that all human beings *"have been created to carry forward an ever-advancing civilization."* This requires everyone, of every gender, ethnicity, and faith tradition, to work alongside each other to build a global society rooted in justice and characterized by unity – a society in which individuals see their outward differences as a reflection of the beauty and perfection of humanity's full spectrum of diversity.

Working to advance the world toward such an all-encompassing unity also requires developing the virtues that befit human dignity – trustworthiness, forbearance, mercy, compassion, and loving-kindness towards all peoples. These are needed to become the basis for every thought and interaction with others. Humanity's collective evolution has brought us to a point where every single one of us knows for a certainty that things are not the way they could be. Whether we acknowledge it or not, most of humanity seeks unity and belonging more than anything else. We want nothing more than to end our age-old separation and achieve the attainable goal of unity and peace.

This Unitive Age, the potentials of which are yet to become fully apparent, is the consummation of all ages. An ever-advancing civilization, before reaching its full maturation, requires a renewal of the understanding of politics. It is no longer useful or even practical to think of politics as activities aimed at improving the status of just one or a few select individuals. This form of politics perpetuates division, separation, and inequality. Sorely needed is a new unitive politics to bring about unity on all levels. Its hallmark would be community building focused on developing an inclusive approach to conflict resolution and peacebuilding in all spheres of society through capacity building, empowerment, and social coherence.

This would carry forward an ever-advancing civilization by expanding circles of unity to greater and greater levels until unity encompasses the entire planet, reflecting the sacred unity of the planet itself, as 'Abdu'l-Bahá predicts: "*The more the world of humanity develops, the more the emanations of Divinity will become revealed, just as the stone, when it becomes polished and pure as a mirror, will reflect in fuller degree the glory and splendor of the sun.*"

The twin processes of collapse and renewal, that have been repeated many times over in humanity's history, carry the world toward an evolutionary culmination. The breakdown of old, divisive politics and worn-out institutions coupled with the blossoming of new ways of thinking and a deeper commitment to cooperation and collective achievement are evidence of a single trend gaining momentum over the past century: movement toward the realization of the ever-increasing interdependence and integration of humanity.

This trend is observable in multiple spheres, from the fusion of world financial markets encompassing diverse sources of energy, raw materials, and technology, to global systems of communications and transportation, to the scientific understanding of the Earth's interconnected biosphere, to the destructive capacities of modern weapons systems demanding unified response and controls.

Both the constructive and destructive potentialities of this trend are poignant reminders of the iconic Apollo 8 earthrise photograph that showed our swirling planet held precariously in motion, revealing in vivid color that we are a single people living in a common homeland. This is impetus enough to acknowledge that we have reached a turning point in the progress of nations. It is time to forge a world political system that can secure for humanity the possibility of justice, prosperity, and peace.

It is clear, too, that nationalism has outlived its purpose and no longer serves an ever-advancing global civilization. Our time requires an authentic and effective universal framework for addressing the increasingly complex and perplexing global issues, as recognized by many national leaders and agencies of the United Nations alike. Needed now is a new order in which all humanity can live in a state of cooperation, unity, and peace. To achieve this vision, an expansion of consciousness taking in all components of the whole, what amounts to a unitive consciousness-in-action, will need to be in place.

This new culture of peace will be built upon a unitive consciousness, as 'Abdu'l-Bahá reminds us: "*The whole world must be looked upon as one single country, all the nations as one nation.... Religions, races, and nations are all divisions of man's making... before God there are neither Persians, Arabs, French nor English; God is God for all, and to Him all creation is one.*"

Humanity's purpose today is to be agents of change in transforming the widespread discord and separation of the human family into a worldwide reconciliation unifying all the diverse elements of the whole of human society. This process of integration started long ago at the level of the smallest units of society, moving from family to community to nation, is now resistlessly approaching its grandest scale, that of world unity, the crowning glory of human evolution on this planet.

We always have assistance available to us through the release of creative energies that have been providing humanity with the capacity to attain each stage in its organic and collective evolution. Though its pace may be perceived as slow and gradual, its direction is undeniably progressive and commensurate with the degree of social progress achieved by each generation, even though it is ultimately a process occurring in cycles.

An ever-advancing civilization calls for a wider, inclusive loyalty, not conflicting with other loyalties, but inspiring an expansive love which takes in all loyalties while providing a foundation upon which world citizenship can thrive, and the structure of world unity can rest. The world is moving toward this destiny.

THE ETHICS OF GLOBALIZATION

The time for a global ethic was evident at the end of the 20th century on the centennial of the first Parliament of the World's Religions when delegates of the world's religions present in 1993 took a historic step in collaboratively composing the "Declaration Toward a Global Ethic," founded on universal principles and irrevocable commitments that all agreed upon.

Similarly, the United Nations declared the first decade of this century as the International Decade for the Culture of Peace and Non-Violence for the Children of the World in its UNESCO Manifesto 2000, also a declaration of a new global ethic. This expressed a universal desire and commitment to live in a way that promotes peace, stability, and growth for our children and our children's children. Both of these timely and very worthy initiatives provide essential guidelines for peacebuilding, and both call for carrying a global ethic into action in every part of the world.

The spirit of the age emanates from a consciousness of the unity of the human family. This understanding is at the heart of a unitive consciousness.

This is what a global ethic depends upon, a prior and independently arrived at commitment to the well-being of the entire human family. Running parallel to a worldwide process of developing the policies, laws, organization, and infrastructure to support world peace is the emergence of a unitive consciousness that all such advancements rest upon and are inspired by.

The inevitable movement toward globalization is a process requiring a guiding ethic that ensures the betterment of the world. Globalization is the culmination of an evolutionary process that requires our thoughtful and calculated input. As an unstoppable phenomenon, globalization embraces all aspects of human life, from the political realm to a world economy, to cultural values and traditions, to humanity's spiritual heritage and destiny. This is precisely why a global ethic based upon a unitive consciousness is so central to the process. Globalization is as much a cultural and spiritual matter as it is political, economic, social, and legal.

All the unitive principles upon which the way of unity rests must also be central to the process of globalization, as only a world-orchestrated effort to apply each of them in everyday settings at all social levels could overcome the many grave problems and crises plaguing the peoples of the world.

Globalization is well underway, whether we direct it or not. But if humanity can steer the process of globalization toward the greater good, it could become a way to simultaneously deal with multiple crises already threatening the planet and all of its inhabitants. By applying the appropriate unitive principle best suited to resolve a particular crisis, we can ensure that the continued unfolding of globalization will indeed be for the betterment of the world.

All crises are interdependent as interconnected dysfunctional parts of one whole, because each one negatively impacts the collective well-being of humanity. So are the unitive principles interdependent as interconnected healing aspects of the whole. Globalization is the perfect opportunity to apply the all-inclusive unitive ethic and unitive principles we already have in our hands.

The existing Global Ethic, gleaned from the shared wisdom of the world's religious traditions, and from the United Nations International Decade for a Culture of Peace, provides clear answers to the question of how humanity can avoid the worst outcome of an ongoing clash of civilizations. All the values and principles needed for a universal civilization are with us. But this is the question we must ask ourselves: will we choose to apply them?

There are communities around the world already applying these universal, unitive principles, as a global ethic-in-action, expressing a new sense of responsibility and solidarity. They are transforming their own diverse communities into an integrated, balanced wholeness, where the principle of unity is paramount. Beyond this, we should also be heartened by the vast number of women and men from virtually every culture and nation on Earth who choose to carry out the various tasks of the agencies of the United Nations under challenging conditions. Their urge towards world unity, while others resist its flow, represents an endangered planetary "civil service," contributing to the betterment of the world, preparing the way for the coming age of peace.

Balanced globalization represents a vision of world unity, not of uniformity, but of unity-in-diversity fully realized. It is the inevitable outcome of the evolution of human civilization, the gradual arrival of humanity at its stage of maturity. Ethical globalization may best be summed up as a spiritual process in which the inherent moral capacities of the human heart become progressively more evident in all human endeavors.

At the heart of an ethics of globalization lies the commitment to consciously create a global culture of unity. This means bringing in and applying unitive principles as operating principles to bring into realization the unity of the human family. This way of guiding and directing the ethics of the process of globalization would move humanity beyond its existing crises of racism and all other forms of prejudice while also bringing about a deep change in the structure of society by making unitive justice the primary principle of social renewal in creating a culture of peace.

The ethics underlying a guided and focused process of globalization also include an understanding of the inherent interconnectedness of all human lives, across all boundaries and economic strata, such that it would be inconceivable to consider peace a condition characterized simply by worldwide absence of conflict, when millions of people die yearly from starvation, disease, and poverty.

The great age to come, of an undisturbed, universal, and lasting peace, will carry as its highest achievement the fruits of a worldwide reconciliation of hearts and minds upholding a common universal ethical framework of unity-in-wholeness.

UNITIVE GLOBAL GOVERNANCE

To expand on the ninth unitive principle, effective and continuous unitive global governance will not be possible until all the other unitive principles have been realized, or as Bahá'u'lláh indicated, *"unless and until its unity is firmly established."*

As the dynamic process unfolds during the culminating steps to lasting world peace, while the unity of the human family is being firmly established, a multi-level system of global governance will be built out to sustain long-term unity and oversee a harmony of civilizations sharing one planetary homeland.

At the end of the twentieth century, on its fifty-fifth anniversary, the United Nations acknowledged that, "Global governance requires a common core of values, standards and attitudes, a widely felt sense of responsibility and obligations – not just by individuals, but also by governments, corporations and civil society organizations."

The UN also acknowledged that in over fifty years, they and the rest of the world have not been able to achieve the translation of these values into the reality of peaceful living. These values, including the nine unitive principles leading to a fully unified human family, represent the foundation of what will be required to enable a true and full unity-in-diversity to become a reality. True unity must be desired by all and agreed upon as a goal to be achieved. And its counterpart – diversity – must be committed to and celebrated as well.

This gradual unfolding took its first steps in the infancy of the globalization process in 1918 when President Woodrow Wilson put forward the ideas of a uniform world order based on right instead of power, multilateral disarmament, and a system of collective security, some of which came to fruition in the formation of the League of Nations.

During World War II, President Franklin D. Roosevelt expanded international security with the "Four Freedoms" (freedom of speech, freedom from want, freedom from fear, and the freedom of worship), which became important in the creation of the United Nations. Without the stalwart work of the United Nations over the past eighty years, the current pattern for modern international relations may not have been set. Over those critically challenging years, the UN has initiated many global summits to bring national and NGO leaders together, ever closer toward world unity.

At the Summit of the Future in September 2024, the United Nations adopted the *Pact for the Future* which contained a major segment on "Transforming Global Governance." This included many commitments to transforming global governance, reforming and strengthening the Security Council, revitalizing the General Assembly, strengthening the Economic and Social Council, strengthening the Peacebuilding Commission, and strengthening the United Nations system as a whole. Details are yet to come on how this will be implemented.

We can go back to the mid-nineteenth century to find the seeds of this recent progress and growth. Exploring the origin and vision of a unifying global governance will give us further insights into the gradual and dynamic process that is leading to the social and political unity of the world.

In a spiritually based wholistic system of peacebuilding distinguished from any other sacred revelation, Bahá'u'lláh *"laid down the essential prerequisites of concord, of understanding, of complete and enduring unity."* These were designed to lead to *"the peace and tranquility of the world and the advancement of its peoples."* This way of unity is built upon unitive principles meant to bring about peace.

In a series of letters to the rulers of the world in the 1860s, including Queen Victoria, Napoleon III, Czar Alexander II, Pope Pius IX, and the Sultan of the Ottoman Empire, before global summits had been thought of or were possible, Bahá'u'lláh called for a universal, global approach to peace and the institutionalization of global collective security as a necessary means of realizing peace.

He wrote on this subject:

> *"The time must come when the imperative necessity for the holding of a vast, an all-embracing assemblage will be universally realized... The rulers and kings of the earth... must consider such ways and means as will lay the foundations of the world's Great Peace... Such a peace* [demands] *that the Great Powers should resolve, for the sake of the tranquility of the peoples of earth, to be fully reconciled among themselves... This will ensure the peace and composure of every people, government and nation."*

The context for this worldwide urgency was the extensive and unabated discord, disunity, and ongoing wars that have plagued humanity throughout its entire social evolution. Prior to World War 1, 'Abdu'l-Bahá tirelessly promoted universal peace in his travels throughout Europe and North

America, focusing upon the manifold principles that constitute the basis for humanity's harmony and unity. He said:

> *"So long as these prejudices [religious, racial, national, political] survive, there will be continuous and fearsome wars. To remedy this condition there must be universal peace. To bring this about, a Supreme Tribunal must be established, representative of all governments and peoples; questions both national and international must be referred thereto, and all must carry out the decrees of this Tribunal."*

In further describing the details of Bahá'u'lláh's plan, he added:

> *"The national assemblies of each country and nation—parliaments—should elect two or three persons who are the choicest of that nation and are well informed concerning international laws and the relations between governments and aware of the essential needs of the world of humanity in this day. The number of these representatives should be in proportion to the number of inhabitants of that country."*

With all of humanity having a share in the representation of their nation, the "*Supreme Tribunal*" would no longer have any pretext for objecting to an international ruling or in the carrying out of its decisions.

The essential ingredient in making this happen, he said, is when "*a certain number of its distinguished and high-minded sovereigns... shall... arise, with firm resolve and clear vision to establish the Cause of Universal Peace.*" This cause must become "*the object of general consultation*" which would lead to "*a binding treaty and establish a covenant, the provisions of which shall be sound, inviolable and definite*" and "*regarded as sacred by all that dwell on earth.*" This "*Most Great Covenant*" will fix the limits of every nation, underlie the relations between all governments, and determine all international agreements.

'Abdu'l-Bahá set in motion a detailed strategic plan in 1916 to ensure implementation of Bahá'u'lláh's vision of a peaceful world. This task, begun by the American Bahá'í community, gradually spread around the world to all the other local and national Bahá'í communities.

This plan has centered around the building of strong, empowered, and vibrant local and national communities striving to effect the transformation in consciousness and values necessary for the eventual emergence of a world order characterized by justice, unity, and peace, founded upon the prerequisite principles for the creation of durable peace.

As a world community began to emerge in the 1930s, Shoghi Effendi continued to develop the inherent unifying potential of this plan, seeing it as contributing *"an organic change in the structure of present-day society, a change such as the world has not yet experienced..."*

The social transformations needed clearly represent a challenge *"to outworn shibboleths of national creeds..."* and called for *"no less than the reconstruction and the demilitarization of the whole civilized world—a world organically unified in all the essential aspects of its life, its political machinery, its spiritual aspiration, its trade and finance, its script and language, and yet infinite in the diversity of the national characteristics of its federated units..."* This would be *"the consummation of human evolution."*

Shoghi Effendi's 1936 vision of a viable and just global governance system consists of several key elements:

- The unity of the human race, as envisaged by Bahá'u'lláh, implies the establishment of a world commonwealth in which all nations, races, creeds and classes are closely and permanently united, and their autonomy and personal freedom are completely safeguarded.

- This commonwealth will consist of a world legislature, whose members will enact such laws as shall be required to regulate and adjust the relationships of all races and peoples.

- A world executive, backed by an international Force, will carry out the decisions arrived at, apply the laws enacted by the world legislature, and safeguard the organic unity of the whole commonwealth.

- A world tribunal will adjudicate and deliver its compulsory and final verdict in all and any disputes that may arise between the various elements constituting this universal system.

- A mechanism of world inter-communication will be devised, embracing the whole planet, freed from national hindrances and restrictions, and functioning with marvelous swiftness and perfect regularity.

- A world metropolis will act as the nerve center of a world civilization, the focus towards which the unifying forces of life will converge and from which its energizing influences will radiate.

- A world language will either be invented or chosen from among the existing languages and will be taught in the schools of all the federated nations as an auxiliary to their mother tongue.

- A world script, a world literature, a uniform and universal system of currency, of weights and measures, will simplify and facilitate understanding among the nations and races of humankind.

- The press will, while giving full scope to the expression of diversified views, cease to be mischievously manipulated by vested interests and will be liberated from the influence of contending governments and peoples.

- The economic resources of the world will be organized, its sources of raw materials will be tapped and fully utilized, its markets will be coordinated and developed, and the distribution of its products will be equitably regulated.

- National rivalries, hatreds, and intrigues will cease, and racial animosity and prejudice will be replaced by racial amity, understanding and cooperation.

- The causes of religious strife will be permanently removed, the distinction between classes will be obliterated, and destitution on the one hand, and gross accumulation of ownership on the other, will disappear.

- The enormous energy wasted on war will be consecrated to such ends as will extend the range of human inventions, technical development, and scientific research, increase the productivity of humankind, and raise the standard of physical health by exterminating disease and prolonging human life.

- A world federal system will blend and embody the ideals of both the East and the West, in which Force is made the servant of Justice.

This vision embodies the expression and the experience of the fullest *unity-in-diversity* and *diversity-in-unity* possible, affording the optimal conditions for all to realize their highest potential through independent intellectual, spiritual, and aesthetic pursuits.

The unitive action step that currently lies before the peoples of the Earth is to prepare the ground for the transition from the present system of national sovereignty to a system of unitive global governance. In a statement to the United Nations on its 50th anniversary, the BIC reflected on current trends to forge a world political system that can secure for humanity the possibility of peace, justice, and prosperity and offered its perspective on three initial propositions:

- The discussions about the future of the United Nations need to take place within the broad context of the evolution of international order and its direction.

- Since the body of humankind is one and indivisible, each member of the human race is born into the world as a trust of the whole. This relationship constitutes the moral foundation of universal human rights.

- The discussions about the future of the international order must involve *and* excite the generality of humankind, engaging women and men at the grassroots level.

The BIC noted also that it regards the current world confusion and the calamitous condition of human affairs as a natural phase in an organic process leading ultimately and irresistibly to the unity of the human family in a single social order whose boundaries are those of the planet.

There are many evolutionary steps to be taken toward building a more just world order. Among them, suggested the BIC, could be redefining the role for the UN within the emerging international order, consisting of:

- Resuscitating the General Assembly by raising minimum requirements for membership; appointing a Commission to study borders and frontiers; searching for new financial arrangements; making a commitment to a universal auxiliary language and common script; and, investigating the possibility of a single international currency.

- Developing a meaningful Executive Function by limiting the exercise of the veto power; institutionalizing ad hoc military arrangement; applying the notion of collective security to other problems of the global commons; and, retaining successful UN institutions with independent executive function.

- A strengthened World Court by extending the Court's jurisdiction and coordinating the thematic courts.

In addition, the BIC suggested a greater focus on releasing the power of the individual, a critical challenge of the emerging international order. This could be accomplished by:

- Protecting fundamental human rights by strengthening the machinery of the UN for monitoring, implementation and follow-up; encouraging universal ratification of international conventions on human rights; and, assuring respect for the monitoring organs of the UN involved in human rights.

- Advancing the status of women by increasing the participation of women in member state delegations; encouraging universal ratification of international conventions that protect women's rights and improve their status; and, planning ahead for implementation of the Beijing Platform of Action.
- Emphasizing moral development by promoting the development of curricula for moral education in schools.

There is still much work to be done, much direct action to be taken to lay these vital preconditions of unitive global governance in their place. The BIC further noted, "Leaders for the next generation must be motivated by a sincere desire to serve the entire community and must understand that leadership is a responsibility; not a path to privilege... This age demands a new definition of leadership and a new type of leader." The emerging Unitive Age requires leaders committed to bringing about unity.

On the 75th anniversary of the UN, the BIC offered a statement on "Humanity and the Path Toward a Just Global Order." Noting that throughout history, periods of turbulence have presented opportunities to redefine collective values and the assumptions that underly them, the present moment suggests how critical the coming quarter century – to the UN's centenary – will be in determining the fortunes of humanity. With this urgency in mind, they offered many key points, among them:

- The only viable way forward lies in a system of deepening global cooperation.
- At each stage in human history, more complex levels of integration become not only possible, but necessary.
- We find ourselves at the threshold of a defining task: purposefully organizing our affairs in full consciousness of ourselves as one people in one shared homeland.

- A framework that accommodates a diversity of approaches, built on a commitment to unity and a shared ethic of justice, would allow common principles to be put into practice in countless arrangements and formulations.
- True acknowledgement of global interdependence requires genuine concern for all, without distinction.
- The welfare of any segment of humanity is inextricably bound up with the welfare of the whole.
- The starting point for consultation on any program or policy must be consideration of the impact it will have on all segments of society.
- Present conditions demand a more wholistic and coherent approach to analysis and decision-making.

Many other groups and organizations are also working on reforming the UN, creating alternatives, or developing global governance models that are founded upon a unitive knowledge base and framework. One example is the proposal of Augusto Lopez-Claros, Arthur Dahl, and Maja Groff that won the 2018 New Shape Prize of Sweden's Global Challenges Foundation. This led to the book *Global Governance and the Emergence of Global Institutions for the 21ˢᵗ Century* and the creation of the Global Governance Forum.

This model draws upon the Bahá'í vision of a global civilization founded on unity-in-diversity and a balance of the material and spiritual aspects of civilization. It acknowledges our higher human purpose of developing the infinite potential in human consciousness and fosters our spiritual evolution. Its aim is creating a system of global governance that reflects and fosters the organic unity of humanity in all its endeavors while operating at all levels on a system of global justice that brings about and maintains unity, so that every individual has the opportunity to develop their full potential.

The model is focused on reforming the central institutions of the United Nations, which, though clearly not a world government, is humanity's primary forum to discuss and deal with issues and challenges of global significance in an increasingly interdependent world. It proposes significant General Assembly reform, with an interim World Parliamentary Assembly as an advisory body, and advisory mechanisms to support global policymaking; the UN Executive Council, a successor to the outdated Security Council, with heightened Collective Security mechanisms including an International Peace Force; the movement toward systemic disarmament and strengthening international rule of law; updating human rights for the 21st century; and, a new United Nations funding mechanism.

The underlying values featured in this model of global governance acknowledge that:

- Every human being deserves the protection of the whole.
- We have a collective trusteeship for the whole of humanity.
- Power and authority need to be redefined and reconceptualized.
- Members of global governance institutions are responsible to their own moral and spiritual conscience, not to those who elected them.
- There are no individual leaders, therefore no individual power.
- Collective decision-making, through the process and steps of consultation, underly all activities of this global system.
- Change toward this global system is only possible as consciousness is raised among the masses of humanity, so progress will be gradual.
- Institutions cannot be transformed if the people within them have not changed.
- A transformation in global systems of education is required to cultivate the potentials available in each individual and draw out the capacity for honesty, altruism, solidarity, cooperation, and integrity.

Unitive global governance needs to be a process of renewal from both the bottom up and top down that aspires to offer experience and evidence that cannot be denied or overlooked. Working simultaneously, both approaches meet in the middle to inspire and confirm each other. Humanity is now at a moment in our collective evolution where all the principles and values needed to bring about and sustain world unity are known and available to us. They are all on the table, ready to be put into action by the entire world for our harmonious and peaceful existence. The process for their application and realization is known; its stages are clear.

Whether grassroots volunteers or global leaders, in touch with each other or not, we are all needed in co-creating the new structures and mechanisms to transform the world around us. We are all partners in healing a divided humanity. We are all essential to restoring our communities to wholeness. We are the ones building the future we envision.

On the occasion of the 2024 UN Summit of the Future, the BIC noted that we face a profound opportunity and a vital imperative: the tremendous task of centering humanity's interdependence at the heart of a global governance system. Concern is deepening that progress made over decades is in decline, and that the scale and complexity of global challenges rapidly outpace the evolution of the systems designed to respond to them. These trends are symptoms of a deeper ailment: an inability on the part of the global community to fully embrace the reality of humanity's inextricable interdependence.

The deepening divisions in all realms of life and the resulting, interconnected crises that threaten humanity's survival cannot be resolved without collectively choosing to adopt and live by a central organizing principle that will ensure lasting peace and prosperity. In their response to the Summit of the Future, the BIC concluded: "It is our belief that placing the oneness of humanity at the heart of international affairs is a necessary prerequisite to stave off further catastrophe and secure lasting peace and harmony."

At this pivotal moment in our social, cultural, and spiritual evolution, understanding that peace will come in a gradual process of many degrees, according to the Bahá'í teachings, the way to peace must mature through an extensive organic process of evolution, unfolding step by step. By necessity, this process is made up of an indeterminable series of victories and reverses, great challenges, setbacks, and difficulties. Yet, with a clear set of unitive principles guiding the way, and the consecrated efforts of the entire human family, this longed for vision will find its realization gradually and become manifest in the world.

We are approaching the turning point of the 1st stage, a two-part process beginning with the *emergence and establishment* of the universal recognition by all peoples that they are members of one human family. This inclusive awareness results in a longer second part of the process consisting of the *consolidation* of this consciousness, which includes completely reconstructing world relations, based on this primary principle of unity and wholeness, moving humanity gradually and ultimately towards the realization of unitive global governance.

This process will tear down barriers to world unity and forge humanity into a unified body through the crucible of tests and trials. This will produce, however long it takes, the unity of nations, a body that is unified but without the inner and outer life to sustain it. This is referred to in the Bahá'í writings as the Lesser Peace.

The 2nd stage of this process, the task of breathing life into this unified body, of creating true spiritual unity among all peoples, communities, and nations, is a longer process of decades, even centuries, depending on how deeply committed humanity is to carry out this endeavor and have it fully expressed in physical reality. This stage will culminate in the realization of the full achievement of the oneness of humanity, manifested in all levels of interpersonal relationships, society, and government. It will signal the spiritualization of the planet through the fusion of all its peoples, creeds, classes, and nations into one fully functioning whole organism operating under the collectively chosen principles to harmonize all relationships and endeavors. This will complete the preconditions for permanent world peace.

With unitive consciousness as its norm, the depth and breadth of the collective unity of this stage will be characterized and sustained by the local, national, and global mechanisms and infrastructures of a world-embracing Commonwealth. This final piece to be put in place represents the fulfillment of all sacred prophesies relating to the time of peace on Earth and is the central instrument and the chief safeguard of what is referred to in the Bahá'í writings as the Most Great Peace.

With all the prerequisite unitive principles firmly in place, the culmination of this long evolutionary process will also signal the merging of the two great rivers of existence, the Changeless and the changing, resulting in the understanding that reality is one as the norm. The fully realized unity-in-diversity of the human family and all life will be a true reflection of the invisible and indivisible wholeness-in-motion of the entire creation, the sacred unity beyond all appearance.

While the 1st stage of this process is clearly within reach, the consummation of the 2nd stage is an organic process that must follow the laws of nature. Summer follows spring, not winter. The fully blossomed flower appears after its full maturation process, not its planting in the fertile soil.

There are many other factors, known and unknown, determining the flow of this process, whether humanity will yet be assailed with further calamities, what obstacles or opportunities will arise, and when this inexorable process will reach its culmination.

This is the choice before humanity: a much longer, divisive, and more destructive path with unimaginable devastation in its wake, *or* the way of unity, overcoming old patterns of discord and conflict through a collective act of will that consciously embraces and implements unitive principles to lay the foundation for the full and complete renewal of society on all social levels.

The way of unity is the way of binding human hearts for the betterment of the world. By focusing on the greater whole, in all its harmony and balance, we will achieve the greater goal, of peace on Earth.

STUDY GUIDE

Chapter Spotlights
&
Questions for Consultation

Chapter 1

Unity Characterizes the Hidden Wholeness of the Universe

- From its inception, an archetypal unity pervaded the entire Cosmos. On this grandest level, the essence of Creation is seen in its original wholeness. All beings have emerged out of the same elemental substance and are bound together by the same power of attraction.

- Creation itself represents the most exact and meticulous expression of unity there is. The Universe is a living superorganism with no boundaries between any of its parts. A single unifying agency organizes the deep structure of its wholeness.

- The attractive force of unity manifests coherence between all atoms of the component parts of Creation, from mineral to vegetable to the animal kingdom and beyond.

- On the social level, we are born as whole beings into a world characterized by division, where unity is both sought after and always existing.

- To realize on Earth the peace that exists in the vast wholeness-in-motion of the entire Creation, a deep commitment to a long-term process of growth and transformation is required to heal a divided humanity and achieve the inherent potential of unity-in-diversity.

- Unity-in-diversity on a global scale can only exist when the plurality of all things is understood, appreciated, and embraced. The way of unity-in-diversity is the only way to harmony, unity, and peace.

Questions for Consultation:

How and why can the Universe be considered a living superorganism with no boundaries between any of its parts?

Why is a deep commitment to a long-term process of growth and transformation required to realize peace on Earth?

Is it realistic to think that over a lifetime our consciousness can expand to become more inclusive and comprehensive, take on wider and wider perspectives, and eventually grasp the wholeness of all things?

Do you sense that there is a natural evolutionary process and direction to our consciousness that moves us toward unity and wholeness, despite disruptions and divisions that try to keep us apart?

What does unity mean to you, and from your own experience or perspective, how is inner unity interdependent with outer unity?

Why does unity, and unity-in-diversity, not mean uniformity or sameness, and how does unity embrace our uniqueness?

How do we grasp the unitive nature of Reality?

"He is a true believer in Divine unity who, far from confusing duality with oneness, refuses to allow any notion of multiplicity to becloud his conception of... the Divine Being as One Who... transcends the limitations of numbers."
Bahá'u'lláh

Chapter 2

Unity Is the Source and Direction of Evolution

- Evolution's trajectory is guiding us toward a re-awakening of our original wholeness, to complete a cycle of renewal and fulfill an age-old vision.

- The grandeur and perfection of the entire Creation carries with it an invisible power of divine love that sustains all things. Polar tensions are resolved with a higher level of consciousness than created them; in unitive consciousness there is no differentiation.

- Biology mirrors cosmology. An innate peacefulness exists in the organic harmony of the wholeness-in-motion within us and all around us.

- The evolutionary flow of Creation is built upon repeating cycles of birth, growth, maturity, decline, and renewal. The form and duration of each cycle is interdependently determined by the intermingling of human receptivity and resistance to the process.

- The inherent nature of all living things is to grow, develop, and change. There is a movement and sequence in all things that is determined by a universal attractive force.

- Humanity's spiritual evolution is directed toward unity. Its apex of consciousness will be reached when we collectively reflect the perfect harmony, unity, and wholeness already existing in all the diversity of creation. Unity of purpose is central to the evolutionary impulse.

Questions for Consultation:

Why are seeming differences and distinctions irrelevant in unitive consciousness?

What are some ways biology mirrors cosmology, and vice versa, and how is this a characteristic of Creation itself?

How and why is humanity's progress dependent upon cycles of renewal?

Is there a direction to humanity's spiritual evolution, and, if so, how will its destination be reached?

How are you directing your own spiritual evolution, and what do you envision as your own spiritual destination?

What is the natural outcome of unity expressed to its fullest
extent in the world?

"Universal peace is the destination towards which
humanity has been moving throughout the ages…
Now… the human race stands on the threshold of its maturity…
However, though world unity is possible—nay, inevitable—
it ultimately cannot be achieved without
unreserved acceptance of the oneness of humankind."
Universal House of Justice

Chapter 3

A Trinity of Unitive Principles

- Unity of purpose is central to the evolutionary impulse.

- Our overarching challenge in healing the false separation which causes all suffering is making a complete shift in how we relate to reality. By focusing on the one reality, which is complete, whole, and always unified, we connect ourselves to the peace already inherent in this grand unity all around us.

- Many of the world's wisdom traditions foretell a time of unity, harmony, and peace on Earth. To get to this promised time, we will need to go through the transformative process leading us to unity and wholeness.

- A wholistic look at the entirety of cultural evolution, including what is yet to come, reveals a process of three essential steps: moving from unity to plurality, and, at some point, back to unity, or *wholeness* followed by *duality* followed by *wholeness*.

- A wholistic view sees the whole first, and evolution as a single great process encompassing the entire creation. A big picture view of evolution notices its ups and downs and acknowledges it does not happen in a straight, smooth, linear fashion.

- A *unitive consciousness* is the natural outcome of fulfilling our own potential. But this depends upon the initiative we take to actively investigate reality on our own. Inherent in this process are myriad distractions that capture our attention and pull us in other directions, away from where our evolving consciousness would naturally take us.

Questions for Consultation:

How do we connect ourselves to the peace already inherent in the grand unity all around us?

How could purposeful evolution be anything other than a single great process encompassing the entire Creation?

What can we undertake ourselves that could expand our consciousness the most?

How is a unitive consciousness the natural outcome of fulfilling our own potential?

Do you see your own consciousness evolving toward wholeness?

How does the wholeness of creation govern evolution and consciousness?

"... all beings are linked together like a chain;
and mutual aid, assistance, and interaction are among their intrinsic
properties,
and are the cause of their formation, development and growth...
every single thing has an effect and influence upon every other,
either independently or through a causal chain."
"Nature is subject to a sound organization, to inviolable laws,
to a perfect order, and to a consummate design...
all are subject to one universal law from which they never depart."
'Abdu'l-Bahá

Chapter 4

The Emerging Unitive Age

- The tumult of the present moment, rather than a reason for despair, is but the earliest dawn of a collective coming of age. This inspires us toward the undertaking of building a peaceful world, such as never before known.

- The ongoing evolutionary flow of spiritual cycles ensures the forward movement of progress while bringing about periodic leaps of consciousness.

- Unity in all realms of being and doing is the overarching, all-encompassing principle that all progress in the world depends upon. Unity is the natural outcome of an organic process of restoring seemingly opposing forces to their inherent wholeness. This will result in the healing of an ailing humanity.

- The *way of unity* is ushering in the Unitive Age. All great "Ages" have taken centuries to play out through a transformative cyclical process that defines evolution and human history. It is through these cycles that the fullest expression of their potential is reached.

- If one universal law governs the entire creation and its evolution, then the same law would govern the evolution of spirituality. How different would our sense of meaning and purpose be if we saw religion as part of evolution?

- In the Unitive Age, the culmination of humanity's long evolution, a unitive consciousness, or a consciousness that brings about unity, will become the norm, the standard by which all things are seen and responded to.

Questions for Consultation:

What is hidden behind the tumult of the present moment?

What does the ongoing evolutionary flow of spiritual cycles ensure us of?

Imagine one universal law governing all of creation and its evolution, including the evolution of spirituality. How would this shift your view of humanity's spiritual evolution?

What are your thoughts and reflections on what the Unitive Age will be like when a unitive consciousness becomes the norm?

Is there a primary role the messengers of the Creator should be seen as playing?

"Prophets of God should be regarded as physicians
whose task it is to foster the well-being of the world and its peoples,
that, through the spirit of oneness,
they may heal the sickness of a divided humanity...
*"*Bahá'u'lláh

Chapter 5

Peace Is the Natural Outcome of the Way of Unity

- Coinciding with the collective development of humanity, unity has progressed through the stages of unity of family, of tribe, of city-state, and nation. These stages of unity have all been necessary preparation for the stage of world unity.

- The central organizing principle – *humanity is one family sharing the entire planet with all life* – requires a set of interdependent unitive principles to guide the dynamic process of creating the preconditions for peace on Earth.

- In our time, instant communication and easy, swift travel have merged the continents of Earth into one landscape, making the unity of the entire human family not only achievable but also within reach.

- This central theme – the oneness of humanity – is only going to be possible by building out a set of unitive principles that will support and sustain such a new level of unity-in-diversity in our time.

- The way of unity, with its unitive principles guiding each step, offers a powerful process leading humanity out of its current crises – from strained family relations to the multiple conflicts and wars characterizing international relations – and into their resolution of once and for all healing the many ills of a divided humanity.

- The set of unitive principles described in this chapter are seen as one whole, yet with many critical and necessary component parts, like cells and organs in the human body, each contributing to and essential for the well-being and optimal functioning of the entire body, the whole of humanity, and Earth. Our current crises cannot be dealt with separately, but only as a deeply interconnected, interdependent whole.

Questions for Consultation:

Why is a central organizing principle, like *humanity is one family sharing the entire planet with all life*, required to build out a set of unitive principles and guide humanity toward creating the preconditions for peace on Earth?

Why do our current global social, economic, and environmental crises need to be dealt with as an interconnected whole, rather than as separate issues?

Why would universally embracing the central organizing principle of the oneness of humanity be something that could help ensure the development of a sense of confidence about the future?

How are you integrating this central organizing principle into your life?

How critical to achieving world peace is implementing the principle
of the oneness of humanity?

"World order can be founded only on an unshakable consciousness
of the oneness of humankind,
a spiritual truth which all the human sciences confirm...
Recognition of this truth requires abandonment of prejudice
—prejudice of every kind—
race, class, color, creed, nation, sex, degree of material civilization,
everything which enables people to consider themselves superior to others.
Acceptance of the oneness of humankind
is the first fundamental prerequisite for
reorganization and administration of the world
as one country, the home of humankind.
Universal acceptance of this spiritual principle
is essential to any successful attempt to establish world peace.
It should therefore be universally proclaimed,
taught in schools, and constantly asserted in every nation
as preparation for the organic change
in the structure of society which it implies."
Universal House of Justice

Chapter 6

Unity-in-Action for the Betterment of the World

- There is no greater, more sacred, purpose than to become the cause of peace and well-being in the world. As spiritual traditions affirm, love is a universal, timeless elixir, the supreme force through which we can achieve wholeness and coherence on Earth.

- Thousands of communities worldwide are striving to apply unitive principles in their daily lives and community activities by working together to achieve a common goal and purpose: to bring about harmony, balance, and unity – the conditions for peace – within their community.

- With the common good as their organizing principle and adopting the overarching principle of the unity of the human family, these communities are empowering themselves to flourish through capacity building activities intended to ensure the equitable, balanced, harmonious, and unified functioning of their communities.

- A fully effective international commitment to unitive change may seem like a long way off. Yet, the only way to realize the completion of the transformation already in progress is to begin to center our wider deliberations on finding, agreeing to, and committing to carry out a shared vision. The current dichotomies need not slow us down.

- When capacity building initiatives are undertaken to release inner potential on a community or collective level, and a framework for collaborative learning is followed, the results are empowering and transformative.

- The ultimate goal of peace on Earth necessitates not only the full development of the spiritual and material aspects of society but also coherence and balance between them to enable all to enjoy the fruits of a prosperous global society.

Questions for Consultation:

Why would a universal commitment to unitive change be an effective way to realize the completion of the global transformation process already under way?

Why is the freedom to choose one's own destiny essential to both individuals and communities?

How would applying unitive principles in daily life and community activities create the conditions for peace in one's local setting?

What are some ways to build capacity, empower, and create coherence within your own community?

What are some ways a process of collaborative learning can be implemented in your neighborhood, community, or city?

What is it that will guarantee the well-being of humanity?

*"The supreme agency for the enlightenment and the redemption of the world
is love, fellowship, and unity among all the members of the human race.
Nothing can be effected in the world…
without unity and agreement."*
"If unity be gained, all other problems will disappear of themselves."
'Abdu'l-Bahá

Chapter 7

The Way of Unity to Inner Peace

- True inner peace is all our component parts functioning as a smoothly run unit, as a unified whole, in which all work together for the benefit of the whole. If we are not united within ourselves, or at peace as an individual, we will be ill-prepared to contribute to the wider peace around us.

- Personal coherence begins in the heart and is experienced as inner peace. This is the state that harmoniously unites our mind, body, and spirit in cooperation and flow, to assist each other in manifesting their innate unity and wholeness.

- Individual inner peace depends upon our considering the welfare of the entire human family as our own. Every person is a cell in the body of humanity, and every nation a vital organ in the body of humanity.

- Turn inward to ensure that all our relations with others are helping to bring about unity. Stand with confidence against those divisive forces attempting to sway society; in their place offer acts of service to promote the general welfare and common good of all.

- Spiritual distinction is the way to inner peace which is the way to interpersonal and world peace. Coming into a world divided and torn apart, achieving any peace at all depends upon us remembering we come from wholeness and are on a journey of returning to wholeness.

Questions for Consultation and a Practice:

What is inner peace to you, and why is it needed to contribute to outer peace?

Why does inner peace depend upon our consideration of the welfare of the entire human family as our own?

How does offering acts of service to others contribute not only to the common good, but also to our own inner peace?

To experience directly the potential of the love already in our hearts, that we may not even be aware of, gaze into someone's eyes. Try this practice with a partner to open the heart to feeling the love that always resides there. Stand or sit in front of someone, even better someone you do not know, and gaze directly into each other's eyes, with a concentrated, conscious focus on the other's eyes for 40 seconds. Then, reflect on the conditions this can create for love to be deeply felt, and how knowing you have an open heart, filled with love, can be a way to change the world into a more loving, peaceful place.

In what ways is the heart the receptacle of the divine love
that brings peace to the world?

"Thy heart is My home; sanctify it for My descent..."
"In the garden of thy heart plant naught but the rose of love..."
"The candle of thine heart is lighted by the hand of My power..."
"Sow the seeds of My divine wisdom in the pure soil of thy heart,
and water them with the water of certitude,
that the hyacinths of My knowledge and wisdom
may spring up fresh and green in the sacred city of thy heart..."
Bahá'u'lláh

Chapter 8

The Way of Unity to Interpersonal Peace

- Becoming a source of social good is living out the twofold moral purpose of simultaneously transforming our own characters while contributing to the advancement of society.

- Unitive relationships at all levels bring into existence civilization-building powers by reflecting the cooperation and reciprocity that governs the Universe. All social action endeavors applying unitive principles to a social need improve the collective life of all involved.

- The practice of consultation can be a primary all-purpose tool for fostering unity, strengthening social coherence, and peacebuilding at all levels. Consultation is the way to arrive at unity of thought, and the only sure way that can lead to unity of action.

- Consultation is a way to gain unexpected insights from a range of perspectives and seemingly irreconcilable views that end up finding new common ground. Consultation is designed to unlock the capacity of each individual and group to contribute most effectively to constructive social change.

- Social coherence, brought about and supported by social justice, is an absolute necessity for world unity and world peace. Both are the result of social action, which is designed to bring about the advancement of civilization and the prosperity of all.

- The way of unity necessitates the abandonment of prejudice of every kind – race, class, color, gender, creed, nationality, age, economic status, mental health – anything that people have used to place themselves above others and deny others any kind of human resource.

Questions for Consultation:

How does becoming a source of social good fulfill our twofold moral purpose?

How is social action applying unitive principles to a social need creating conditions for peace?

How and why is the art and practice of consultation a primary all-purpose tool for fostering unity and leading to unity of action?

Why would love-in-action be considered the sacred activism of our time?

What are some community building efforts to implement in your own community that might lead to world peace?

What are some community building efforts to implement in your own community that might lead to world peace?

What are some ways we can become a source of social good?

"Be worthy of the trust of thy neighbor, and look upon him with a bright and friendly face.

Be a treasure to the poor, an admonisher to the rich, an answerer of the cry of the needy...

Be as a lamp unto them that walk in darkness, a joy to the sorrowful,

a sea for the thirsty, a haven for the distressed,

an upholder and defender of the victim of oppression.

Let integrity and uprightness distinguish all thine acts.

Be a home for the stranger, a balm to the suffering, a tower of strength for the fugitive.

Be eyes to the blind, and a guiding light unto the feet of the erring.

Be an ornament to the countenance of truth, a crown to the brow of fidelity,

a pillar of the temple of righteousness, a breath of life to the body of mankind..."

Bahá'u'lláh

Chapter 9

The Way of Unity to World Peace

- A sustainable, lasting peace on Earth must be built upon a foundation of unifying principles that are designed to bring about and maintain unity on all levels of relational interactions, from family, to community, to city, to region, to nation, and the entire planet.

- To carry forward an ever-advancing civilization, everyone, of every gender, ethnicity, and faith tradition, will need to work side by side to build a global society, rooted in justice and characterized by unity, in which humanity reflects the beauty and perfection of its full range of diversity.

- Witnessing the twin processes of collapse and renewal, we are all agents of change needed to transform the widespread discord and separation of the human family into a worldwide reconciliation unifying all the diverse elements of human society. Creative energies have been released by divine sources to assist us all in this essential endeavor.

- As the final step to lasting world peace, after the unity of the human family has been firmly established, a multi-level system of global governance designed to sustain long-term unity will oversee a harmony of civilizations sharing one homeland.

- The long-promised peace on Earth, brought about by the establishment of a global commonwealth in which all nations, creeds, and backgrounds will be closely and permanently united, will be sustained by a world legislature, a world executive, and a world tribunal that are interconnected by a world inter-communication system embracing the whole planet and free from national restrictions, a world language, a universal system of currency, and an equitably regulated unitive economic system.

- The emergence of this unitive system of global governance will have also seen the reconstruction and demilitarization of the whole world in all the essential aspects of life, representing the consummation of human evolution.

Questions for Consultation:

Why does a sustainable, lasting peace on Earth need to be built upon a foundation of unitive principles?

Why does an ever-advancing civilization leading to a peaceful world need the full participation and voice of all people of all backgrounds working side by side as agents of change?

What do you view as the essential components of a system of unitive global governance that will truly represent the entire human family and that will be able to sustain a peaceful world?

How would you describe the full maturation process of the long-promised time of peace on Earth, what this is characterized by, and what stages this process will involve?

Could the intention of God be to bring about peace on Earth?

"God's purpose is none other than to usher in,
in ways He alone can bring about,
and the full significance of which He alone can fathom,
the Great, the Golden Age of a long-divided, a long-afflicted humanity.
Its present state, even its immediate future, is dark, distressingly dark.
Its distant future, however, is radiant, gloriously radiant
—so radiant that no eye can visualize it."
Shoghi Effendi

KEYS TO THE EVOLUTIONARY PROCESS LEADING TO PEACE ON EARTH

We have all the principles, tools, and processes needed to complete the global transformation well underway that will bring about peace. All that remains is to follow the central organizing process of *knowledge*, *volition*, and *action*.

This unitive process beginning with *knowledge* of the relevant principles, combined with the understanding of their necessity for peace, is followed by the will, or *volition*, to commit to their conscious implementation in the world, and culminates in the well-thought-out *action* required to bring the vision inspired by the principles into reality.

Completing this process fulfills our shared responsibility of implementing the transformation of words and ideas into deeds, or action steps that bring about unity. The instability in the world calls for leaders who will overcome the prevailing paralysis of will and lead in a movement from words to deeds.

Here are the key challenges in carrying out an ongoing evolutionary process toward peace:

Understanding the natural order, harmony, and wholeness of the Universe

- An inherent and organic unity pervades the Universe. All the planets are in perfect alignment with each other. All the cells and organs in the human body are created to be in perfect alignment with each other. All beings are bound together by the power of attraction.

Harmony, unity, wholeness, and peace make up the essential nature of the Universe.

- Knowing all things to be one leads to the feeling of belonging to all things. This sense of deep connection arises from a unitive consciousness and assures us that all things are tied together in an infinite web of life throughout the Cosmos.

- *World peace depends upon our reflecting the natural state of the Universe all around us.* Our work in bringing about this greater unity-in-diversity is peacebuilding. Expanding our consciousness, having it become more inclusive, taking on wider and wider perspectives, and finally living at peace in the wholeness of all things, is what will merge the changing and Changeless orders of reality into one.

Aligning our will with the flow and direction of evolution

- The inherent nature of all living things is to undergo cycles of birth, growth, maturity, decline, and renewal. Evolution's trajectory is not a straight path. A dynamic process of renewal takes us through ongoing cycles of transformation, leading us toward the promised time of unity, harmony, and peace on Earth.

- Social evolution, with its many cycles of crisis and victory, is directed toward the Golden Rule writ large, a new moral standard for a global community. If we can remember just one thing, let it be what we know to be true in our hearts: consciousness is intended to evolve toward unity and wholeness. This may be the most critical key to remaining firm in our commitment to peacebuilding.

- *World peace depends upon aligning our will with the flow and direction of evolution.* Our role is turning this knowledge of the wholistic direction of evolution into social action toward unity and wholeness. We are always being assisted by evolution itself in this effort. Tapping into these society building powers continuously released to transform human hearts, shape new social institutions, and expand circles of unity is what sustains our hope and optimism.

Adopting an all-inclusive identity

- The forces propelling new forms of global interconnection and interdependence demand that we widen the circle of our belonging to transcend oppositional identities of "us" and "them" that breed mistrust and reinforce competition. Our true nature leaves no excuse to exclude anyone from any circle of unity. Unity-in-diversity rests upon the sacredness of all beings.

- Our time calls for a new, all-human identity, a wider loyalty broadening affiliations. Without giving up any legitimate allegiances, we can transcend national interests for the greater good of the whole. Our primary identity is belonging to one human family. This all-inclusive identity solidifies our place and role in our local, national, and international community.

- *World peace depends upon our adopting an all-inclusive identity.* Our eternal, changeless identity is two-fold: we are both global citizens and expressions of a boundless sacred unity. Our role is to ensure the flowering of our unitive consciousness, embrace all in our common identity, and act accordingly in all circumstances.

Living by a central organizing principle and adopting a plan for achieving the necessary global transformational change

- Humanity is passing through its turbulent adolescence approaching its long-awaited maturity. The next step in our evolution is clear. Building out an infrastructure of families, communities, societies, nations, and global governance is required to realize the oneness and wholeness of human relationships, where there is no "other" left to exclude from the circle of all life.

- The central organizing principle guiding a set of core unitive principles toward global renewal is *humanity is one family sharing the entire planet with all other life*. To achieve this level of global unity needed to sustain world peace, a plan is necessary for global transformation that is scalable to all levels of society, local to regional to national to global. Such a plan has been implemented by thousands of communities around the world for over a century to create the foundation and framework for a peaceful and creative world.

- *World peace depends upon our living by a central organizing principle and carrying out a plan for achieving the necessary global transformational change.* Our role in this process centers around the building of strong, empowered, and vibrant local communities wherever we are that will contribute to the transformation in consciousness and values regionally, nationally, and globally that are necessary for the emergence of world unity characterized by global justice.

Living by a set of supporting core unitive principles that will create the conditions for maintaining unity on all levels

- As the Unitive Age continues to unfold, the following unitive principles, representing the way of unity, will become recognized as guiding a dynamic process leading humanity out of its current crises and into the realization of its oneness manifested by its inherent unity-in-diversity:

    - **Unitive Consciousness** – consciousness that brings about unity.

    - **Unitive Education** – education that brings about unity.

    - **Unitive Relationships** – relationships that bring about unity.

    - **Unitive Justice** – justice that brings about unity.

    - **Unitive Economics** – economics that brings about unity.

    - **Unitive Global Development** – development that brings about unity.

    - **Unitive Language** – language that brings about unity.

    - **Unitive Narratives** – narratives that bring about unity.

    - **Unitive Global Governance** – governance that sustains world unity.

- *World peace depends upon our living by a set of core unitive principles.* Our role is keeping our focus on the wholeness of all things. As we strive to bring these unitive principles into reality, we will usher in the promise of peace on Earth.

Independently investigating reality

- We arrive at a unitive consciousness by independently investigating truth. Through the process of an unfettered search, we encounter limited, divisive, and exclusive forms of consciousness. As we transcend and let go of these, we adopt a consciousness that brings about unity.

- This inner quest can eliminate one of the main sources of conflict in the world today – the inability or unwillingness to distinguish truth from falsehood, right from wrong. It is the prevalence of disinformation that makes seeking a unitive consciousness one of the only ways that can save us from a make-believe realm of concoction. We have an inherent urge to understand reality. A fundamental obligation of our humanity, of our sacred nature, is to seek to fulfill this capacity and responsibility embedded within us. Our pursuit of truth leads us to the understanding that truth is one.

- *World peace depends upon our independent investigation of reality.* Our role is to consciously reflect on all the life experiences, opinions, and views that come to us, to deeply engage in the process of weighing all sides of an issue, and to choose to enact in every realm of our lives that which will bring about unity and wholeness. This will ensure our potential of achieving a unitive consciousness.

Undertaking coordinated social action to build vibrant communities

- Large scale change happens through small-scale change being achieved over and over. Unity is globally scalable. An example of such unity-in-action to achieve deep change worldwide is found in the

Bahá'í international community. Together with friends, colleagues, and citizens from every walk of life, they have been gaining experience promoting peaceful and prosperous communities through applying unitive principles in everyday life and shared situations.

- Representing a true cross-section of humanity, these efforts, guided by all levels of institutional support, are carried out in consultative spaces of villages and neighborhoods that invite community members, irrespective of background or belief, to better understand their social reality and devise appropriate responses to the challenges they face. Their purpose is to support empowerment, ensure the freedom to choose one's own destiny, and bring about harmony, balance, and unity to create conditions for peace within the community and the world.

- The lessons learned from these experiences in culturally diverse settings are profound, far-reaching, and fully resonant with humanity's needs in this moment. The experience of this global community is offered as a living example of the expanding unity in the world, as a model for study, and for reinforcing hope in the unity of the human family.

- *World peace depends upon our social action for building vibrant, peaceful communities.* Our role in this profound global effort is our commitment to contribute, relative to our own capacity and strengths, wherever we are, what will assist humanity in realizing its collective maturity through its full unity-in-diversity.

Following a collaborative learning process to achieve social coherence at all levels

- Unitive principles applied locally in communities around the world through relationship-based activism has been carried out in Bahá'í-inspired social action initiatives for over a century. With the common good as its organizing principle, this method embraces a collaborative learning process consisting of:
  - **study** of a chosen topic or need of the group, with relevant guidance;
  - **consultation**, following a set process of defined steps;
  - **social action**, based on the consultative will of the group; and,
  - **reflection**, adding resources, learning lessons, making modifications.

- This complete process can be repeated as needed to ensure sustainable growth and maintain a continuity of learning and action. Rather than being "top-down" *or* "bottom-up," this approach built upon reciprocity and interconnectedness incorporates both and leads to transformation through a meeting-in-the-middle of the two approaches.

- *World peace depends upon our undertaking a collaborative learning process to achieve social coherence at all levels.* Our role in initiating, carrying out, or participating in this method in our own community or neighborhood is vital to achieving the long-term, overall goal of global unity.

Scaling the art and practice of consultation for the international stage

- Consultation is a primary, all-purpose tool for fostering unity, strengthening social coherence, and peacebuilding. Consultation is the surest way to achieve unity of thought and undertake unity-in-action. Through a group process of seeking truth, identifying relevant principles, exchanging differing views and opinions in a dignified and unattached manner while respecting the full range and diversity of thought to build consensus, a common understanding is reached and decisions are made for a collective course of action. As in a flower garden, individual strengths and differences contribute to the betterment of the whole.

- Consultation for addressing large-scale problems can be scalable to international settings. Participants who enter a consultative space first as human beings, and second as representatives of their organization, nation, or constituency, not bound to a particular position, and without attachment to a desired outcome, can genuinely pursue solutions founded upon truth and create an opportunity for a search for common ground. This approach of adopting a posture of learning, while following the respectful conditions underlying the process, ensures that participants see themselves as active agents in a collaborative endeavor to achieve a commonly arrived at solution while becoming more committed to its success.

- *World peace depends upon our scaling consultation for international practice.* Our role is to help integrate the art of consultation into as many settings as we are in, whenever possible, that can benefit from a process designed to bring about unity while respecting and honoring the views and opinions of all involved.

A Meditation for Peacebuilding

All around me, everything was created in harmony,
unity, wholeness, and peace.
All things within me were created for harmony,
unity, wholeness, and peace.
May my every thought and action reflect this
harmony, unity, wholeness, and peace,
by being directed toward building loving and kind relationships.
May these relationships be woven into the fabric
of vibrant and thriving communities.
May these communities become links in a chain,
contributing to the harmony, unity, and wholeness
of peace on earth.

ACKNOWLEDGMENTS

Peace has been a thread woven in and out of the tapestry of my life since my first breath, though this was not always evident to me. For their indispensable role in this book coming into being, I owe my deepest gratitude to my parents, Helen and Leon Atkinson.

It was only within the last decade that I realized peace had to be brought to the forefront in my life and remain there until its completion. While peace was behind the curtain in my other books, it was always waiting to come front and center. So, for this book, I'd like to thank once again all my mentors, guides, and students throughout my life, mentioned by name in my previous books, who have, in various ways, guided me toward and helped keep my focus on the big picture of all things and what the reality of wholeness is ultimately leading us toward. Developing the concept for this book, extending its scope and reach, and fleshing it all out, with each component having its own deep interconnectedness with all other components, has been a greatly rewarding experience for me.

I have called upon many friends and colleagues to help shape this book. I am extremely grateful to all the early readers of the manuscript, Ann Boyles, Phyllis Edgerly Ring, Glenn Nerbak, Elena Mustakova, Daniel Perrell, Carl Murrell, Deborah Moldow, Dana Sawyer, Jude Currivan, Julie Krull, Beth Tener, and Wendy Ellyatt for their thoughtful feedback, insights, and encouragement when it was still in rough form. It was also very rewarding to receive the input and feedback from the members of the New Generation Leaders for an Awakening World Synergy Circle of the Evolutionary Leaders,

Tatiana Speed, Scott Catamas, Simon Ester, Laura Pals, Maggie LaCosta, and Dominick Delgado Diaz.

It has been a continuing pleasure to collaborate with my friend and colleague Kurt Johnson and the entire Light on Light Press team, Karuna, Sandra (Chamatkara) Simon, and Nomi Naeem, as well as with Ariel Patrica and Sacred Stories Publishing for a third time.

I could not be more pleased to have been able continue my collaboration with Kate Sheehan Roach, an accomplished, expert editor who, in our third book project together, knows exactly what I want to say, and why, better than I do sometimes.

It is always very confirming to receive the endorsements of many respected leaders in the field. To Ervin Laszlo, Andrew Harvey, Jude Currivan, Jack Canfield, Deborah Moldow, Dot Maver, Emily Hine, and Julie Krull, I am extremely grateful for taking the time to read and offer their thoughts on this book

Most of all, and as always, my deepest appreciation and lasting gratitude goes to my first and most important reader, Cynthia Atkinson, who is always there with her honesty, understanding, wisdom, and encouragement.

ENDNOTES &
ADDITIONAL RESOURCES

Frontispiece

Bahá'u'lláh, *Gleanings from the Writings of Bahá'u'lláh*. Wilmette, IL: Bahá'í Publishing Trust, 1952/1976, #131. **https://www.bahai.org/r/877770890**

Preface

vii Creating the World Anew: see **https://www.bic.org/sites/default/files/creating_the_world_anew_bic_csw63_statement_2.pdf**

vii Unity not the ultimate goal: Universal House of Justice. **https://www.bahai.org/r/907575070**

Introduction

ix The First Peoples: Peggy Beck, Anna Lee Walters, and Nia Francisco, *The Sacred: Ways of Knowledge, Sources of Life*. Tsaile, AZ: Navajo Community College Press, 1992, 57-61.

x Jude Currivan, "A Radical Guide to Reality." **https://www.youtube.com/watch?v=6GkLM8o4RXc**

xiv Knowledge, volition, and action: Abdu'l-Bahá, *The Promulgation of Universal Peace*, #47.10.
https://www.bahai.org/r/467723418

xiv Bahá'í tradition: From the earliest times to the present, the world's great spiritual traditions have "driven leaps in human progress. These outpourings of creativity have resulted in some of humanity's most impressive and enduring achievements in the arts, architecture, governance, law, literature, and science," (p. 1) spanning the entire scope of cultural, social, and technological change.

"Members of the Bahá'í Faith… see humanity as standing on the cusp of just such a great societal shift – one that will be global in scope. The next and necessary stage in humanity's continuing ascent is the unification of all nations and peoples in a peaceful and just global civilization – one that welcomes and honors all, benefitting from the unique cultural and religious heritage each brings to the whole." (p. 1)

Bahá'ís believe that such a unifying plan is offered in the writings of Bahá'u'lláh (1817-1892), the Founder of the Bahá'í Faith, who "revealed a profound spiritual vision, revolutionary principles, and practical approaches to lead humanity through its treacherous adolescence into maturity." (p. 1) This prescription for peace is centered on the fundamental principle of the oneness of humanity.

Originating in Persia (now Iran) in the mid 1800s, the Bahá'í Faith is present in every country in the world, with members from virtually every national, ethnic, religious, and tribal background. Bahá'u'lláh's coming was heralded by the Báb (1819-1850), meaning "the Gate." (p. 12)

'Abdu'l-Bahá (1844-1921), son and successor of Bahá'u'lláh, was the perfect exemplar of the Faith's spirit and teachings. He was a champion of social justice and an ambassador for international peace. (p. 75) Shoghi Effendi (1897-1957), his grandson and successor, was the Guardian of the Bahá'í Faith, the authoritative interpreter of its sacred writings, and the administrator of its growing world community. (p. 80) The current international governing body, the Universal House of Justice, was first elected in 1963. (p. 81)

The Bahá'í international community is committed to "working systematically" to "build new patterns of individual and community life and new organizational structures" (p. 95) for sustaining world peace. *The Bahá'ís: Contributing to an Emerging Global Civilization.* New York: Bahá'í International Community, 2017.

Chapter 1 ~ Unity Characterizes the Hidden Wholeness

1 The cause of existence: 'Abdu'l-Bahá, *The Promulgation of Universal Peace.* Wilmette, IL: Bahá'í Publishing Trust, 1922-1925/1982, #89.7. **https://www. bahai.org/r/367824701**

3 The Hermetic Principle of the Law of Correspondence is one of seven Hermetic principles seen in nature and expressed in the Emerald Tablet and the Corpus Hermeticus from the teachings of Hermes Trismegistus, widely referred to in many spiritual traditions.
https://en.wikipedia.org/wiki/Hermes_Trismegistus
https://en.wiktionary.org/wiki/as_above,_so_below

3 Plato, *The Republic*. Translated by F. M. Cornford. New York: Oxford University Press, 1951, 319.

4 Elena Mustakova, *Global Unitive Healing: Integral Skills for Personal and Collective Transformation*. New York: Light on Light Press, 2021, chapters 2 and 4.

5 Robert Atkinson, *A New Story of Wholeness: An Experiential Guide for Connecting the Human Family*. New York: Light on Light Press, 2022.

5 Tikkun Olam: **https://www.myjewishlearning.com/article/tikkun-olam-repairing-the-world**

6 Perfect unity and love: 'Abdu'l-Bahá, *The Promulgation of Universal Peace,* ibid, #104.3. **https://www.bahai.org/r/622154911**

6 Jude Currivan, *The Story of Gaia: The Big Breath and the Evolutionary Journey of Our Conscious Planet*. Rochester, VT: Inner Traditions, 2022, 2, 6, 7.

6 Guy Murchie, *The Seven Mysteries of Life: An Exploration of Science and Philosophy*. Boston: Houghton Mifflin, 1978, chapter 14.

7 David Bohm, *Wholeness and the Implicate Order*. London: Routledge, 1980.

8 This endless universe: 'Abdu'l-Bahá, *Some Answered Questions*. Wilmette, IL: Bahá'í Publishing Trust, 1930/1987, #69.3. **https://www.bahai.org/r/802753808**

8 Divine Unity: 'Abdu'l-Bahá, *Some Answered Questions*, ibid, #81.6.
https://www.bahai.org/r/565874658

8 The Upanishads: Andrew Harvey, *The Essential Mystics: Selections from the World's Great Wisdom Traditions*. San Francisco: Harper, 1996, 38.

8 The Great Spirit: Black Elk, *The Sacred Pipe*. New York: Penguin, 1980, xx.

9 The Buddha: Paul Carus, *The Gospel of the Buddha*. Chicago: Open Court Publishing, 1915, 142.

9 Divinity in all things: Nader Saiedi, *Logos and Civilization*. Bethesda, MD: University Press of Maryland, 2000, 96.

9 Identity of unity: Nader Saiedi, *Logos and Civilization*, ibid, 94.

12 Regard the world: Bahá'u'lláh, *Gleanings from the Writings of Bahá'u'lláh*, ibid, #120. **https://www.bahai.org/r/727412649**

14 Human unity, spiritual unity: 'Abdu'l-Bahá, *The Promulgation of Universal Peace,* ibid, #69. **https://www.bahai.org/r/335968653**

14 Greater love has no one: John 15:13.

15 The means to prevent further splintering: Robert Stockman, *The Bahá'í Faith: A Guide for the Perplexed*. New York: Bloomsbury Academic, 2013, chapter 2.

16 The Covenant: **www.bahai.org/r/523393849**

17 Erik Erikson, "Remarks on the Wider Identity," in *A Way of Looking at Things*. New York: Norton, 1986, 498-501.

18 Widen the circle of our belonging: Bahá'í International Community, **https://www.bic.org/statements/embracing-interdependence-foundations-world-transition**

19 Diversity in the human family: 'Abdu'l-Bahá, *Paris Talks*. London: Bahá'í Publishing Trust, 1912/1971, #15.7. **https://www.bahai.org/r/268841058**

19 What all find their highest wish realized in: 'Abdu'l-Bahá, *Selections from the Writings of 'Abdu'l-Bahá*. Wilmette, IL: Bahá'í Publishing, 1978, #227.25. **https://www.bahai.org/r/242821225**

19 Diversity-in-unity: Suheil Bushrui, *Retrieving Our Spiritual Heritage: Bahá'í Chair for World Peace Lectures and Essays, 1994-2005*. Wilmette, IL: Bahá'í Publishing, 2012, 57-9.

Chapter 2 ~ Unity Is the Source and Direction of Evolution

21 Mysterious web of interdependency: Suheil Bushrui, *Retrieving Our Spiritual Heritage*, ibid, 26.

22 I loved thy creation: Bahá'u'lláh, *Hidden Words*. Wilmette, IL: Bahá'í Publishing Trust, 1975, Arabic, #4. **https://www.bahai.org/r/486363123**

22 The greatest bestowal: 'Abdu'l-Bahá, *The Promulgation of Universal Peace*, ibid, #6.5. **https://www.bahai.org/r/764990976**

22 Absolute order: 'Abdu'l-Bahá, *The Promulgation of Universal Peace*, ibid, #35. **https://www.bahai.org/r/513146375**

22 Each an expression of the other: 'Abdu'l-Bahá, *The Promulgation of Universal Peace*, ibid, #110.3. **https://www.bahai.org/r/376247249**

24 In every age: Bahá'u'lláh, *Gleanings*, ibid, #26. **https://www.bahai. org/r/987953771**

24 Perpetual motion: 'Abdu'l-Bahá, *Some Answered Questions*, ibid, #14.12. **https://www.bahai.org/r/307813157**

24 The law of motion: 'Abdu'l-Bahá, *Paris Talks,* ibid, #29. **https://www. bahai.org/r/982255238**

24 Degrees of perfection: 'Abdu'l-Bahá, *Some Answered Questions*, ibid, #64. **https://www.bahai.org/r/376816491**

25 Thich Nhat Hanh, *Cultivating the Mind of Love.* Berkeley, CA: Parallax Press, 1996.

25 Law of attraction: 'Abdu'l-Bahá, *Paris Talks,* ibid, #42.6. **https://www. bahai.org/r/593841904**

26 A threshold has been crossed: Universal House of Justice, April, 2002. **https://www.bahai.org/r/633856349**

27 Michael Bernard Beckwith, "Is World Peace Possible?" in *Our Moment of Choice: Evolutionary Visions and Hope for the Future.* Edited by Robert

Atkinson, Kurt Johnson, and Deborah Moldow. New York: Atria/Beyond Words, 2020, 33-38.

28 A great unity: 'Abdu'l-Bahá, *The Promulgation of Universal Peace*, ibid, #82. **https://www.bahai.org/r/971819005**

28 James O'Dea, "The Great Map of Peace," in *Our Moment of Choice*, ibid, 3-10.

28 Universal House of Justice, *The Promise of World Peace*, 1985, 1. **https://www.bahai.org/r/883867984**

29 The hallmark: Shoghi Effendi, "World Unity the Goal," *The World Order of Bahá'u'lláh*. Wilmette, IL: Bahá'í Publishing Trust, 1936. **www.bahai.org/r/194770170**

Chapter 3 ~ A Trinity of Unitive Principles

32 Pierre Teilhard de Chardin, *The Human Phenomenon*. Translated by Sarah Appleton-Weber. Portland, OR: Sussex Academic Press, 2003, 29.

32 Deepak Chopra, "Wholeness is What We Are," in *Our Moment of Choice*, ibid, 157-163.

33 No balance: C.G. Jung, *Memories, Dreams, Reflections*. New York: Vintage, 1963, 345.

34 Longest way: C.G. Jung, *Collected Works of C.G. Jung*, V.12. Princeton: Princeton University Press, 1980, 6.

34 Long-awaited coming of age: Universal House of Justice, *The Promise of World Peace*, 1985, #9. **https://www.bahai.org/r/883867984**

35 Desmond Tutu and Mpho Tutu, *Made for Goodness*. New York: Harper One, 2010, 7.

36 Ken Wilber, *The Marriage of Sense and Soul*. New York: Broadway Books, 1998, Ch. 8.

37 Unity to plurality: Robert Atkinson, *The Story of Our Time: From Duality to Interconnectedness to Oneness*. Delray Beach, FL: Sacred Stories Publishing, 2017, 43-46.

37 Charles Darwin, *The Descent of Man*. New York: Penguin Classics, 2004, 147.

38 Growth and development: 'Abdu'l-Bahá, *Some Answered Questions*, ibid, 1987, 198-9. **https://www.bahai.org/r/771160088**

38 Ethen Siegal, "What is the Most Astounding Fact About the Universe?" in *Forbes/Science*, April, 2016.

39   Hans Küng, editor, *A Global Ethic: The Declaration of the Parliament of World Religions*. New York: Continuum, 1993, 34-5.

40 Elizabeth Gilbert, *Eat, Pray, Love*. New York: Penguin, 2007, 154.

41 The collective unconscious: C.G. Jung, *Psychological Reflections*. Princeton: Princeton University Press, 1973, 22, 29-31.

41 Seek and ye shall find... He who approaches...: quoted in Jeffrey Moses, *Oneness: Great Principles Shared by All Religions*. New York: Ballentine Books, 2002, 91-93.

42 If we investigate: Abdu'l-Bahá, *The Promulgation of Universal Peace*, ibid, #56. **https://www.bahai.org/r/270449351**

42 William Blake, "Auguries of Innocence," in *The Complete Poetry and Prose of William Blake*. New York: Anchor, 1982.

43 The personality desires: C.G. Jung, *Memories, Dreams, Reflections*, ibid, 3-5.

44 Evelyn Underhill, *Mysticism*. New York: Dutton, 1911/1961, 445.

Chapter 4 ~ The Emerging Unitive Age

47 tumult... despair... unifying social structures: Universal House of Justice, *The Promise of World Peace*, 1985, Intro, #9-10. **https://www.bahai. org/r/883867984**

48 The earth is but: Bahá'u'lláh, quoted in Shoghi Effendi, *The Promised Day is Come*. Wilmette, IL: Bahá'í Publishing Trust, 1941/1996, 186-7.

49 Wayne Teasdale, *The Mystic Heart: Discovering a Universal Spirituality in the World's Religions*. Novato, CA: New World Library, 1999, 4-7, 23.

50 Andrew Harvey, *The Essential Mystics*, ibid.

51 Leaves of one branch: Bahá'u'lláh, *Tabernacle of Unity*. Bahá'í eBooks, #1.15. **https://www.bahai.org/r/197380154**

52 Turn your faces: Bahá'u'lláh, *Tabernacle of Unity*, ibid, #1.10. **https://www.bahai.org/r/971263797**

52 Unity is necessary: 'Abdu'l-Bahá, *Paris Talks*, ibid, #42.5. **https://www.bahai.org/r/471776836**

52 Stephen Prothero, *God is Not One*. New York: Harper, 2010.

53 The All-Knowing Physician: Bahá'u'lláh, *Tabernacle of Unity*, ibid, #1.4. **https://www.bahai.org/r/553038498**

54 The distinguishing feature: Bahá'u'lláh, *Gleanings*, #43.10. **https://www.bahai.org/r/902862713**

54 Karl Jaspers, **https://www.commentary.org/articles/karl-jaspers/the-axial-age-of-human-historya-base-for-the-unity-of-mankind**

56 Continuing nature of divine Revelation: *The Bhagavad Gita*. Translated by Eknath Easwaran. Berkeley: Nilgiri Press, 2007, 119; Isaiah, 62.2; Buddha, quoted in Paul Carus, ibid, 217; John 16: 12-13; Qur'an, 11:105, 13:39.

57 Chosen ones: Bahá'u'lláh, *The Kitáb-i-Íqán (The Book of Certitude)*. Wilmette, IL: Bahá'í Publishing, 1950, Pt 1.13. **https://www.bahai.org/r/042414512**

57 Treasuries of divine knowledge: Bahá'u'lláh, *The Kitáb-i-Íqán*, ibid, Pt 2.5. **https://www.bahai.org/r/077907308**

57   Outer expression: Abdu'l-Bahá, *The Promulgation of Universal Peace*, ibid, #52.2. **https://www.bahai.org/r/841894042**

58   Changeless faith: Bahá'u'lláh, *Gleanings*, ibid, #70. **https://www.bahai.org/r/538672141**

59 Universal House of Justice, *The Promise of World Peace*, 1985, Pt 1, #2. **https://www.bahai.org/r/883867984**

59   Bonds of unity: Abdu'l-Bahá, *The Promulgation of Universal Peace*, ibid, #47.3. **www.bahai.org/r/266767615**

59   The universal Golden Rule: Universal House of Justice, *The Promise of World Peace*, 1985, Pt 1, #5. **https://www.bahai.org/r/883867984**

59   Samuel P. Huntington, *The Clash of Civilizations and the Remaking of World Order*. New York: Simon & Schuster, 2011, 320.

59   Hans Küng, *A Global Ethic*, ibid, 17-35.

59   Ervin Laszlo, *The Inner Limits of Mankind: Heretical Reflections on Today's Values, Culture, and Politics*. Oxford: One World Publications, 1989, 65-67, 120-128.

60   Interreligious dialogue: Suheil Bushrui, *Retrieving Our Spiritual Heritage*, ibid, 101-110.

Chapter 5 ~ Peace Is the Natural Outcome

65   Peace has been the universal goal: Jeffery Moses, *Oneness*, ibid, 36.

66   H.H. the 14th Dalai Lama: **https://www.scu.edu/mcae/architects-of-peace/Dalai-Lama/essay.html#:~:text=Peaceful%20living%20is%20about%20trusting,our%20being%2C%20we%20desire%20contentment**

67   Candles of Unity: *The Bahá'ís*, ibid, 91. See also, **https://www.bic.org/statements/preparation-life-peace**

68   Merged the continents: 'Abdu'l-Bahá, *Selections from the Writings of 'Abdu'l-Bahá*. Wilmette, IL: Bahá'í Publishing, 1978, #15. **https://www.bahai.org/r/355125495**

71   Universal peace: 'Abdu'l-Bahá, *Selections from the Writings of 'Abdu'l-Bahá*, ibid, #227. **https://www.bahai.org/r/966924488**

71   A set of principles: Hoda Mahmoudi and Janet Khan, *A World Without War: 'Abdu'l-Bahá and the Discourse for Global Peace*. Wilmette, IL: Bahá'í Publishing, 2020, 133-6;

72   Consciousness of oneness: Universal House of Justice, *The Promise of World Peace*, Pt 3, #2. **https://www.bahai.org/r/883867984**

73   Teaching world citizenship: Universal House of Justice, *The Promise of World Peace*, #2.10. **https://www.bahai.org/r/108290894**

73   Education for Unity: Suheil Bushrui, *Retrieving Our Spiritual Heritage*, ibid, 111-130.

75   Albert Einstein, *The Einstein Reader*. New York: Citadel, 2003, 23.

75   Spawned many books, for example: Kelly James Clark, *God and the Brain*. Eerdmans, 2019; Carolyn Myss, *The Science of Medical Intuition*. Sounds True, 2002; Francis S. Collins, *The Language of God*. Free Press, 2006; Stuart A. Kauffman, *Reinventing the Sacred*. Basic Books, 2008; Brian Greene, *The Elegant Universe*. Vintage Books, 2001; Frank J. Tipler, *The Physics of Immortality*. Knopf, 1997; and, Bernard Haisch, *The God Theory*. Weiser Books, 2009.

75 Paul Davies, *The Mind of God: The Scientific Basis for a Rational World*. New York: Simon & Schuster, 1993.

75 Peace education programs: **https://nationalpeaceacademy.us/news**

75   Culture   of   peace: **https://pathwaystopeace.org/wp-content/ uploads/2018/12/Culture-of-Peace-Description-Open-Use.pdf**

75   Spirit of peace in the community: **https://www.bic.org/statements/ education-peace**

76   Conscious   agents: **https://www.bic.org/statements/new-delivery-systems-basic-education**

77 Complementary roles: *The Bahá'ís*, ibid, 94.

77 Passed on through the family: Universal House of Justice, *The Promise of World Peace*, Pt 2, #9. **https://www.bahai.org/r/883867984**

77 Two wings: 'Abdu'l-Bahá, *Selections from the Writings of 'Abdu'l-Bahá*, ibid, #227.18. **www.bahai.org/r/040813728**

77 Full equality: Universal House of Justice, *The Promise of World Peace*, Pt 2, #9. **https://www.bahai.org/r/883867984**

78 No distinction is evident: **https://www.bahai.org/r/365983525 https://www.bic.org/perspectives/spiritual-reality-equality-prerequisite-peace**

78 Katuyola, Zambia, **https://www.bic.org/statements/reimagining-role-institutions-building-gender-equal-societies**

79 Women are less likely to sanction war: see Abdu'l-Bahá, *The Promulgation of Universal Peace*, ibid, #62.7. **https://www.bahai.org/r/986057314**

79 A virtue and a right: **https://www.bic.org/statements/spiritual-basis-equality**

80 Values, attitudes, and behaviors: **https://www.bic.org/statements/rights-child**

80 UN Pact for the Future:
https://www.un.org/sites/un2.un.org/files/sotf-pact_for_the_future_adopted.pdf

81 Transforming the foundations of community life: **https://www.bic.org/statements/rising-generations-weaving-new-tapestry-community-life**

81 Meaningful engagement: **https://www.bic.org/news/youth-and-future-generations-heart-summit-future**

83 The inescapable duty: *A Unifying Vision in Action: An Introduction to the Bahá'í Faith*. Evanston, IL: Bahá'í Publishing, 2023, 19.

84 Racism: Universal House of Justice, *The Promise of World Peace*, Pt 2, #5. **https://www.bahai.org/r/883867984**

84 Power of unity and love: *A Unifying Vision in Action*, ibid, 13.

84 Justice is a powerful force: Bahá'u'lláh, *Epistle to the Son of the Wolf.* Wilmette, IL: Bahá'í Publishing Trust, 1969, para. 55. **https://www.bahai. org/r/937961309**

84 The purpose of justice: Bahá'u'lláh, *Tablets of Bahá'u'lláh.* Wilmette, IL: Bahá'í Publishing Trust, 1988, #6.6. **https://www.bahai.org/r/549730774**

85 A system of unitive justice: see: **https://cssp.org/2019/11/honoring-the-global-indigenous-roots-of-restorative-justice**

85 Declaration of the Parliament: Hans Küng, *A Global Ethic*, ibid, 17-35.

86 Elena Mustakova, *Global Unitive Healing*, ibid.

87 Oxfam report: **https://en.wikipedia.org/wiki/Distribution_of_wealth**

87 Humanity's collective life suffers: **https://www.bahai.org/r/934375828**

87 Best use of wealth: *A Unifying Vision in Action*, ibid, 17.

88 Inordinate disparity: Universal House of Justice, *The Promise of World Peace*, Pt 2, #6. **https://www.bahai.org/r/883867984**

88 Incompatibility of poverty: **https://www.bic.org/perspectives/efforts-eradicate-poverty-we-all-depend-each-other**

88 Notion of prosperity: *The Bahá'ís*, ibid, 93.

90 Capacity to think globally: **https://www.bic.org/statements/global-action-plan-social-development**

90 Systems that empower: **https://www.bic.org/perspectives/perspective-understanding-why-purpose-development**

90 Well-being and happiness: **https://www.bic.org/perspectives/development-human-happiness-and-challenge-distinguishing-means-ends**

90 Balance of material and spiritual needs: **https://www.bic.org/statements/toward-development-paradigm-21st-century**

91 World citizenship: **https://www.bic.org/statements/world-citizenship-global-ethic-sustainable-development**

91 Indisputable interdependence: Universal House of Justice, *The Promise of World Peace*, Pt 2, #7. **https://www.bahai.org/r/883867984**

92 Feel less foreign: **https://bahaiteachings.org/why-global-second-language-should-be-first-priority/?fbclid=IwAR1f0W3jwAYaL2J-oWq5QpHutjjzlF5vDG1YkBF5PPmSW_SLIT7AecAOADA**

93 The cause of unity: **https://www.bahai.org/r/262982422**

93 As an auxiliary: Abdu'l-Bahá, *The Promulgation of Universal Peace*, ibid, #82.12. **https://www.bahai.org/r/618799911**

93 One great unit: Joseph Campbell, **https://www.jcf.org/learn/joseph-campbell-four-functions-of-myth**

96 *Creating an Inclusive Narrative.* Australian Bahá'í Community, 2020. **https://www.oea.bahai.org.au/inclusive-narrative-project**

97 The physical realm we exist in: **https://evolutionaryleaders.net/unitivenarrative**

98 Evolutionary progress: **https://noetic.org/blog/why-a-unitive-narrative-now**

99 One country: Bahá'u'lláh, *Gleanings*, ibid, #117. **https://www.bahai.org/r/696472436**

99 UN SDGs: **https://www.un.org/en/common-agenda/sustainable-development-goals**

100 IDGs: **https://innerdevelopmentgoals.org**

101 Identify the principles: Universal House of Justice, *The Promise of World Peace*, Pt 2, #13. **https://www.bahai.org/r/883867984**

102 Shoghi Effendi, "The Principle of Oneness," *The World Order of Bahá'u'lláh*, ibid. **https://www.bahai.org/r/431364656**

102 Protect distinctive expressions: *Creating an Inclusive Narrative*, ibid, 38. **https://www.oea.bahai.org.au/inclusive-narrative-project**

104   David Gershon, **https://empowermentinstitute.net/transformative-social-change**

106   Where we derive our greatest meaning: **https://www.bic.org/news/assumptions-about-human-nature-shape-design-ai-technology**

106   Ensuring AI data is bias-free: **https://www.bic.org/news/beyond-technology-ai-opens-new-perspectives**

107   Peter Block, *Activating the Common Good: Reclaiming Control of Our Collective Well-Being*. Oakland, CA: Berrett-Koehler Publishers, 2024. **https://www.google.com/books/edition/Activating_the_Common_Good/3LTIEAAAQBAJ?hl=en&gbpv=1&printsec=frontcover**

108   Leaders who will overcome the paralysis of will: Bahá'í International Community, **https://www.bic.org/statements/embracing-interdependence-foundations-world-transition**

108   Leadership style designed to foster connection and cooperation: **https://www.a4uj.org/uj-leadership**

109   A unitive pattern can be consciously built: *The Bahá'ís*, ibid, 94.

Chapter 6 ~ Unity-in-Action for the Betterment of the World

111   Cause of peace and well-being: Abdu'l-Bahá, *The Secret of Divine Civilization*. Wilmette, IL: Bahá'í Publishing Trust, 1990, 3. **https://www.bahai.org/r/614945684**

111   Knowledge, volition, and action: Abdu'l-Bahá, *The Promulgation of Universal Peace*, ibid, #47.10. **https://www.bahai.org/r/467723418**

112   Plan established by Bahá'u'lláh: **https://www.bic.org/statements/ promise-disarmament-and-peace**

112 100,000 localities: **https://www.bahai.org/national-communities**

113 A model for study: Universal House of Justice, *The Promise of World Peace*, Pt 4, #4. **https://www.bahai.org/r/883867984**

113 An enterprise of infinite complexity: **https://www.bahai.org/library/authoritative-texts/the-universal-house-of-justice/messages/20121126_001/1#994173812**

113 Long-term process... build vibrant communities: *A Unifying Vision in Action*, ibid, 12, 15-16.

113 Peter Block, *Activating the Common Good*, ibid. **https://www.google.com/books/edition/Activating_the_Common_ Good/3LTIEAAAQBAJ?hl=en&gbpv=1&printsec=frontcover**

114   Social development... Bahá'í-inspired development process: *For the Betterment of the World: The Worldwide Bahá'í Community's Approach to Social and Economic Development*. New York: Bahá'í International Community, 2003/2023, 6-13. **https://dl.bahai.org/bahai.org/betterment-world-standard-quality.pdf**

116 Bahá'í International Development Organization:
https://www.bahai.org/library/authoritative-texts/the-universal-house-of-justice/messages/20231128_001/1#729554670

116 Unity-in-action:
https://www.bic.org/statements/unity-action-reclaiming-spirit-sustainable-development-agenda

117 Release universal capacity: **https://www.bic.org/statements/billions-arising-releasing-universal-capacity-transformative-social-change**

118 Need for action is urgent: **https://www.bic.org/perspectives/statement-daniel-perell-our-common-agenda-and-enhancing-international-cooperation**

120 Bani Dugal, **https://www.bic.org/perspectives/building-trust-and-relationships-sustain-society-commitments-actions**

120 Social action: **https://www.bahai.org/r/422509899**

120 Arthur Dahl: **https://iefworld.org/ddahl23t_governance**

122 Structures of a new civilization: *For the Betterment of the World*, ibid, 8. **https://dl.bahai.org/bahai.org/betterment-world-standard-quality.pdf**

123 Study, consultation, action, and reflection: **www.bahai.org/r/368569116**

123 Visions and strategies are re-examined: *For the Betterment of the World*, ibid, 13.
https://dl.bahai.org/bahai.org/betterment-world-standard-quality.pdf

125   Attitudes toward youth: **https://www.bic.org/perspectives/building-compelling-vision-future-0**

125   A bird with two wings: **https://www.bic.org/statements/toward-prosperity-role-women-and-men-building-flourishing-world-civilization**

126   A method of empowerment: **https://www.bic.org/statements/empowerment-mechanism-social-transformation**

127   Within the last decade: **https://www.bic.org/statements/embracing-interdependence-foundations-world-transition**

127   Training institutes: **https://www.bahai.org/action/involvement-life-society/social-action**

128-30   Social action projects: *For the Betterment of the World*, ibid, 18-33. **https://dl.bahai.org/bahai.org/betterment-world-standard-quality.pdf**

132   Ditalala, DRC: "A Vision of Peace," **https://news.bahai.org/story/1233**

134   United States: **https://www.bahai.us/beliefs/building-community**

136   The objective: Hoda Mahmoudi and Janet Khan, *A World Without War*, ibid, 3.

136   There was no separating peace: Hoda Mahmoudi and Janet Khan, "'Abdu'l-Bahá Champion of Universal Peace," in *The Bahá'í World: A Selection of Articles on Justice, Unity and Peace*. Bahá'í International Community: Bahá'í

eBooks Publications, 2022, 10. **https://www.bahaiebooks.org/publications/ justiceunityandpeace**

Chapter 7 ~ The Way of Unity to Inner Peace

142 Thich Nhat Hanh, *Cultivating True Peace: Ending Violence in Yourself, Your Family, Your Community, and the World.* New York: Free Press, 2003, 5.

142 Black Elk, quoted in Andrew Harvey, *The Essential Mystics*, ibid, 14.

142 Arnold Toynbee, quoted in Suheil Bushrui, *Retrieving Our Spiritual Heritage*, ibid, 39.

143 Ervin Laszlo, quoted in Suheil Bushrui, *Retrieving Our Spiritual Heritage*, ibid, 259.

143 HeartMath: **https://www.heartmath.org/gci**

143 Every good habit: 'Abdu'l-Bahá, *Paris Talks*, ibid, #18. **www.bahai. org/r/165303977**

144 The human spirit: Universal House of Justice, *The Promise of World Peace*, Pt 1, #1. **https://www.bahai.org/r/883867984**

144 The power of thought: Hoda Mahmoudi and Janet Khan, in *The Bahá'í World: A Selection of Articles on Justice, Unity and Peace*, ibid, 7. **https://www. bahaiebooks.org/publications/justiceunityandpeace**

145 The expressions of the soul: *The Bahá'ís*, ibid, 42, 44, 92.

145   Meditation and prayer: Universal House of Justice, **www.bahai. org/r/503933298**

146   Unity within self: **https://www.bic.org/statements/preparation-life-peace**

146   Tara Brach, **https://www.tarabrach.com/peace-work-audio**

147   John Keats, *Selected Letters*. New York: Oxford University Press, World Classics, 2009, 232.

147   With joy and radiance: Bahá'u'lláh, **http://www.bahai.org/r/253167976**

147   One hour's reflection: Bahá'u'lláh, **http://www.bahai.org/r/269100132**

147   Divine inspiration: 'Abdu'l-Bahá, *Paris Talks*, **http://www.bahai. org/r/359367592**

148   In thought and attitude: 'Abdu'l-Bahá, **http://www.bahai. org/r/269778803**

148   Care for the stranger: Abdu'l-Baha, *Selections from the Writings of 'Abdu'l-Bahá*, ibid, #16.5.
https://www.bahai.org/r/117959446

149 The rehabilitation of the world: Bahá'u'lláh, *Tablets of Bahá'u'lláh*, ibid, #11.27, 35. **https://www.bahai.org/r/625781508**

149 Deeds that are pure: Bahá'u'lláh, *Hidden Words*, ibid, Persian #76.
https://www.bahai.org/r/358991785

149 Lamp of divine guidance: *Selections from the Writings of 'Abdu'l-Bahá*, ibid, #12.3. **https://www.bahai.org/r/305304502**

149 Center of attraction: *Selections from the Writings of 'Abdu'l-Bahá*, ibid, #35.5. **https://www.bahai.org/r/456225810**

149 Become eminent: *Promulgation of Universal Peace*, ibid, #68.4. **https://www.bahai.org/r/331882631**

150 Turning inward: Shoghi Effendi, quoted in *Excellence in All Things*, #35. **https://bahai-library.com/pdf/compilations/excellence_all_things.pdf**

150 Honor and distinction: **https://www.bic.org/statements/preparation-life-peace**

150 Deepak Chopra, *Peace is the Way: Bringing War and Violence to an End.* New York: Three Rivers Press, 2003, 115, 122.

150 Circle of unity: *Paris Talks*, ibid, #15.12. **https://www.bahai.org/r/317342905**

151 The divine religions: *The Promulgation of Universal Peace*, ibid, #41. **https://www.bahai.org/r/416614145**

151 To know inner peace: Jeffery Moses, *Oneness*, ibid, 204.

Chapter 8 ~ The Way of Unity to Interpersonal Peace

153 Peter Block, *Activating the Common Good*, ibid. https://www.google.com/books/edition/Activating_the_Common_Good/3LTIEAAAQBAJ?hl=en&gbpv=1&printsec=frontcover

154 Thich Nhat Hanh, *Cultivating True Peace*, ibid, 133-36.

154 The cause of peace: 'Abdu'l-Bahá, *The Secret of Divine Civilization*, ibid, 1. https://www.bahai.org/r/006593911

154 Twofold moral purpose: *The Bahá'ís*, ibid, 11.

154 Let your thoughts: Bahá'u'lláh, *Gleanings*, ibid, #43.4. https://www.bahai.org/r/998953432

154 Strive that your actions: 'Abdu'l-Bahá, *Paris Talks*, ibid, #26.7. https://www.bahai.org/r/144066038

155 Hardships and suffering: *Pause and Reflect: Meditations for Change*. Evanston, IL: One Voice Press, 2023, 49.

155 Voice of peace: *Pause and Reflect*, ibid, 70-1.

155 Essential relationships: *Pause and Reflect*, ibid, 72.

156 fiftieth cousins: Guy Murchie, ibid, 345; https://www.scientificamerican.com/article/humans-are-all-more-closely-related-than-we-commonly-think

156 Civilization-building powers: *Pause and Reflect*, ibid, 86.

156 Shared identity: *Pause and Reflect*, ibid, 87.

157 Field of service: **https://www.bahai.org/r/640866959**

157 Relationship with the divine: *Pause and Reflect*, ibid, 131.

158 Make a cooperative effort: David Bohm, *On Dialogue*. Routledge, 1996.

158 No predefined purpose: **https://en.wikipedia.org/wiki/Bohm_Dialogue**

159 Not a format for the struggle for power: Nader Saiedi, *Logos and Civilization*, ibid, 357.

160 Ideas belong not to the individual: *Creating an Inclusive Narrative*, ibid, 34-6.

160 The shinning spark: 'Abdu'l-Bahá, quoted in *Social Action: A Compilation Prepared by the Research Department of the Universal House of Justice*. Wilmette. IL: Bahá'í Publishing, 2020, #163.

160 A contribution to the consensus: *The Promulgation of Universal Peace*, ibid, #31.2. **https://www.bahai.org/r/507894527**

160 Identifying the spiritual principles: *The Promise of World Peace*, Pt 2, #13. **https://www.bahai.org/r/883867984**

161 Effective consultation: *Social Action*, ibid, #168.

161   Primary steps: John S. Hatcher, *The Ascent of Society: The Social Imperative in Personal Salvation.* Wilmette, IL: Bahá'í Publishing, 2007, 243.

162   All that is needed: **https://www.bic.org/perspectives/consultation-effective-action-reflections-road-summit-discussion-series**

163   To achieve peace: *The Promise of World Peace*, Pt 3, #10. **https://www.bahai.org/r/883867984**

163   Communities that cross boundaries: **https://www.bahai.us/beliefs/building-community**

164   A world organically unified: **https://www.bahai.us/public-affairs/focus-areas/race**

165   Learning to apply spiritual principles: **https://www.bahai.us/wp-content/uploads/2021/03/unity-social-justice**

166   Everyone has a part to play: **www.bahai.org/r/417390190**

166   Peace must first be established: *Selections from the Writings of 'Abdu'l-Bahá*, ibid, #201. **https://www.bahai.org/r/168340975**

Chapter 9 ~ The Way of Unity to World Peace

168   Ever-advancing civilization: Bahá'u'lláh, *Gleanings*, ibid, #109. **https://www.bahai.org/r/994085186**

168   Characterized by unity: **www.bahai.org/r/082258886**

169 An inclusive approach to conflict resolution: Suheil Bushrui, *Retrieving Our Spiritual Heritage*, ibid, 227-8.

169 The more the world: 'Abdu'l-Bahá, *The Promulgation of Universal Peace*, #24.3. **https://www.bahai.org/r/566743659**

170 Reached a turning point: **https://www.bic.org/statements/turning-point-all-nations**

170 Effective universal framework: *The Promise of World Peace*, Pt 2, #1-4. **https://www.bahai.org/r/883867984**

170 The whole world: 'Abdu'l-Bahá, *Paris Talks*, ibid, #40.16. **https://www.bahai.org/r/560996260**

171 Creative energies: Shoghi Effendi, *The Promised Day is Come*, ibid, 192-4.

171 Wider, inclusive loyalty: Shoghi Effendi, *The Promised Day is Come*, ibid, 199-201.

171 Moving toward this destiny: Universal House of Justice, **https://www.bahai.org/r/949130994**

171 Hans Küng, *A Global Ethic*, ibid.

171 Culture of peace: Thich Nhat Hanh, *Cultivating True Peace*, ibid, 207.

172 Inevitable movement toward globalization: Suheil Bushrui, *Retrieving Our Spiritual Heritage*, ibid, Chapter 11.

173 Planetary "civil service": Universal House of Justice,
https://www.bahai.org/library/authoritative-texts/the-universal-house-of-justice/messages/19851001_001/1#910323081

173 A spiritual process: Suheil Bushrui, *Retrieving Our Spiritual Heritage*, ibid, 262.

173 A global culture of unity: **https://www.bic.org/statements/one-same-substance-consciously-creating-global-culture-unity**

174 Absence of conflict: **https://www.bic.org/statements/peace-and-development**

174 Great age to come: Shoghi Effendi, *The Promised Day is Come*, ibid, 192.

174 United Nations: **https://hdr.undp.org/content/human-development-report-1999**

175 True unity: Suheil Bushrui, *Retrieving Our Spiritual Heritage*, ibid, 230.

175 Uniform world order: Suheil Bushrui, *Retrieving Our Spiritual Heritage*, ibid, 231-8.

175 UN Pact for the Future:
https://www.un.org/sites/un2.un.org/files/sotf-pact_for_the_future_adopted.pdf

176 The essential prerequisites: Bahá'u'lláh, *Gleanings*, ibid, #43.10. **https://www.bahai.org/r/902862713**

176 Peace and tranquility: Bahá'u'lláh, *Tablets of Bahá'u'lláh*, ibid, #11.
https://www.bahai.org/r/200685474

176 Global approach to peace: Nader Saiedi, "Replacing the Sword with the Word: Bahá'u'lláh's Concept of Peace," in *The Bahá'í World: A Selection of Articles on Justice, Unity and Peace*, ibid, 135. **https://www.bahaiebooks.org/publications/justiceunityandpeace**

176 All-embracing assemblage: Bahá'u'lláh, *Gleanings*, ibid, #117. **https://www.bahai.org/r/696472436**

177 Supreme tribunal: 'Abdu'l-Bahá, *Selections from the Writings of 'Abdu'l-Bahá*, ibid, #202.11. **https://www.bahai.org/r/190839078**

177 National assemblies: 'Abdu'l-Bahá, *Selections from the Writings of 'Abdu'l-Bahá*, ibid, #227.31. **https://www.bahai.org/r/036338180**

177 The cause of universal peace: 'Abdu'l-Bahá, *The Secret of Divine Civilization*, ibid.
https://www.bahai.org/r/605810522; **www.bahai.org/r/413673867**

178 Strategic plan: Hoda Mahmoudi and Janet Khan, *A World Without War*, ibid, 94. See also 'Abdu'l-Bahá, *Tablets of the Divine Plan*. Wilmette, IL: Bahá'í Publishing Trust, 1993. **https://www.bahai.org/r/531491243**

178 An organic change: Shoghi Effendi, "The Principle of Oneness," *The World Order of Bahá'u'lláh*, ibid. **https://www.bahai.org/r/264008982**

178-80 World commonwealth: Shoghi Effendi, "World Unity the Goal," *The World Order of Bahá'u'lláh*, ibid. **www.bahai.org/r/213721999**

180   Optimal conditions: Suheil Bushrui and Mehrdad Massoudi, *The Spiritual Heritage of the Human Race: An Introduction to the World's Religions*. Oxford: One World Publications, 2010, 390.

180-81 Statement on the 50th Anniversary of the UN: **https://www.bic.org/ statements/turning-point-all-nations#V**

182   Statement on the 75th Anniversary of the UN: **https://www.bic.org/ statements/governance-befitting-humanity-and-path-toward-just-global-order**

183 Global Governance Forum: **https://globalgovernanceforum.org**

185   A vital imperative: **https://www.bic.org/statements/embracing-interdependence-foundations-world-transition**

185 An organic process of evolution: Universal House of Justice, **https:// www.bahai.org/r/975935253**

186   Emergence and establishment… consolidation: from a talk by Ali Nakhjavani, Bahá'í Summer School, Acuto, Italy, 1999, referring to Shoghi Effendi's explanation regarding the stages leading to the Lesser Peace and the Most Great Peace. (p. 47 of Question Time at the Italian Sumer School with Mr. Ali Nakhjavani, Acuto, Italy, August 22-28, 1999, published by Casa Editrice Bahá'í, 2006). Personal communication from Ann Boyles, 12/14/23.

186 The Lesser Peace: Universal House of Justice, 1976. **https://www.bahai. org/r/284971064**

187 Most Great Peace: Shoghi Effendi, *The World Order of Bahá'u'lláh*, ibid. **https://www.bahai.org/r/784120322**

187 Whether humanity will yet be assailed: **www.bahai.org/r/417390190**

Study Guide

193   Divine unity: Bahá'u'lláh, *Gleanings*, ibid, #84. **https://www.bahai.org/r/333537962**

197 Universal peace: Universal House of Justice, 2019. **https://www.bahai.org/r/544819830**

201   All beings are linked: 'Abdu'l-Bahá, *Some Answered Questions*, ibid, #46.6. **https://www.bahai.org/r/725713286**

201 Nature is subject: 'Abdu'l-Bahá, *Some Answered Questions*, ibid, #1.2. **https://www.bahai.org/r/854608442**

205 Regarded as physicians: Bahá'u'lláh, *Gleanings*, ibid, #34.6. **https://www.bahai.org/r/186183494**

209 World order: Universal House of Justice, *The Promise of World Peace*, Pt 3, #2-5. **https://www.bahai.org/r/883867984**

213 The supreme agency: 'Abdu'l-Bahá, *The Secret of Divine Civilization*, ibid, 23. **https://www.bahai.org/r/872311141**

213 If unity be gained: 'Abdu'l-Bahá, *Selections from the Writings of 'Abdu'l-Bahá*, ibid, #15. **https://www.bahai.org/r/870877966**

217 Thy heart: Bahá'u'lláh, *Hidden Words*, ibid, Arabic, $59, Persian #3, 32, 33.

221 Be as a lamp: Bahá'u'lláh, *Gleanings*, ibid, #130. **https://www.bahai. org/r/174232426**

225 The Golden Age: Shoghi Effendi, *The Promised Day is Come*, ibid, 190. **https://www.bahai.org/r/563821072**

Additional Resources

Miguel Santesteban Gil, *The Concept of Peace in the Baha'i Faith*. Oxford: George Ronald, 2022.

Peace: A Compilation of Extracts from the Bahá'í Writings. Bahá'í Publications Australia: Bahá'í International Community, 1990/2021. **www.bahaibooks. com.au**

A Spiritual Path to Unity & Social Justice: The Bahá'í Faith in America. Wilmette, IL: National Spiritual Assembly of the Bahá'ís of the United States, 2021.   **https://www.bahai.us/wp-content/uploads/2021/03/unity-social-justice/index.html**

Consultation: A Compilation of Extracts from the Bahá'í *Writings*. Bahá'í Publications Australia: Bahá'í International Community, 1978/2020. **www. bahaibooks.com.au**

Forging a Path to Racial Justice: A Message from the Baha'is of the United States. Wilmette, IL: National Spiritual Assembly of the Baha'is of the United States, 2020. **www.bahai.us/path-to-racial-justice**

Christopher Buck, "Fifty Bahá'í Principles of Unity," *Bahá'í Studies Review*, Vol. 18, 2012/2017.

"Peace – Words from 'Abdu'l-Bahá's Paris Talks" **https://www.youtube.com/watch?v=5qBxYbeUSwA**

Sarah Farmer, "A Life Dedicated to Peace" **https://vimeo.com/900310295**

Bahá'í World News Service **https://news.bahai.org**

Bahá'í International Community **https://www.bic.org**

A Global Community **https://www.bahai.org/national-communities**

Peace: A Compilation of Bahá'í Writings
https://www.bahai.org/library/authoritative-texts/compilations/peace/peace.pdf?21403856

Universal Principles and Action Steps **https://issuu.com/lightonlight/docs/universal_principles_and_action_steps**

Universal Peace Quotations **https://www.bahai.org/beliefs/universal-peace/quotations**

The Ruhi Institute for a Global Process of Learning **https://www.ruhi.org/en**

Unitive Justice

Bahá'í International Community, "Building a Just World Order"
https://www.bic.org/statements/building-just-world-order

Bahá'í International Community, "Transforming Collective Deliberation: Valuing Unity and Justice **https://www.bic.org/statements/transforming-collective-deliberation-valuing-unity-and-justice**

Bahá'í International Community, "Striving Towards Justice" **https://www.bic.org/statements/striving-towards-justice-transforming-dynamics-human-interaction**

Bahá'í International Community, "Freedom to Believe" **https://www.bic.org/statements/freedom-believe**

Bahá'í International Community, "Combating Racism" **https://www.bic.org/statements/combating-racism**

Bahá'í International Community, "Eliminating Racism" **https://www.bic.org/statements/eliminating-racism**

Unitive Justice.com **https://unitivejustice.com**

Unitive Economics

Bahá'í International Community, "In Efforts to Eradicate Poverty, We All Depend on Each Other" **https://www.bic.org/perspectives/efforts-eradicate-poverty-we-all-depend-each-other**

Bahá'í International Community, "Towards a Just Economic Order" **https://www.bic.org/statements/towards-just-economic-order-conceptual-foundations-and-moral-prerequisites**

Bahá'í International Community, "Eradicating Poverty: Moving Forward as One"
https://www.bic.org/statements/eradicating-poverty-moving-forward-one

Bahá'í International Community, "Guiding Principles on Extreme Poverty and Human Rights"
https://www.bic.org/statements/guiding-principles-extreme-poverty-and-human-rights

Bahá'í International Community, "A New Framework for Global Prosperity"
https://www.bic.org/statements/new-framework-global-prosperity

Bahá'í International Community, "The Realization of Economic, Social, and Cultural Rights"
https://www.bic.org/statements/realization-economic-social-and-cultural-rights

U.S. Bahá'í Office of Public Affairs, "Wealth Must Serve Humanity"
https://www.bahai.us/public-affairs/focus-areas/economic-justice

Unitive Narratives

Bahá'í International Community, "Where is Investment Needed for Sustainability? In New Narratives" **https://www.bic.org/perspectives/where-investment-needed-sustainability-new-narratives**

Bahá'í International Community, "New Narratives in the Quest for Equality"
https://www.bic.org/perspectives/perspective-new-narratives-quest-equality-elites-and-everyone-else

SDG Thought Leaders Circle, "Unitive Narrative"
https://sdgthoughtleaderscircle.org/unitive-new-narrative

Unitive Narrative Synergy Circle, "A Unitive Narrative Grounded in Unitive Consciousness"
https://www.unitivenarrative.org/resource-papers/unitive-consciousness

IONS, "Why a Unitive Narrative Now?"
https://noetic.org/blog/why-a-unitive-narrative-now

Psychology Today, "The Evolution of Narratives"
https://www.psychologytoday.com/us/blog/hope-and-the-consciousness-journey/202212/the-evolution-narratives

Unity Earth, "Unity and a Unitive Narrative"
https://www.youtube.com/watch?v=55-bEkwCt48

Unitive Age Research Collaborative, "Restoring a Unitive Worldview and Narrative for a Flourishing World" **https://www.unitiveage.net**

Unitive Education

Bahá'í International Community, "The Determining Factor of a Quality Education for All"
https://www.bic.org/statements/teachers-situation-determining-factor-quality-education-all

Bahá'í International Community, "Re-imagining Education"
https://www.bic.org/perspectives/re-imagining-education-perspective-piece-educational-systems-current-and-future-global-challenges

Bahá'í International Community, "The Human Side of Learning" **https://www.bic.org/perspectives/human-side-learning-why-expertise-isnt-enough**

Bahá'í International Community, "Education and Training for the Betterment of Society" **https://www.bic.org/statements/education-and-training-betterment-society**

Unitive Education Collaborative **https://www.unitiveeducation.org**

Alliance for Unitive Justice, "Unitive Education" **https://www.a4uj.org/unitive-education**

Unitive Relationships

Gender Equality, Honoring Children and Youth

Bahá'í International Community, "Reimagining the Role of Institutions in Building Gender-Equal Societies" **https://www.bic.org/sites/default/files/pdf/bic-2024-csw_0.pdf**

Bahá'í International Community, "In Full Partnership: Women's Advancement as a Prerequisite for Peaceful Societies" **https://www.bic.org/statements/full-partnership-womens-advancement-prerequisite-peaceful-societies**

Bahá'í International Community, "Advancement of Women and Girls Featured at Major Forum on Development" **https://www.bic.org/news/advancement-women-and-girls-featured-major-forum-development**

Bahá'í International Community, "Reorganizing the Women's Movement for the Next Steps Forward" **https://www.bic.org/perspectives/reorganizing-womens-movement-next-steps-forward**

Bahá'í International Community, "Building Communities Free of Gender-Based Violence"
https://www.bic.org/perspectives/building-communities-free-gender-based-violence-constructive-role-religion

Bahá'í International Community, "The Eradication of Violence Against Women and Girls"
https://www.bic.org/statements/eradication-violence-against-women-and-girls

Bahá'í International Community, "Transforming Values to Empower the Girl Child"
https://www.bic.org/statements/transforming-values-empower-girl-child

Bahá'í International Community, "The Role of Men and Boys in Achieving Gender Equality"
https://www.bic.org/statements/role-men-and-boys-achieving-gender-equality

Bahá'í International Community, "The Greatness Which Might Be Theirs: Protection of Women's Rights" **https://www.bic.org/statements/greatness-which-might-be-theirs-protection-womens-rights**

Bahá'í International Community, "Women and Men in Partnership"
https://www.bic.org/statements/women-and-men-partnership

Bahá'í International Community, "Preparation for Life in Peace: The Contribution of Women"
https://www.bic.org/statements/preparation-life-peace-contribution-women

Bahá'í International Community, "Women and the Peace Process"
https://www.bic.org/statements/women-and-peace-process

Bahá'í International Community, "Youth and Future Generations at the Heart of the Summit of the Future" **https://www.bic.org/news/youth-and-future-generations-heart-summit-future**

Bahá'í International Community, "Rising Generations: Weaving a New Tapestry of Community Life" **https://www.bic.org/statements/rising-generations-weaving-new-tapestry-community-life**

Bahá'í International Community, "Effective Models of Communication and Interaction"
https://www.bic.org/perspectives/effective-models-communication-and-interaction

Bahá'í International Community, "Preparation for Life in Peace: The Role of Youth"
https://www.bic.org/statements/preparation-life-peace-role-youth

Bahá'í International Community, "The Contribution of Youth to World Peace"
https://www.bic.org/statements/contribution-youth-world-peace

Bahá'í International Community, "The Spirit of Youth in Action"
https://www.bic.org/perspectives/spirit-youth-action

Humanity's Relationship with the Natural World
Bahá'í International Community, "A Call for a New UN Pillar on Preserving and Protecting the Earth" https://www.bic.org/perspectives/unea-6-here-lets-use-it-call-new-un-pillar-protecting-and-preserving-earth

Bahá'í International Community, "Putting Values to Work in an Age of Climate Change"
https://www.bic.org/perspectives/putting-values-work-age-climate-change

Bahá'í International Community, "Building a Global Community One Generation of Youth at a Time" https://www.bic.org/perspectives/perspective-building-global-community-one-generation-youth-time

Bahá'í International Community, "Reason and Morality as a Bridge to Climate Action"
https://www.bic.org/perspectives/transcending-materialism-reason-and-morality-bridge-climate-action

U.S. Bahá'í Office of Public Affairs, "The Natural World is a Divine Trust"
https://www.bahai.us/public-affairs/focus-areas/environment

International Environment Forum, "Resources on Environment and Sustainable Development"
https://iefworld.org/resource.htm#STATEMENTS

Unitive Global Development

U.S. Bahá'í Community, "Building Community: Love in Action" **https://www.bahai.us/beliefs/building-community**

Universal House of Justice, "Social Action"
https://www.bahai.org/library/authoritative-texts/the-universal-house-of-justice/messages/20121126_001/1#617215432

Bahá'í International Community, "Empowerment as a Mechanism for Social Transformation"
https://www.bic.org/statements/empowerment-mechanism-social-transformation

Bahá'í International Community, "Unity in Action: Reclaiming the Spirit of the Sustainable Development Agenda" **https://www.bic.org/statements/unity-action-reclaiming-spirit-sustainable-development-agenda**

Bahá'í International Community, "A Wider Perspective on Human Nature and Development"
https://www.bic.org/perspectives/perspectives-beyond-economic-man-wider-perspective-human-nature-and-development

Bahá'í International Community, "Reflections on the 62nd Commission for Social Development"
https://www.bic.org/perspectives/view-interns-reflections-62nd-commission-social-development

Bahá'í International Community, "Strengthening the Foundations of Social Development"
https://www.bic.org/statements/collective-learning-collective-will-strengthening-foundations-social-development

Bahá'í International Community, "Sustainable Development: The Spiritual Dimension"
https://www.bic.org/statements/sustainable-development-spiritual-dimension

Bahá'í International Community, "Valuing Spirituality in Development"
https://www.bic.org/statements/valuing-spirituality-development

Bahá'í International Community, "Conservation and Sustainable Development in the Bahá'í Faith"
https://www.bic.org/statements/conservation-and-sustainable-development-bahai-faith

Bahá'í International Community, "Understanding Why: The Purpose of Development"
https://www.bic.org/perspectives/perspective-understanding-why-purpose-development

Bahá'í International Community, "Right to Development"
https://www.bic.org/statements/right-development

Bahá'í International Community, "Peace and Development"
https://www.bic.org/statements/peace-and-development

Bahá'í International Community, "Social and Economic Development: The Bahá'í Contribution"
https://www.bic.org/statements/social-and-economic-development-bahai-contribution

Bahá'í International Community, "Global Action Plan for Social Development"
https://www.bic.org/statements/global-action-plan-social-development

Bahá'í International Community, "World Citizenship: A Global Ethic for Sustainable Development"
https://www.bic.org/statements/world-citizenship-global-ethic-sustainable-development

Bahá'í International Community, "Shared Vision, Shared Volition: Choosing Our Global Future Together"
https://www.bic.org/statements/shared-vision-shared-volition-choosing-our-global-future-together

Bahá'í International Community, "The Bahá'í International Community and World Peace"
https://www.bic.org/statements/bahai-international-community-and-world-peace

Unitive Global Governance

Education Synergy Circle of the Evolutionary Leaders, "Universal Principles and Action Steps"
https://issuu.com/lightonlight/docs/universal_principles_and_action_steps

Earth Governance, "Strengthening Earth Governance to Protect the Environment" **https://earthgovernance.org**

Global Governance Forum, "Global Governance and the Emergence of Global Institutions for the 21st Century" **https://globalgovernanceforum.org/wp-content/uploads/2020/10/Global-Governance-and-the-Emergence-of-Global-Institutions.pdf**

Global Governance Forum, "A Second Charter: Imagining a Renewed United Nations" **https://globalgovernanceforum.org/wp-content/uploads/2023/08/SecondCharter_Imagining-Renewed-United-Nations.pdf**

IntegraLight Institute, "Unitive Earth Governance Collaborative" **https://integralight.org/unitive-earth-governance-collaborative**

Bahá'í International Community, "Turning Point for All Nations" **https://www.bic.org/statements/turning-point-all-nations#V**

Bahá'í International Community, "The Role of the Environment in the Future of Global Governance" **https://www.bic.org/news/role-environment-future-global-governance**

Bahá'í International Community, "Global Governance Must be an Unfolding Generational Process" **https://www.bic.org/perspectives/global-governance-must-be-unfolding-generational-process**

Bahá'í International Community, "The Prosperity of Humankind" **https://www.bic.org/statements/prosperity-humankind**

Bahá'í International Community, "Restructuring International Order"
https://www.bic.org/statements/restructuring-international-order

Bahá'í International Community, "The Earth Charter/Rio De Janeiro Declaration and the Oneness of Humanity"
https://www.bic.org/statements/earth-charterrio-de-janeiro-declaration-and-oneness-humanity

Bahá'í International Community, "The Promise of Disarmament and Peace"
https://www.bic.org/statements/promise-disarmament-and-peace

Bahá'í International Community, "The Common Goal of Universal Peace in Buddhism and the Bahá'í Faith"
https://www.bic.org/statements/common-goal-universal-peace-buddhism-and-bahai-faith

Bahá'í International Community, "One Same Substance: Consciously Creating a Global Culture of Unity"
https://www.bic.org/statements/one-same-substance-consciously-creating-global-culture-unity

Bahá'í International Community, "Toward the 21st Century and Peace"
https://www.bic.org/statements/toward-21st-century-and-peace

SDG Thought Leaders Circle, "The Unitive Cluster at the United Nations"
https://sdgthoughtleaderscircle.org/the-unitive-cluster-at-the-un

ABOUT THE AUTHOR

Robert Atkinson, PhD, award-winning author, educator, and developmental psychologist, is a 2020 Gold Nautilus Book Award winner as co-editor of *Our Moment of Choice: Evolutionary Visions and Hope for the Future*, a 2023 Silver Nautilus Book Award winner for *A New Story of Wholeness: An Experiential Guide for Connecting the Human Family*, and a 2017 Silver Nautilus Book Award winner for *The Story of Our Time: From Duality to Interconnectedness to Oneness*. He is also the author or co-editor of nine other books including, *Year of Living Deeply: A Memoir of 1969* (2019), *Mystic Journey: Getting to the Heart of Your Soul's Story* (2012), *The Life Story Interview* (1998) and *The Gift of Stories: Practical Applications of Autobiography, Life Stories, and Personal Mythmaking* (1995).

He received his B.A. in philosophy and American Studies from Southampton College of Long Island University, an M.A. in American Folk

Culture from SUNY, Cooperstown, an M.A. in counseling from the University of New Hampshire, and his Ph.D. from the University of Pennsylvania in cross-cultural human development, with a post-doctoral research fellowship in adolescent development at the University of Chicago. He is professor emeritus at the University of Southern Maine, an internationally recognized authority on life story interviewing, a pioneer in the techniques of personal myth making and soul making, and founder of StoryCommons. His books on life storytelling have been translated into Japanese, Italian, and Romanian and are widely used in personal growth and life review settings. He is a member of the Evolutionary Leaders Circle, a project of the Source of Synergy Foundation, a recipient of a Lifetime Achievement Award as a Visionary Leader from the Visioneers International Network, and founder of One Planet Peace Forum. **www.RobertAtkinson.net**

MESSAGE FROM THE PUBLISHER

Light on Light Press produces enhanced content books spotlighting the sacred ground upon which all religious and wisdom traditions intersect; it aims to stimulate and perpetuate engaged interspiritual and perennial wisdom dialogue for the purpose of assisting the dawning of a unitive consciousness that will inspire compassionate action toward a just and peaceful world.

We are delighted to publish The Way of Unity because there is nothing more important right now than peace and harmony on the planet. This book addresses this most vital of needs in the broadest and most inclusive of ways. One of its distinctive features, very much in line with the interspiritual messaging of Light on Light, is highlighting the great diversity of social and transformative projects around the world, in so many countries, across so many ethnic groups and thematic arenas, being carried out by the Bahá'í international community that demonstrate vividly how an interspiritual foundation framed by universal principles put into action for the good of the whole can have such an exemplary global impact.

The Way of Unity builds out a vision of harmony and wholeness to illustrate how an organic renewal process can be followed that, by its very nature, purpose, and approach, is at the same time putting in place the preconditions for world peace to unfold naturally in its intended way. This is a book we feel will become a standard reference for what the Bahá'í tradition has brought to the world in our planet's ongoing visioning of global transformative change and, ultimately, world peace.

We consider this book an essential guide with all the needed signposts for navigating our way through the process of global transformation currently spreading across the planet. We are extremely pleased to bring forth this watershed book when the world so needs it.

Managing Editors—

Kurt Johnson, PhD
Robert Atkinson, PhD
Chamatkara (Sandra Simon)
Nomi Naeem, MA